PAN AMERICAN CLIPPERS

THE GOLDEN AGE OF FLYING BOATS

"Someday a Clipper flight will be remembered as the most romantic voyage in history."

— Clare Boothe Luce, 1941

PAN AMERICAN
CLIPPERS

THE GOLDEN AGE OF FLYING BOATS

JAMES TRAUTMAN

CHINA CLIPPER

PAA

The BOSTON
MILLS PRESS

Dedicated to   *Tina, Amy, and Alyssa*

A BOSTON MILLS PRESS BOOK

Library and Archives Canada Cataloguing in Publication

Trautman, James, 1946-
Pan Am Clippers : the golden age of flying boats /
James Trautman.

Includes bibliographical references and index.
ISBN-13: 978-1-55046-476-4
ISBN-10: 1-55046-476-0

1. Pan American World Airways, Inc. -- History.
2. Seaplanes -- United States -- History.
3. Transpacific flights -- History. I. Title.

TL684.T73 2007   387.7'06573   C2007-902855-1

Publisher Cataloging-in-Publication Data (U.S.)

Trautman, James, 1946-
Pan Am Clippers : the golden age of flying boats /
James Trautman.
[272] p. : ill. (some col.) ; cm.
Summary: An illustrated history of Pan American Airways
Clipper flying boats, including the key role they played
in the evolution of transoceanic flight.

ISBN-13: 978-1-55046-476-4
ISBN-10: 1-55046-476-0
1. Pan American Clipper (seaplane). 2. Pan American Airways
Corporation -- History.   3. Seaplanes -- American -- 1930-1940.
3. Transatlantic flights -- History. I. Title.

629.13347 dc 22   TL684.2.T737 2007

Published by
Boston Mills Press, 2007
132 Main Street, Erin, Ontario N0B 1T0
Tel 519-833-2407 • Fax 519-833-2195

In Canada:
Distributed by Firefly Books Ltd.
66 Leek Crescent, Richmond Hill
Ontario, Canada L4B 1H1

In the United States:
Distributed by Firefly Books (U.S.) Inc.
P.O. Box 1338, Ellicott Station
Buffalo, New York, USA 14205

Design: Chris McCorkindale and Sue Breen
McCorkindale Advertising & Design

Printed in China

The publisher gratefully acknowledges the financial support for our publishing program by the Government of Canada through the Book Publishing Industry Development Program.

(Cover) Pan Am Clipper travel poster of the romantic South Pacific commissioned by Pan Am and painted by Paul George Lawler.
art.com and the Swann Galleries of New York City

(Back jacket above) December 7, 1941. Pan American World Airways poster "Routes of the Flying Clipper Ships," commissioned by Pan Am and painted by L. Helguera. Author's Collection

(Back jacket below) May 10, 1939. Pan Am *China Clipper* approaching the water for landing in San Francisco Bay.
Clyde Sunderland, Pacific Aerial Surveys, HJW Geospatial Inc.

(Page 1) S-42 *Brazilian Clipper* on the water at the Dinner Key Terminal.
University of Miami, Richter Library, Pan Am Collection

(Page 2) Juan Trippe and his famous aircraft, the S-48 and the B-314.
San Diego Aerospace Museum

(Page 3) *China Clipper* on the water undergoing regular maintenance.
University of Miami, Richter Library, Pan Am Collection

(Page 4) Early Pan Am luggage sticker. Author's Collection

(Page 5) Two Pan Am Clippers riding at anchor with the PanAir boat alongside.
Greg Young Publishing

INTRODUCTION

"Let me tell you about the very rich. They are different from you and me. They possess and enjoy early, and it does something to them, makes them soft where we are hard, and cynical where we are trustful, in a way that, unless you were born rich, it is difficult to understand. They think, deep in their hearts, that they are better than we are because we had to discover the compensations and refuges of life for ourselves. Even when they enter deep into our world or sink below us, they still think that they are better than we are. They are different."

— F. Scott Fitzgerald

ONE MAY CHALLENGE THE ABOVE QUOTE, but the early years of aviation in the 1920s would fit nicely into *The Great Gatsby* and its old wealth mixing with the new self-made millionaires of the Roaring Twenties. Much of this new wealth had been made through war production during World War I. World War II would alter civilian aviation and create a climate for the expansion of cheaper air travel for the masses. But that was in the future, and in the 1920s and 1930s, international air travel would be for the more elite. The early days of civilian air travel had only one type of passenger class: first class.

Juan Trippe would take over the fledgling Pan American Airways and turn it into a worldwide airline. His family was old wealth, having made their money in the great Clipper sailing ships of the 1800s.

Another key figure in the formative years of aviation and Pan American Airways was Harry Guggenheim, who would become Charles Lindbergh's mentor. The two met prior to Lindbergh's solo flight across the Atlantic to Paris. Guggenheim told Lindbergh they would get together once he returned from his epic venture. Whether he believed that Lindbergh would make it back or not is open to debate. The Guggenheim family made their wealth in mining and reinvested in the future of the United States by establishing many foundations, including the Guggenheim Fund for the Promotion of Aeronautics. This foundation would be responsible for the development of blind instrument flying, the establishment of the Safe Aircraft Competition and, most importantly, the establishment of major centers of aeronautical engineering throughout the United States.

Early 1929 Pan Am ad focused on the elite business-class traveler.
University of Miami, Richter Library, Pan Am Collection

(Left) Passengers boarding European-bound Pan Am Clipper at the Marine Air Terminal, New York City. Clyde Sunderland, Pacific Aerial Surveys, HJW Geospatial Inc.

Harry Guggenheim was true to his word, and Lindbergh was introduced to the wealthy and connected of the United States at parties in the Hamptons, people like Dwight Morrow and Thomas Lamont of the J. P. Morgan bank, Juan Trippe, Orville Wright, John D. Rockefeller Jr., Theodore Roosevelt Jr., and Herbert Hoover. The groups that met at the parties were the foundation that would push the development of American aviation, including the concept of passenger travel. Dwight Morrow would eventually become Lindbergh's father-in-law, and Harry Guggenheim would appoint Lindbergh as a consultant to the Guggenheim Aeronautical Fund at a salary of $25,000 per year.

Juan Trippe would operate Pan American Airways until his retirement in 1968, experiencing years that would bring glory and almost total defeat. At a Pan American Airways board meeting on March 14, 1939, Trippe would lose most of his power. The *China Clipper* routes were in the red and the board was not sold on the Atlantic routes to Europe. Eventually, Trippe would take back his power, but the routes would continue to be money losers. At some times, more flights were cancelled due to inclement weather than were flying.

The arrival of World War II and the end of the Golden Age of Flying Boats may have been a blessing to Pan American Airways.

Charles and Mrs. Lindbergh, Juan Trippe and his wife, Captain Musick, and others on an early flight.

University of Miami, Richter Library, Pan Am Collection

Charles Lindbergh in a Sikorsky
S-38 opening the route to the
Panama Canal Zone.

Map of the Clipper Atlantic
route: New York - Shediac,
New Brunswick - Botwood,
Newfoundland - Foynes, Ireland
- Southampton, England.
Author's Collection

(Opposite) 1929 ad for Pan Am
Airways Inc. Author's Collection

THE MOST WATCHED-FOR SHIP IN THE WORLD!

LONDON CALLING

"When does the next Clipper leave Lisbon?"

WASHINGTON CALLING

"Who was on yesterday's Clipper?"

HAVANA CALLING

"Reserve four seats on the first Clipper"

BUENOS AIRES CALLING

"Rush shipment by Clipper"

MANILA CALLING

"Decision awaits arrival of Clipper"

At this very minute in half a hundred far-flung countries, Pan American Clippers are helping to shape history. They carry the hopes of democracy everywhere.

Upon their prompt arrival hinge decisions and events of world importance. And regularly as clockwork the Flying Clippers speed their vital cargo of men, mail, materials and merchandise along 75,556 miles of routes. By other means of transport this cargo would be many days or weeks longer in arriving.

Today, Pan American Clippers provide a quick, direct and certain link between the United States and Europe. They bind North and South America together, as well as Alaska and the U. S.

They bring the distant Orient and Australasia within days of our shores, instead of weeks.

In providing these two-way bridges the Clippers are more than U. S. emissaries of trade. They are Uncle Sam's ambassadors of good will. They carry America's traditions of freedom to 55 lands. They strengthen our ties, build our prestige with these neighbors. And finally they serve as this country's lifelines of defense, linking our island outposts and bases in one strategic network.

AMERICA'S MERCHANT MARINE OF THE AIR

Travel PAA

PAN AMERICAN AIRWAYS *System*

CHAPTER 1

THE HISTORY OF THE PAN AMERICAN CLIPPER FLYING BOATS (1931-1946):

The Roaring Twenties and Flying the Mail

THE END OF WORLD WAR I CREATED the social, political, and economic conditions for the Golden Age of Aviation. The perfect environment for the rapid advancement of commercial aviation was created in the 1920s and 1930s. During the war, Allied flying boats searched for enemy submarines and ships. To counter these aircraft, the Germans developed twin-float fighter planes. Prior to the entry of the United States in World War I, there were only a few hundred aircraft, and flying was for the very wealthy or carnival performers. The war created the first boom in the manufacture and training of pilots and ground staff. Advancements were made rapidly in aerodynamics. There were new airframes, engines, equipment, and even new pilots to fly the aircraft. Almost every day a new plane appeared on the front pages of the newspapers across the country.

By 1919, planes manufactured for war were reconverted into the first large civilian aircraft. Shortly before entering World War I, the United States Congress appropriated $100,000 to begin operation of an experimental air service to deliver the mail. The first flights operated by the United States Army and the Postal Service were on a small, limited schedule. On May 14, 1918, the first mail flight departed Belmont, Long Island. On the first day it reached Philadelphia, and on the second it reached Washington, where President Woodrow Wilson was on hand to greet this wonderful new service.

World War I had created a massive supply of surplus aircraft. The next step in the plan was for the U.S. Postal Service to spread the mail service across the continental United States. The first flights were from Chicago, Illinois, to Cleveland, Ohio. By September 1920, the mail flights were able to cross the Rocky Mountains and could now span from coast to coast. There was one major problem: the aircraft could not fly at night. The country did not have a navigation system established to allow night flights. Aircraft would fly the mail as far as their reach, but only until darkness. Then the mail was unloaded and placed onto trains to complete the journey. Even with this crude, rudimentary system, the United States Postal Service was able to cut 22 hours from coast-to-coast deliveries.

Piloting a mail plane was a dangerous and, in many instances, deadly business. Slowly, however, the U.S. Government and aviators recognized that in order to continue to fly

(Left) Late 1930s-early 1940 ad for the Pan Am Clippers – "The Most Watched - For Ship in the World!" Author's Collection

(Below) 1st day cover celebrating June 1, 1923 – First Airmail Flight, Albany, New York, to Buffalo, New York, and 1st day cover celebrating May 15-21, 1938, National Airmail Week. Author's Collection

1918 NCI Glenn Curtis
flying boat.

San Francisco Airport Museums, Mitch Mayborn Collection

the mail safely, a navigation system had to be implemented across the country. Finally, in 1921, rotating beacons spaced 80 miles apart were put into operation on the Columbus to Dayton flights in Ohio. The beacons rotated and were visible to pilots. This meant the mail flights could continue into darkness. Eventually, a coast-to-coast system would be established, and the mail would not require transfer to railroad trains. Transcontinental eastbound mail could be delivered in 29 hours, while westbound mail took an extra five hours due to the prevailing winds.

By 1925, the United States Post Office aircraft were flying 2.5 million miles and delivering 14 million pieces of mail. Republican President Calvin Coolidge wanted to move the government out of the airmail business and turn it over to the private sector. This suited the business community, since contributions had been made to the Republican Party for that purpose. The 1920s and early 1930s became the perfect time for businessmen to move into aviation through the mail contracts. The Administrations of Calvin Coolidge and Herbert Hoover believed that the private sector could deliver the mail more efficiently. A second committee was appointed to make recommendations in the matter of standards for civilian aviation. The committee was chaired by a senior partner in the J. P. Morgan investment bank, Dwight Morrow. The 1920s were the starting point for the relationship between the wealthy and the new aviators. As a direct outcome of the Contract Mail Act (1925) and the recommendations of the Morrow board, flying the mail would create competition among the new aviators and the many companies that entered the market. The first company to be granted a mail license was the Ford Motor Company. Henry Ford had been one of the first successful bidders to carry mail from Chicago to Detroit to Cleveland. Ford was already employing aircraft to carry automobile parts to his various assembly plants more quickly and more cheaply. He even developed his own aircraft, the Ford Trimotor. The Trimotor was large enough to carry 12 passengers and roomy enough for them to be able to walk around the cabin.

On April 15, 1926, Charles Lindbergh tossed mail bags into the belly of a DH-4, jumped into the cockpit and roared down the runway of Lambert Field in St. Louis and headed to Chicago. As a prelude to crossing the Atlantic Ocean solo, he was making history as the pilot of the first mail flight for Robertson Aircraft. Before reaching Chicago three and a half hours later, he made stops in Springfield and Peoria.

Passenger service was also expanding and growing at a rapid rate. By 1930, over 400,000 passengers were flying on U.S. carriers. In 1926, civilian passenger aircraft had carried 6,000 people. With the popularity of flying increasing, aviation schools appeared in almost every town. Barnstormers crossed the country and demonstrated daredevil flying for the paying public. Rides were offered at a nominal price to take the curious onlookers up into the clouds.

The Inman Brothers Flying Circus was one famous barnstorming troupe. They operated a 20-passenger Boeing 80A aircraft, which was billed on their advertising billboards as the "Boeing Clipper — America's Largest Trimotor." The Inman Brothers had a smaller aircraft that also operated with the circus. Their aircraft were the same type employed on the early mail and passenger air routes. For 50 cents, an individual daredevil would be taken aloft, and if one paid a dollar, the flight would be longer. The Inman Brothers introduced thousands of people to the safety, comfort, and novelty of air travel. The other major attraction of the show was the famous parachute jump: "4,000 foot parachute jump — weather permitting — collection taken for the jumper" read the billboard ad.

The Inman Brothers are, in a way, part of the Pan American story, since they employed the term Clipper before Juan Trippe and Pan American Airways. However, in 1931, the Clipper trademark was registered by Juan Trippe and Pan American Airways for their new fleet of S-40s. The Inman Brothers had to launch a lawsuit to be allowed to continue to use the "Boeing Clipper — America's Largest Trimotor" in their flying circus advertising.

1920s Inman Brothers Flying Circus Poster.

Swann Galleries of New York City

Barnstormers were the most exciting daredevils of the day. Remember, it was the Roaring Twenties. There may have been Prohibition, but good times were on, and almost everyone was aching for excitement and fun after the horrors of World War I. Stunt pilots and aerialists were performing almost any known trick or maneuver, as well as new tricks to bring excitement to the crowd below. Many barnstormers had been World War I fliers and were able to purchase their aircrafts for a few hundred dollars. When World War I ended, there was a surplus of aircraft available, and they were sold cheap. The U.S. Government had purchased hundreds of the famous Jenny biplanes for $5,000 each, but the usual surplus price was $200 after the war. Barnstorming flourished due to the lack of government regulations in the early days of flight.

The Curtiss JN-4D Jenny was the major civilian aircraft of the 1920s. It was an early aircraft that was a product of trial and error. The OX-5 engine was very temperamental and difficult to keep cool. Doing so meant cutting away much of its leather-strapped cowling. The very short exhaust pipes would usually throw hot fumes and oil in the face of the pilot. At times the hot fumes and oil could become so hot the dope on the aircraft fabric would cause a fire. Even with all the flaws, the Curtiss Jenny was important to the advancement of early aviation.

Barnstorming and sponsored air races were the rage of the public in the 1920s and early 1930s. This allowed the public a glimpse of civilian aviation, although of a limited kind. Pilots had to be creative and solve problems, often in emergency situations. Failure could result in death or serious injury. The Wright brothers and Glenn Curtiss had early exhibition teams touring the countryside. In the very early days, these performances advertised the company's aircraft. There were hundreds of aviation companies hoping to sell their product, but most of these companies did not survive.

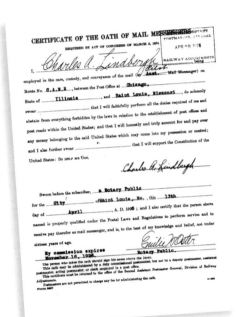

Charles Lindbergh's first contract to fly the United States mail. Author's Collection

A barnstorming show had a familiar pattern. Advance people would travel ahead and put up the advertising posters and meet with people to promote the show that was on its way. This was the same sales technique that the circuses that crisscrossed America employed with great success for many years. One or more pilots would appear and fly over the target area to get the attention of the local citizens. The aircraft would land on someone's farm (hence the name barnstorming) and ask the farmer how much money he wanted to allow them to set up for the show.

Once the site was secured, an aircraft would usually fly over the town and drop out handbills (miniature billboard posters) to give the public information about the troupes and the dates of the shows. Each touring group had a specialty or two that set it apart from the other shows, such as a wing walker, a special aerial dive, a parachutist, or skywriting. The crowds would usually then follow the path of the aircraft to the farm field where the show would be getting ready to start.

It's hard to imagine today, but in some towns all the shops and businesses would come to a halt. The stunt pilots performed daring dives, spins, barrel rolls, and the famous loop de loop. Audiences saw aerialists walking the wings of the aircraft, stunt parachuting, and even the most daring midair transfers of personnel, including pilots.

One barnstormer, Eddie Angel, performed the "Dive of Death," a nighttime free fall from 5,000 feet while holding a pair of flashlights. The famous groups included Douglas Davis, Jimmy and Jessie Woods (a husband-and-wife team), and the Five Blackbirds, an all-African-American group.

The Ivan Gates troupe was the most traveled, visiting every state and traveling internationally. On one occasion, when rides were offered to the public at a dollar a passenger, 980 people were taken aloft. During the Golden Age of Barnstorming, the Ivan Gates Flying Circus took an estimated one million passengers in the air. The circus had a perfect safety record, which included saving aviator Rosalie Gordon when her parachute became tangled in the tail of their aircraft. Clyde Pangborn left his cockpit to free Rosalie.

Many famous fliers received their start by barnstorming, including Charles Lindbergh, Roscoe Turner, Bessie Coleman (the first licensed African-American female pilot) and Wiley Post. Roscoe Turner became a famous race pilot and could be seen with his flight companion, Gilmore the lion cub. Roscoe Turner's sponsor was the Gilmore Gasoline company of California, and Gilmore the lion cub was the company advertising mascot. The lion cub wore a small parachute when it traveled in the aircraft. Roscoe Turner and Gilmore were seen on the red carpet in Hollywood in Martin Scorsese's film *The Aviator*.

Barnstorming began to disappear by the late 1920s and had almost completely disappeared by the mid-1930s. There was a brief resurgence with the surplus aircraft from World War II. Once again, barnstormers visited and took the general public up for joyrides in the air.

The public's fascination moved into aviation's next step for adventure: speed racing. Speed races became almost a weekly event. The races not only provided money, trophies, and prestige to the winner, but also stimulated rapid advancements in aviation. The new engines, new fuselages, and new flying techniques that were developed were eventually transformed into the emerging passenger air services of the day.

Charles Lindbergh made his fame and fortune by becoming the first aviator to cross the Atlantic nonstop, accomplishing a feat where many others had failed. Many fliers had died in the attempt to be the first. A new first was accomplished, and another aviator became famous seemingly every day. For many, the fame was short-lived, and they were never to be seen or heard of again.

In August 1927, shortly after conquering the Atlantic Ocean, Lindbergh received an offer from James Dole, of the Dole pineapple fortune, to participate in a race from California to the Hawaiian Islands. The prize was $35,000. He turned down the offer, but 15 other eager aviators accepted the challenge and the possibility to become the new Charles Lindbergh.

Three were killed in crashes getting ready for the race, and one plane was not even allowed to take off when it was discovered that its flight instruments were so miscalibrated that

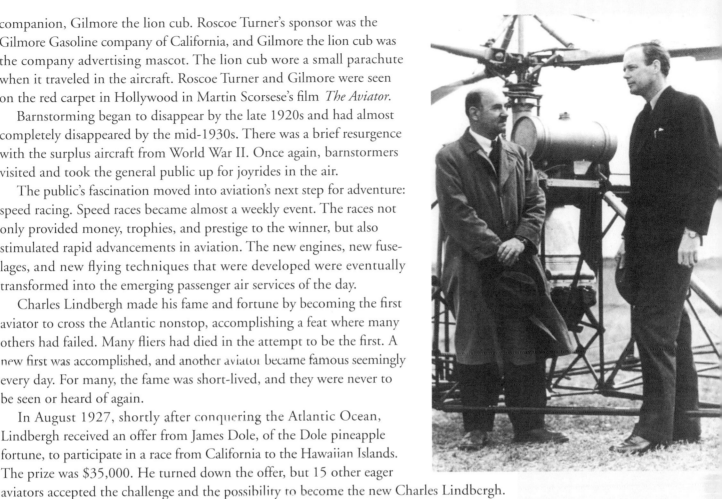

Igor Sikorsky and Charles Lindbergh standing next to an early Sikorsky helicopter. Besides designing flying boats, the Sikorsky Company would become one of the largest manufacturers of helicopters in the world. Igor Sikorsky Historical Archives

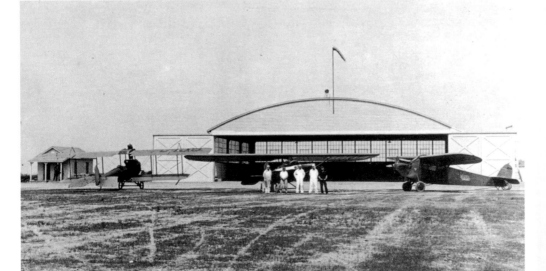

1920s photo of the new Scarborough, Maine, Airport. During the "Roaring Twenties" it seemed almost every town had an airport. The glamour and romance of aviation was everywhere. Author's Collection

Charles Lindbergh and the *Spirit of St. Louis,* the man and plane that accomplished the first solo flight across the treacherous Atlantic Ocean.
National Air and Space Museum

the aircraft had no chance of finding the Hawaiian Islands. Another was grounded due to the fact that the aircraft would not have enough fuel in its tanks to reach the islands. The remaining aircraft were a mixed flying group that included a female passenger in one aircraft (it appeared the pilot had not considered that every extra pound of weight would necessitate more fuel). Several of the others had no understanding of what was required to fly across a large ocean and find a little speck of land and then the airfield. Two crashed on takeoff, one turned back before the point of no return with engine trouble, and the fourth turned his plane around after the wind ripped the canvas fabric on the aircraft.

Art Goebel was granted a winner's welcome when he became the first to cross from Oakland, California, to Honolulu's Wheeler Field in the time of 26 hours, 6 minutes, and 33 seconds. He had received assistance from the new radio beacon system and also had more experience than other pilots, as he was working in Hollywood as a stunt flier on aviation movies. The 1920s and 1930s were the time when aviation translated onto the silver screen, first in silent films and then in the talkies.

In 1920, the National Air Races had started in a very small way. By 1922, the National Aeronautic Association was founded, eventually becoming the sanctioning body for the races. Aviation races were becoming more organized on a national scale, and the rewards and crowds larger. One of the early awards was the Pulitzer Trophy Race prize.

Amelia Earhart, Paul Collins, Jack Sheehan, Captain Milton Anderson, Laurence F. Whittemore, and Phillip Payson standing in front of a Stinson SM6000 Trimotor aircraft. Norm Houle

By the late 1920s, the U.S. Government began to employ the races as a testing ground for various new types of fighter pursuit planes that were in the development stage. When the government announced that it was interested in a new fighter pursuit aircraft, the various aviation companies sprang into action with plans for the plane that fit the government specifications. The National Air Races became not only the testing ground for the new aircraft, but the forum to demonstrate the capability of each competing company's aircraft.

In the 1929 race, organizer Clifford Henderson had designed a closed course of 50 miles that pitted the civilian aircraft against the military pursuit aircraft. The civilian aircraft had been designed and constructed by the new generation of builders. Most of the new builders operated from small shops, not unlike the first Wright brothers' shop. Funding was still critical for the advancement of not only military aviation, but also the newly emerging civilian airlines.

Juan Trippe was getting Pan American Airways off the ground and requesting various companies to provide Pan American with an aircraft of a specific type and design to meet the company's requirements. Many of the companies were beginning to meet the challenge of the expanding aerial environment. The biplane model aircraft began to disappear, due to the requirement for more speed. Companies began to hire more technically trained employees. By the late 1920s, the newly trained technical staff and engineers from the myriad number of training colleges began to move into the companies and airlines. The aviation industry, including the passenger industry, was becoming more specialized and organized.

As Pan American Airways expanded and its requirements evolved, Juan Trippe would become a major factor in requesting various companies to submit proposals for aircraft. He would not use just any aircraft, and the various companies — Sikorsky, Martin, Boeing and Ford — would respond to his expectations.

Hundreds of aviation companies sprang up and disappeared. Shareholders made and lost fortunes in the 1920s and 1930s. The U.S. Government realized that aircraft could bring the country closer together by delivering the mail quickly. In addition, aircraft could be employed as a means to project power and prestige.

Pan American stock certificate for less than 100 shares.
Author's Collection

(Left) Juan Trippe on the February 1929 cover of *US Air Services* magazine.
Author's Collection

Under the directorship of Juan Trippe, Pan American Airways demonstrated that the mail could be delivered and passenger travel made glamorous. For a brief period in aviation history, the most majestic and beautiful planes ever to fly appeared on routes from the United States to Central and South America, the Orient, and Europe. The Golden Age of Aviation brought forth the S-40, S-42, Martin 130, and the Boeing 314, aircraft that would forever become known as the Clippers, giant flying boats that did not require a large landing field. The vast seas and oceans of the world were the landing fields.

The aircraft carried the mail to far-off, exotic destinations and assisted in establishing bases that would become famous in the annals of World War II: Hawaii, Midway, Wake Island, and Hong Kong. The Clippers would convert from civilian use prior to World War II to workhorse aircraft during the war.

Tragically, the same circumstances that created the aviation boom of the 1920s and 1930s would result in the demise of the flying boats. Many were destroyed during the war and several given to the British Government. At the end of World War II, the United States offered to return the Clippers to Pan American. Pan American declined, however, as aviation had made great strides and the days of the giant flying boats were over. Pan American and Juan Trippe's goal after World War II was to create inexpensive travel for the masses. The Clippers of the 1930s had been for the wealthy, but the future was the mass public.

Hundreds of new airfields remained as consequences of the war. New aircraft had been designed and were surplus to the military's requirements. Aircraft could be purchased inexpensively, just as at the end of World War I. Juan Trippe's concern was always the bottom line. The Clippers were majestic but too expensive to operate. The new aircraft, such as the Lockheed Constellation, were larger, more fuel efficient, and could carry more cargo and passengers. Juan Trippe envisioned a new age of cheap air travel across the oceans that did not require island hopping.

The tragedy of the story of Pan American's Clippers is that none have survived. The Sikorsky S-42s, Martin 130s, and the Boeing 314s, the majestic, magnificent flying boats that had opened the door to delivering the mail worldwide and carrying passengers in fantastic splendor to exotic places have passed into the mists of aviation history.

In May 1919, newspaper headlines featured the exciting journey of the three NC-4 United States Navy seaplanes and their flight across the Atlantic. The famous British team of John Alcock and Arthur Brown had not yet made their Atlantic crossing. The three Navy flying boats took off from Trepassey Bay in Newfoundland. The aircraft were headed on a journey that would take the planes to Plymouth, England, before their ultimate destination, the Azores. The NC-4 piloted by A. C. Read made the 2,775-mile journey and became the first aircraft to complete a transatlantic crossing. The other two flying boats met a tragic end. One became the first airplane to sink in the Atlantic Ocean, and the other was hit by a large wave and ended its flight.

Ford Trimotor of Maddox Airlines. Author's Collection

Americans followed the progress of the flight adventure and became more fascinated with not just the airplane but the individuals that flew them. A new class of celebrity was established. Newfoundland, at the time a colony of Great Britain, would play a major role in other historic flights. It would become the landing field for a fleet of 24 Italian flying boats commanded by General Italo Balbo on their journey to and from the 1933 Chicago Century of Progress World's Fair. Charles Lindbergh and his wife, Anne Morrow, would stop in Newfoundland as part of one of their flights that searched for and surveyed routes for Pan American's Clipper planes. Charles and Anne Lindbergh would make two important survey flights. The first, in 1931, would take them across the Arctic to Japan and China. In 1933, a survey flight in their two-seater Lockheed Sirius monoplane fitted with pontoons would take them on a journey reaching Europe, Russia, Africa, and South America. Newfoundland would play a large part in the flights of the *Atlantic Clippers* and even in 2005 serves as a stopover point for transatlantic flights.

The 1920s was the decade of rum-running, jazz, and the expansion of consumer spending in the United States. By the early spring of 1922, radio, like aviation, had become a craze. With affluence and the rise of the middle class came the explosion of consumer goods. Every home had a radio to keep in touch with entertainment and the current events of the country and the world. Aviation would be linked to the radio. The exploits of aviators could also be seen at the local movie theater through movies and the twice-weekly news-reel. The publicity of each new first or record surpassed was reported to a public that was interested in living each event.

A hard-core group of fliers saw the Roaring Twenties as the dawn of a new age. Aviation opportunities were everywhere. These were men who were addicted to flying and could never seem to get enough of it. One group, the traveling barnstormers, thrilled crowds

Charles Lindbergh and his wife, Anne Morrow, on the Lockheed Sirius floatplane. On one of the legs of surveying routes across the North Atlantic.

Botwood, Newfoundland, Museum

23

with their feats of flying, wing walking and acrobatics. Magazines were filled with ads for training and positions: "See Life — Win Applause — Thrills — Big Money." Ads listed the job-training opportunities available and various positions that would become available in the aircraft industry: "Airplane Repairman — Flier — Airplane Mechanician — Airplane Inspector — Airplane Salesman — Airplane Assembler — Airplane Builder — Airplane Pilot — Airplane Instructor — Airplane Contractor — Airplane Engineer — Airplane Photography — Aerial Advertising."

A second group viewed aviation as the new arena to set records. Speed records, distance records, solo flights, records to be set or broken, first flights, air races with rich cash prizes. Any unknown individual could immediately make a name for him- or herself with one record or feat. Fame and fortune awaited the successful who survived those early days of flying. The 1920s thrived on heroes. After World War I, the public wanted to forget the horrors of the war and dwell on heroes, aviation, sports, and the movies. Almost any flight was carried on the front page of the newspapers. The main goal of any publisher is to sell more papers, and selling more papers means more advertising. Advertising for flying lessons, aircraft, and air travel became one of the main income generators for newspapers.

World governments recognized that aviation was a way to bring out nationalist feelings in their citizens. Competition between aviators was one aspect of this, and governments began to feed into the idea of projecting their country into the eyes of other nations through aviation.

Every small aircraft manufacturer envisioned building their aircraft in a barn, winning the big air race, and becoming a millionaire overnight. Almost every day new airplane manufacturers or airline companies issued stock offerings to the aviation-crazy public. The majority of companies and shareholders usually met the same fate: bankruptcy. The Roaring Twenties was a time of new aircraft manufacturers and fledgling airlines selling shares to an aviation-hungry public. Companies worth millions of dollars on paper one day were worthless the next. Shareholders were left with little or nothing. It was the decade of the Wild West.

Although Juan Trippe became synonymous with Pan American Airways, he was not the original founder of the company. Pan American Airways Incorporated was officially founded on March 14, 1927, by Captain J. K. Montgomery, and incorporated in the State of New York. The company's plan was to develop a base of operations in Florida and eventually to become a worldwide commercial airline. Captain Montgomery had strong financial backers, including Richard Bevier, the son-in-law of the famous banker Lewis Pierson. Pan American Airways hoped to win an airmail contract to carry the mail to South America by way of the West Indies.

Besides J. K. Montgomery, two other groups were in competition for the coveted route to South America to deliver the mail. Reed Chambers and World War I flier Eddie

(Left) Series of photos of the Lockheed Sirius floatplane. One with locals assisting and the second of the aircraft in the water. Botwood, Newfoundland, Museum

1928 Robertson Cessna Cabin monoplane arriving in Chicago on a flight from St. Louis carrying the United States mail. Author's Collection

1950s photo of a stewardess and pilot reading the historical plaque located in Key West, Florida, marking the first flight on October 28, 1927.

Rickenbacker, the founders of Florida Airways, and Juan Trippe, founder of the Aviation Corporation of America, led these groups. J. K. Montgomery and Pan American were victorious in the first round, winning the coveted Miami to Havana airmail run.

Pan American almost lost the coveted airmail route in October 1927, due to its inability to secure aircraft to fly to Cuba. Close to 30,000 pieces of mail needed to be delivered from Florida to Havana, and at stake was the $25,000 deposit. If an aircraft was not available, then the contract would become null and void and the money lost. At the very last minute, a small Fairchild FC-2 from West Indian Aerial came to the rescue. The pilot, Cy Caldwell, had been approached and offered the princely sum of $145.50 to fly the mail and secure the route for J. K. Montgomery and Pan American.

First passengers boarding the Pan Am Fokker Trimotor at Key West, Florida, for a flight to Havana, Cuba, on January 16, 1928.

University of Miami, Richter Library, Pan Am Collection

1st day cover carried on the first flight from Key West, Florida, to Havana, Cuba, on October 19, 1927. Front of letter signed by Pilot Cy Caldwell. Author's Collection

Cy Caldwell had been a prominent test pilot for the Glenn L. Martin Company. He and his mechanic, Calvin Rouse, had arrived in Miami with a leaking oil tank that required repair. Caldwell departed Miami at 1:15 p.m. on October 18, 1927, for Key West. He landed at Key West's old Navy ramp an hour and 50 minutes later. Although Prohibition was still in effect, it was easy to find liquor in Key West, and a good time was had by all. The mail was loaded aboard the Fairchild FC-2 the next morning. The weight of the mail was so great that the weight restrictions required the mechanic to be left behind. The aircraft departed at 8:04 a.m. with a big send-off.

Caldwell landed the FC-2, *La Nina*, an hour and two minutes later in Havana. Calvin Rouse, the mechanic, had to take the steamer and meet the aircraft in Havana.

Commencing on October 28, 1927, was a regular mail flight from Key West to Havana each day. The mailbags were shipped on the Florida East Coast Railway and, upon arrival, were loaded into the spanking new Fokker C-2 aircraft. Pan American now had an official hangar and regular mail flights. The Florida East Coast Railway would play an essential part in the development of Pan American Airways in those early days. Besides carrying the mail each day, the Florida trains were one of Pan American Airways' first advertising tools. Ads

were placed in their regularly scheduled trains departing New York City for Florida. This would pave the way for the first passenger flights from Key West to Havana.

The first passenger service started on January 16, 1928, and in that first month, Pan American Airways carried 71 passengers, 23,292 pounds of mail, 1,572 pounds of cargo,

A Fairchild FC-71 of
Pan American Airways.
Bill Thompson Collection

631 pounds of excess baggage, and 1,683 pounds of Cuban mail on the return trips. A one-way passenger ticket cost $50 — steep, but in that first year, over 1,100 tickets were sold.

Florida was becoming the hot vacation area. The 1920s were the boom time for Florida real estate and tourism. Even the famous Marx Brothers were caught up in the Florida "Gold Rush." The plot of their 1929 film *Coconuts* concerned the Florida "Gold Coast" and the wealth that was pouring into the state.

"Home, Sweet Florida — Go to Florida, where enterprise is enthroned, where you sit and watch at twilight the fronds of the graceful palm, latticed against the fading gold of the sun kissed sky — where sun, moon and stars at eventide stage a welcome — where the whispering breeze springs fresh from the lap of the Caribbean and woos with elusive cadence like unto a mother's lullaby."

With the Florida boom, Juan Trippe began to slowly expand Pan American Airways into the Caribbean and Latin America. The flying boats made their way onto the stage. Not the magnificent S-40s or S-42s, but the Sikorsky S-38. The S-38s would provide the Caribbean service until adequate airfields were constructed and large aircraft appeared on the scene.

CY CALDWELL

Cy Caldwell was born in Bridgetown, Nova Scotia, Canada. In 1912, he worked for the Bank of Nova Scotia and then ran one of the first movie theaters in the province. When Canada entered World War I in 1914, he joined the Royal Flying Corps to fulfill his goal of learning to fly and finding adventure in a foreign land. Cy Caldwell became a well-known and recognized aviation journalist after his tenure with Pan American Airways. He wrote for various publications, including the famous *Aero Digest*. One of his best-known pieces was a critique of *Tailspin Tommy*, the famous comic strip of the 1930s that dealt with early aviation. He eventually became an American citizen.

Juan Trippe had a price for saving the contract, and it was to take majority control of Pan American Airways. Trippe was able to raise $300,000 in capital from Grover C. Loening, W. Averill Harriman, William H. Vanderbilt, Edward O. McDonnell, Sherman M. Fairchild, John Hay Whitney, William A. Rockefeller, and Seymour H. Knox. The parent company would become Aviation Corporation of the Americas. For the next 40 years, Trippe would lobby, manipulate the Board of Directors, and do everything within his ability to increase the power and prestige of Pan American. When competition stood in the way, he would threaten to put them out. The airline grew on its own and through takeovers. It would become his airline. Every mail contract that Juan Trippe bid on, Pan American Airways won. The company did not lose one contract that it wanted. Trippe also employed his family and school and business connections. In the years of Republican administrations, he was even allowed to assist in drafting the new airmail legislation and determining the fees that the U.S. Government would pay for every bag of mail. By October 1941, Pan American Airways and its various subsidiaries had made $83 million on flying the mail.

Early 1930s Pan Am advertising poster. Posters focused on travel to exotic and romantic destinations, such as Cuba, Mexico, Central and South America, the Caribbean. Early travel attracted the wealthy and business class.
Greg Young Publishing

JUAN TRIPPE

Juan Trippe's original career path was very different; he was expected to be employed in his family's investment firm. Trippe was born on June 27, 1899, in Seabright, New Jersey, to a wealthy family that had made their fortune from the old Clipper sailing ships of the mid-1800s. Like so many of his generation, however, Trippe was a man with a dream to build a worldwide airline company and become one of the new rich.

His family had been lucky in making their fortune from the Clipper sailing ships, and he would make his own fortune with the newest mode of transportation: the airplane. Juan was named after his mother's Cuban stepfather. He never liked the name, although it would open many doors in Latin America in the coming years. Latin America would be the first step on the road to a global airline.

Trippe's early ancestors may not have been wealthy, but they could trace their history back to the Norman Conquest. The Trippes of Canterbury served the King and God, and they produced a long line of soldiers and clergymen. In 1663, a Lieutenant Henry Trippe emigrated to the colonies and set up a tobacco plantation. Trippe Creek, on the Eastern Shore of Maryland, is named for the family.

In 1805, Lieutenant John Trippe was wounded fighting the Barbary pirates in Tripoli and received the highest award that the United States could bestow: the Congressional Medal of Honor. A Navy destroyer was named for him 100 years later. The family continued to prosper and receive honors and gain influence.

Later photo of the brains behind Pan American Airways, Juan Trippe. San Diego Aerospace Museum

Juan Trippe entered Yale in 1917. Yale University was for old money and old immigrants to the New World. It was the university that offered a perfect education for a young man who desired wealth, position, and status. It was the school for the very select elite to attend. The student body was male, white, Anglo-Saxon and Protestant. The political background was mostly Republican.

He entered Yale as World War I was raging in Europe. Like many of his ancestors, he wanted to become involved in the military, especially in aviation. He immediately joined Yale's ROTC Program and played on the freshman football team. After the victory over archrival Harvard, he and seven teammates decided to join the Marine Corps as flying cadets.

Unfortunately, he failed his physical exam due to his inability to pass the eye test. Perfect 20/20 vision was required, and he was not able to attain that standard. His father was able to pull some strings by contacting the Assistant Secretary of the Navy, Franklin D. Roosevelt. Given another chance, he passed the test by memorizing the lines on the eye chart. Trippe was assigned to ground school instruction and taught to fly in Miami. He made his first solo flight in a Jenny at Hampton Roads, Virginia, and was commissioned an ensign in the United States Naval Reserve. With more training, he could have qualified as a night bomber pilot, but the Armistice was signed on November 11, 1918, while he was on his way to New York City to board a ship for France.

Trippe returned to his studies at Yale in 1919, fulfilled with the knowledge that he had performed his duties as a Yale man. He formed the Yale Flying Club and began to write for the university newspaper, *The Graphic*. His love of aviation appeared in print when the United States hoped to have three flying boats cross the Atlantic. Trippe wrote a glowing piece on the aircraft: "If our naval seaplane is the first to get across, and needless to say, all Americans hope she will be, her pilots will have doubly distinguished themselves, for they will have been not only the first to fly across the Atlantic Ocean but also the first to demonstrate that a flight across the Atlantic Ocean is a perfectly safe and sane commercial proposition and not a gigantic game in which the prospective transatlantic pilot or passenger has big odds against his safe arrival in the United States." He was already at a young age plotting his ideas for not only transoceanic flights, but also an airline that would become the national airline of the United States. He would spend his entire life attempting to make his airline become the American "chosen instrument." His selling point was the fact that his airline was 100 percent American. In the beginning, though, it was only a dream, as the reality was that he found himself working on Wall Street.

He found working on Wall Street to be a stifling experience. In many ways, it was like a small Yale. He was surrounded by Yale men and other Ivy League graduates. Most days, the salesmen sold bonds and securities in the morning, usually to friends and relatives, and then, after lunch, made for the golf course and other business ventures. Upon learning in 1922 that the United States Navy had several surplus seaplanes for sale, he and a friend, John Hambleton, purchased several at $500 each. An air charter service, Long Island Airways, was launched, flying the wealthy in from the Hamptons to party in New York City. During the day, the planes were employed in the movie industry. In the early 1920s, New York City was a hub of moviemaking. The Astoria Studio in Queens was flourishing. The movie-viewing public clamored for movies with aviation themes, featuring real pilots flying real planes. Phony backdrops would not do. In the Roaring Twenties, life was exciting and lived quickly.

October 1929, *Popular Mechanics* magazine featuring the Dornier three-deck flying boat. The inside article stated it had 12 engines, which propelled the 137-foot aircraft, a wing spread of 157 feet, and could fly at a rate of 155 miles an hour. The craft could carry 100 persons and had salons and luxurious sleeping accommodations for 60.
Author's Collection

CHAPTER 2

THE PAN AMERICAN CLIPPERS

Juan Trippe had enjoyed his time in the military and used a military model in his design for the operation of Pan American Airways. This did not only apply to the administrative and hiring aspects, but also right down to the uniforms and employee protocol and behavior. Late in 1930, Andre Priester ordered the pilots' uniforms to be changed from white trousers and a dark blue coat to an all-navy-blue uniform with white hats. The standard tie was adopted at the very same time, replacing the previously acceptable bow tie and four-in-hand knot.

A standard color scheme was adopted for every Pan American Airways aircraft: dark blue stripes just below the company name, with a hemisphere logo on the nose and rear tail. A red line was painted along the waterline on flying boats.

The public could observe the entire crew march onto the aircraft, a military-precision marching unit. Trippe wanted the public to begin to recognize the logo and become

(Left) Color drawing of the S-42 arriving in Hong Kong.

John T. McCoy Jr., University of Miami, Richter Library, Pan Am Collection

Pan Am Clipper crew marching to their aircraft. The crew wore all-navy blue uniforms with white hats. Juan Trippe modeled every aspect of the airline on his experiences as a naval aviator during World War I.

University of Miami, Richter Library, Pan Am Collection

repeat flyers of Pan American Airways. The airline projected an image with clean, orderly personnel. It was recognized that passengers paid very good money to fly and wanted to be treated as first-class passengers. Sloppy attire and manners would lead the public to question the company that operated the aircraft that they were flying on.

Four different types of aircraft were employed during the brief history of Pan American Airways. Each new aircraft type was larger and more advanced than the previous type. The common factor was each aircraft type became more luxurious than the previous one. Although Juan Trippe recognized that the flying public would expand, the Clippers were the champagne of modern aviation. The passengers would pay a premium to fly across the oceans, and for that price they would receive royal service. The earliest Clipper was the four-engine Sikorsky S-40, followed by the four engine Sikorsky S-42. Next were the Martin 130, manufactured by the Glenn L. Martin Company, and the Boeing 314.

The American public fell in love with the Clipper flying boats. The name was chosen for its strong connections to the family of Juan Trippe. Juan had always loved anything connected to the ocean and sailing. He was nautical-minded and realized that the Pan American flying boats were the 1930s version of a fast sailing ship.

Each aircraft received a name, just as though it were a sailing ship. Trippe believed that the public would want to travel on his aircraft if each plane could be marketed as a romantic destination spot. Each individual steamship of the 1930s had a name of its own. What prevented an aircraft from being named? In addition, each name would be connected to one of the airline's faraway destination spots. The name of each aircraft became a marketing tool.

The Clipper ships of the 1800s were the fastest sailing vessels. In 1851, Clipper ships were described thus: "Such a passage as this is more than a local triumph and ensures the reputation not only of the builders of the ship and her enterprising owner, but of the United States. It is truly a national triumph and points clearly to the preeminence upon the ocean which awaits the United States of America." Juan Trippe envisioned his airline, Pan American Airways, to one day become the national airline of the United States.

(Left) "The *Yankee Clipper* Sails Again," poster of the B-314 Clipper flying over an 1840s sailing ship known as the Clipper. The Pan Am Clipper name was taken from the first sailing ships to "open the Orient."
Gordon Grant

S-38 and S-39 in flight. Two of Igor Sikorsky's early aircraft.
Igor Sikorsky Historical Archives

With short-term and long-range plans in hand, he sat down with the famous aviation engineer Igor I. Sikorsky to discuss an over-the-water passenger aircraft. Juan was methodical in his planning. He kept sensitive material in an old rolltop desk in his New York City office. First, the mail routes and passenger service to Latin America, next, a transpacific route to China, and finally, the ultimate test, a transatlantic route. The Atlantic would be tackled last in the long-range plan due to the unpredictability of the weather conditions in the Atlantic Ocean region.

Juan Trippe (left) and Charles Lindbergh in front of a Pan Am Airways Trimotor.

University of Miami, Richter Library, Pan Am Collection

In 1929, Juan Trippe contracted with Igor Sikorsky to commence the design of an enlarged four-engine version of the Sikorsky S-38. The original contract called for a four engine over-the-ocean aircraft. Two were to be designed and built for Pan American Airways at a cost of $125,000 per aircraft. Later, a third S-40 would be optioned. The S-40 became the first aircraft manufactured to the exact specifications of an airline. In the coming decades, Juan Trippe would continue to do business in this manner, tendering out the specifications for a type of aircraft and then letting the aircraft manufacturers come forward with their plans for meeting Pan American's requirements.

During the winter of 1930, Igor Sikorsky made several trips from his aircraft plant in Stratford, Connecticut, to Juan Trippe's three-room New York City office, located at 100 West 42nd Street. With the blueprints placed on a long table, four men huddled and studied the S-40 project: Juan Trippe, Igor Sikorsky, Charles Lindbergh, and Andre Priester.

Andre Priester was hired by Trippe in 1927 to become Head Chief Engineer for the company. Eventually, his role would be expanded to include all of Pan American's operations. Priester became very visible around Pan American's head office and wherever Pan American had operations. He become responsible for the specifications and design of each Pan American aircraft. He hired and fired staff. Priester reported to Trippe but was usually left alone to make major decisions.

Priester wrote the manuals, checklists, and procedures to be followed. Every pilot and employee would be required to act in the Pan American way: fly, dispatch, and maintain their airplanes in an orderly, efficient manner. Priester would become known for his "safety first" approach, and crew members were to always bear in mind the comfort of the passengers: "Handle your aircraft and regulate your flight as to accomplish maximum comfort for them and to inspire their confidence in yourself, your aircraft, and in air transportation."

Priester stressed in his aviation manual that "bumpy air is psychologically disturbing

Sikorsky S-38 in flight over College Point Harbor, 1929.

Igor Sikorsky Historical Archives

to passengers and should be avoided whenever practicable." How to accomplish the goal was spelled out in detail in the manual: by flying above clouds when they are sufficiently broken to permit glimpses of land and water; by not flying in clouds; by flying at high altitudes when smooth air can be found; by flying over the water when air is rough over land, provided a too great deviation from the regular course or too great increase of time required for the flight does not result; and give rain squalls and local disturbances a wide berth when practicable.

Also studying the S-40 blueprints and diagrams was Juan Trippe's other recruiting coup. In 1929, he had convinced Charles Lindbergh to become a consultant to Pan American Airways. After his solo flight across the Atlantic in 1927, Lindbergh had been flooded with offers to star in motion pictures, endorse many types of commercial products, and make appearances on the lecture circuit.

Lindbergh signed a four-year contract in 1929, intrigued by Juan's ideas for the future of American aviation. He would act as a consultant and receive $10,000 per year, plus options on 10,000 shares of Pan American stock at $15 per share and another 10,000 shares at $30 per share. His duties would include the surveying of new routes, contributing to the development of new aircraft, and flight-testing new aircraft.

Lindbergh wanted the S-40 to encompass the new developments in aviation in 1930. Lindbergh had envisioned a clean, sleek airframe with fully cowled engines and cantilevered wings, in one with the four engines. He was disappointed by the aircraft he referred to as a "flying forest." Ultimately, the S-40 simply resembled a four-engine version of the S-38. It was a maze of struts, flying wires, braces, and outriggers. The S-40's appearance resembled a boat hull that had been slung underneath an aircraft.

There were disagreements on the design of the S-40. Priester and Sikorsky believed that the refinements wanted and requested by Lindbergh were not yet possible. Each was costly in the amount of weight that would be created, and the four Hornet engines would simply not be able to handle such weight. Trippe was not totally satisfied, but agreed with Priester and Sikorsky. He wanted the aircraft to expand Pan American's service area and continue on the road to his long-term blueprint for the future. There was a realization that, in 1931, aircraft engines had not been designed and manufactured to handle the items Lindbergh envisioned.

Sikorsky did agree to one major alteration pointed out on the aircraft by Lindbergh. The S-40 was a flying boat outfitted with brass nuts on an aluminum framework. Salt was a maintenance problem on a flying boat. The combination of brass nuts on aluminum would result in white powder, the end product of electrolysis, forming overnight.

Other alterations were made to the cockpit. Lindbergh believed that the cockpit should be located forward, not higher as the design indicated. A high cockpit located in the center section of the wing allowed water kicked up by the propellers to fly up into the cockpit window, resulting in limited visibility.

Though designed as a flying boat, the S-40 would have landing gear. Sikorsky believed that the S-40 was designed to fly over large tracts of landmass in Latin America, so a landing-gear system would be required. It had become a critical engineering problem that no landing-gear system had been employed on such a large aircraft. Eventually, Sikorsky noticed the large gears employed on train cars, and once modified, the S-40 had a new landing-gear system.

"Aboard a Flying Clipper" – interior of the S-40. Teak paneling. Men smoking a cigarette and doing a puzzle. Little girl playing. A steward serving passengers refreshments.
Author's Collection

Aboard a "Flying Clipper Ship"

After several meetings of the Sikorsky, Priester, Trippe, and Lindbergh team, the S-40 design was compete, and in the spring of 1931, the S-40 neared completion. When it was rolled out of the large hangar, Sikorsky told his employees, "Once again, we could feel gratified in watching one more ambitious dream materialized. It was grand to stand before a nearly completed airplane, and attempt to recall the impressions created by the early ideas and sketches of the ship before it was built, or even designed."

The cabin of the S-40 had been designed to carry 40 passengers sitting four abreast in comfort. Each compartment held eight passengers with four abreast facing fore and aft and separated by a main aisle. The lounge would sit eight persons. The S-40's interior was beautiful. The walls and ceiling were made of polished walnut paneling and the lounge was finished in a very dark stain. The passenger chairs were designed in a Queen Anne style. Designed for comfort, the chairs were low and upholstered in blue and orange. Blue carpet covered the entire floor area of the passenger compartments. The rectangular windows were equipped with blinds of heavy rope and textured in gray silk with winged "S" chrome latches. There were many game tables so that the passengers could enjoy entertainment while flying. The game section included backgammon, cards, puzzles, checkers, and chess. The smokers' lounge had large ashtrays very similar to those found on ocean liners.

For safety, exposed life preservers hung in the lounge. The compartments had four handcrafted, inlaid wood pictures depicting the hunting of wild game and other stages of man's advancement through the ages. Walnut could be seen throughout the aircraft. The stewards had been provided with extra space to prepare meals and snacks.

The aircraft had a flying range of 500 miles, but would increase to 950 miles if only 24 passengers were carried. The four Hornet engines, supplying 950 horsepower, would allow the aircraft to travel at 115 miles per hour.

Once Sikorsky's Chief Test Pilot, Boris Sergievsky, had competed his test series, a few minor modifications were required. Once these modifications were completed, the S-40 was painted in the colors of Pan American Airways and turned over to Captain Basil Rowe. Rowe accepted the aircraft and flew her to Anacostia, Florida.

On Columbus Day, 1931, with Navy and Marine Corps bands playing and two national radio networks broadcasting live, the S-40 was ready for christening. After a short speech

Rollout of the first S-40 from the hangar at the Sikorsky plant in Bridgeport, Connecticut.
Igor Sikorsky Historical Archives

Mrs. Herbert Hoover christening the S-40 with water from the Seven Seas. Juan Trippe looks on. Igor Sikorsky Historical Archives

Pamphlet advertising a Pan Am air cruise to Chile. Author's Collection

by Juan Trippe, Mrs. Herbert Hoover christened the aircraft the *American Clipper*. The bottle was not filled with champagne, but Caribbean salt water.

With Charles Lindbergh at the controls on the inaugural flight, the *American Clipper* left Dinner Key, Miami, and headed for Kingston, Jamaica; Barranquilla, Colombia; and Cristobal in the Panama Canal Zone. Thirty-two passengers were on board, including Igor Sikorsky. Lindbergh and Sikorsky would sit and discuss the design for the next flying boat during overnight stops.

On the stopover at Barranquilla, the *American Clipper* almost met a disastrous fate. The tank overflowed while Lindbergh was standing on the top of the wing supervising the refueling operation. Noticing many spectators on the dock smoking, Lindbergh shouted, "Stop smoking!" The spectators complied by flicking the burning cigarettes into the water. For a few long seconds, Lindbergh held his breath. He was "Lucky Lindy" once again, as the cigarettes did not ignite the gasoline in the water and the S-40 flew on.

Financially, 1931 was a good year for Pan American Airways, as its annual profit reached $105,452 on revenue of $7,913,587. With the new S-40s, mail and passenger services were increasing. The *American Clipper* was followed by sister ships the *Caribbean Clipper* and the *Southern Clipper*. The three would fly the Central and South America routes. The S-40s would fly to Santiago, Buenos Aires, Rio de Janeiro, Bogotá, and Lima. In 1936, the aircraft were equipped with the new, more powerful Hornet TB1 engines, which allowed for 40 passengers.

The S-40 was lumbering, unattractive, and more of a transport than a passenger aircraft. Although successful, the S-40 could only fly in daylight, since it lacked navigation aids and instrumentation for night flying. The S-40 would continue to fly and service the Panama route and remain in service until scrapped during World War II. The

S-40 would be just one aircraft in the slow, methodical approach that Juan Trippe and Charles Lindbergh would employ to make the airline successful in the coming decades. Each new aircraft and route was one small part of an expanding foundation until one day the airline's name would become Pan American World Airways.

Sadly, the S-40, by 1943, could only be seen in a Miami junkyard. The hulk was the major section that remained. Gone were the days of glory and glamour. The S-40 resembled an old ship hull sitting beached, the engines and any other useful item gone. The barely visible name was fading beneath the knocked-out cockpit windows.

The S-40 was the building block that resulted in the S-42. As the story is told, the S-42 first appeared on the back of a hotel menu in Cienfuegos, Cuba. The inaugural flight of the S-40 had resulted in the design of the S-42. Over many meals on the flight, Lindbergh and Sikorsky discussed and drew up what would become the S-42. Lindbergh agreed that he would attempt to sell Trippe on the new aircraft and Sikorsky would sell the plan to United Aircraft, which was the parent company of Sikorsky Aircraft Company.

With foreign competition increasing, Trippe did not require a hard sell. He realized that the French airline Aeorpostale was flying mail from Africa to South America. The Germans were employing the *Graf Zeppelin* on a regular schedule. The *Graf Zeppelin* had made 139 trips across the Atlantic Ocean, carrying 17,591 passengers without an accident, and flew over one million miles before it was retired. Foreign aircraft were providing excellent service and luxury to their passengers, and Trippe was in competition for the Latin American trade.

Whenever a Pan Am Clipper was departing or arriving, large crowds gathered to watch at Dinner Key, Miami.

University of Miami, Richter Library, Pan Am Collection

Pan Am's competitor, British Imperial Airways flying boat *Caledonia,* over New York City.
Memorial University of Newfoundland, Centre for Newfoundland Studies, Robert Tait Collection

Germany was very much interested in the potential for large flying boats to cross the ocean. Germany saw that their flying boats, Zeppelins, had the ability to demonstrate that it was an economic, political, and technological power. The newfound ability to cross the ocean or to fly to other continents had commercial implications but also the ability to influence the destination countries politically. Latin America in the 1930s was an emerging region that Germany, France, and the United States wanted to influence through airline routes. In 1938, a German Focke-Wulf FW-200 landed at Floyd Bennett Field in New York. This milestone, an airliner able to cross the ocean from Germany without any stopovers, was the first indicator that the days of the flying boat would end in the not-too-distant future.

With the growth of Pan American Airways and aviation throughout the United States and new markets opening, other manufacturers attempted to interest Juan Trippe in their product. The Ford Motor Company in 1932 attempted to interest Pan American Airways in their version of a float plane. It was intended to be a high-speed Ford seaplane with Wasp engines. Building upon its successful Trimotor, the Ford float plane would be a more deluxe version with the ability to take off and land on water.

The flying boat was described in a letter to Juan Trippe as having the capability to fly at a cruising speed of 133 to 137 miles per hour. The flying time from Miami to San Juan, a distance of 1,180 miles, would be just over nine hours. The Ford Company believed that a float plane would be safer than a flying boat since the passenger compartments were higher in the water, and in a flying boat, the passengers would receive the impact of a crash or accident and be submerged in a matter of minutes. A float plane had the ability to stay above the water much longer.

Pan American Airways did make a test of the Ford Trimotor and found that the aircraft had excellent takeoff and landing, high maneuverability on the water, freedom from spray and water on the engines, and very good visibility for the pilot. The Ford Trimotor was not chosen by Pan American Airways, however, so Pan American could focus on flying boats.

(Above left) *Graf Zeppelin* over Biscayne Bay near Miami, Florida. The *Graf Zeppelin* and her sister ship the *Hindenburg* made regular trips to South America prior to the start of World War II.
University of Miami, Richter Library, Pan Am Collection

(Below) German Dornier Do-X in flight over Norfolk, Virginia, 1931. Greg Young Publishing

Igor Sikorsky at his desk on October 10, 1945. Model of the famous S-42 on the desk and a painting of the VS-44 on the wall. Igor Sikorsky Historical Archives

Trippe more than ever envisioned Pan American Airways as America's airline and outreach to the world. He envisioned transoceanic travel carried out by Pan American's flying merchant ships.

Pan American Airways placed an order on October 1, 1932, for three Sikorsky S-42s. This was not just any order, for Pan American specified certain customized items. Lindbergh and Trippe saw the S-42 as the next logical step in the development of a transoceanic aircraft.

The design team was put together to design, modify, and eventually build the S-42, "the next step." Added to the team of Lindbergh, Priester, and Sikorsky were individuals from United Aircraft, Pratt & Whitney, and Hamilton Standard. The team represented each component of the aircraft from fuselage to engines to propellers.

Eventually it was decided the S-42 would have four engines mounted directly onto the leading edge of the aircraft. Engine performance was increased by the addition of the new Hamilton controllable-pitch propeller. Designed by Hamilton engineer Frank Caldwell, the new propeller would allow greater control of the engines. The other advanced feature was the new design of the wing. A new long and narrow wing was developed. The new wing would result in less drag and more lift capability. Struts were still required due to the

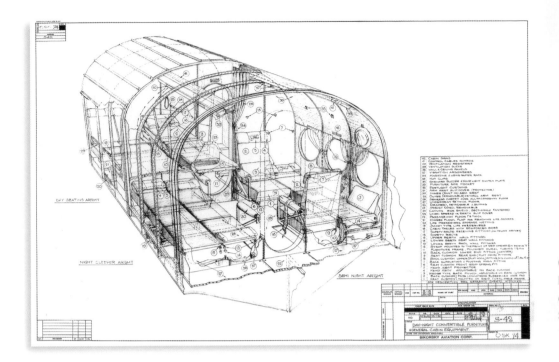

Official Sikorsky Company blueprint of the day/night convertible furniture of the S-42. Igor Sikorsky Historical Archives

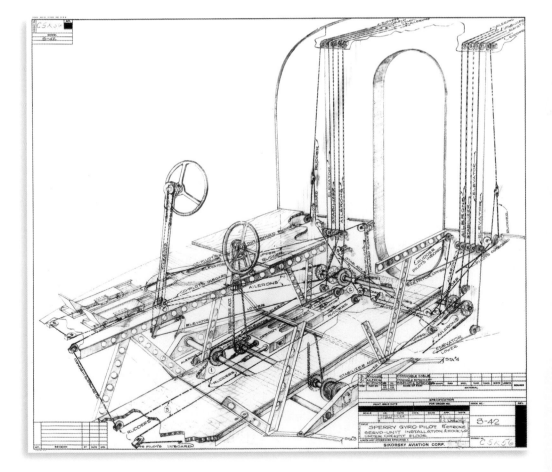

Official Sikorsky Company blueprint of the Sperry Gyro Pilot System of the S-42. Igor Sikorsky Historical Archives

length of the wing. A wing with no external bracing would be too heavy for the aircraft. Two extruded duralumin struts were placed on either side. The S-42 was not larger than the S-40, but it had cleaner lines. Gone were the ungainly tail booms and the mass web of wiring throughout the aircraft. Another important alteration, the S-42 was approximately 40 percent faster than the S-40, and with the increased speed came increased range.

The prototype of the S-42 was completed shortly after Christmas 1933. Unfortunately, a test flight could not be conducted until March 19, 1934, due to the amount of ice on the Housatonic River. Each test flight set a new record. Throughout the spring and summer of 1934, the S-40 set record after record. On April 26, the aircraft lifted over eight tons of payload and on May 17 flew to a record altitude of 20,407 feet carrying a payload of 11,023 pounds.

An astounding eight world records were set on August 1, with test pilot Boris Sergievsky, Charles Lindbergh, and Pan American Chief Pilot, Captain Edwin C. Musick, on board. A 311-mile closed course was laid out, which went from the lighthouse in Stratford, Connecticut, to the George Washington Bridge in New Jersey, over the borough of Staten Island, to Long Island, Point Judith, Rhode Island, and then back to the Stratford light-house. The S-42 began its record-setting flight at 9:24 a.m. She flew four round-trips over the course and was in the air for seven hours, 53 minutes, and 58 seconds. The S-40 put the United States into first place in the number of aviation records held. The S-42's flight on that hot summer day covered 1,242 miles. The distance from Newfoundland to the Azores was 1,240. The day of the transoceanic crossing was one step closer.

The S-42 entered service for Pan American in the fall of 1934. Flying from Dinner Key, Miami, to Buenos Aires and Brazil, she was named the *Brazilian Clipper*. Travel time was reduced from eight days to five days. The S-42s demonstrated that Pan American was now indeed America's airline.

The famous August 1, 1934, test flight with Charles Lindbergh at the controls, Test Pilot Boris Sergievsky, and Captain Edwin Musick. Records set and the distance covered would allow transoceanic travel to move one step closer. Igor Sikorsky Historical Archives

1934 delivery of the S-42 to Pan American Airways. Left to right: Captain Edwin Musick, Andre Priester, Charles Lindbergh, Juan Trippe, Igor Sikorsky, E. Vidal, and F. Nielsen.
Igor Sikorsky Historical Archives

With the S-42s entering service, Juan Trippe also placed a new order with the Glenn L. Martin Company for three M-130 flying boats. Pan American's goal of transoceanic flight continued to move closer to reality. William Stephen Grooch, the Pacific Division Chief of Operations for Pan American, asked an Englishman in mid-1933, "Would you care to make a friendly bet that we won't fly a load of mail across the Pacific two years from now?" Juan Trippe's objective was to launch a mail service to the Far East by the 100th Anniversary of the first China Clipper ship arriving in San Francisco. That meant Pan American would have to be ready by November 22, 1935.

To many, Trippe's goal was more than a dream. A flight from San Francisco to Hawaii would cover 2,402 miles. A flight to Hong Kong was a staggering 8,746 miles. In the decade before Pan American's flight, 13 fliers had perished in 12 single and mass attempts to span the long Pacific distances, many of them on the flight from California to Honolulu.

On June 26, 1931, Pan American had issued a letter to leading aircraft manufacturers with its requirements for a long-range, over-the-water aircraft. The specification list included details regarding increased load carrying, twin-row engines, cowl flaps, the galley, integral fuel tanks, a station for multiple flight crew, engine synchronizer indicators, Bowser totalizing fuel meters, propeller brakes (to stop an engine while in flight), automatic carburetors and constant speed propellers. The cost of each Martin 130 was $417,201.60. The figure included one complete flight unit (hull, engines, propellers, radio, and other equipment), but not the cost of spares.

The Martin 130s were built at the Glenn L. Martin plant in Middle River, Maryland. Work commenced in November 1932, and the keel of the first aircraft was put down in May 1933. The aircraft was designed by Martin's Chief Engineer, Lassiter Milburn; Assistant Chief Engineer and Test Pilot Ken Ebel; and Project Engineer L. D. McCarthy.

The M-130 was a high-wing monoplane flying boat with four engines. The primary function was mail and passenger travel in the Pacific region. The engines were located on

the leading edge of the wing, which was on a vertical semipylon extension above the combination hull and fuselage. A single horizontal and vertical stabilizer was employed. The M-130 had ten large windows that could be opened in flight to provide visibility for the passengers. The 90-foot hull, constructed of riveted 24 stainless aluminum, was divided into six watertight compartments. The wing was a high-wing with a cantilever construction, also constructed with 24 stainless aluminum.

The M-130 was powered by four Pratt & Whitney R-1830 radial aircooled, 4,000-horsepower engines. The cabin on the M-130 was not pressurized, but it did contain an air-conditioned system for passenger comfort. The flight bridge was equipped with dual flight controls and instruments, including a new Sperry Automatic Pilot.

On either side of the hull were two large, single sponsons, or sea wings, to provide stabilization of the craft in the water. The sponsons were employed to support the short X-shaped wing struts and provided a lift capability while the M-130 was in flight.

The cabin interior was approximately 45 feet long and was divided into cabins. Each compartment contained settees convertible to bunks.

The beautiful work on the interior of the three M-130s had been accomplished by Norman Bel Geddes. He worked with the Pan American Airways engineers and other interior experts. Mr. Bel Geddes was a former New York City theatrical set decorator of the 1920s and had become part of the Art Deco movement. He operated his own studio and was credited in some quarters for the origin of the word "streamline" in relation to industrial, architectural, and interior fashions. Bel Geddes was responsible for the M-130 furniture and bulkhead lining, designed for efficiency with zippered seams for quick removal when required. He had provided the upholstery in every compartment and area of the M-130s.

Bel Geddes was even involved in the aircraft's dinnerware. The plates and saucers had a type of vacuum bottom that allowed them to cling to the table. This was critical when the aircraft hit rough weather. Even though the flying boats were modern aircraft, none were pressurized, so the pilot was limited on how high he could take the aircraft to "climb the stairs."

Bel Geddes was hired to work his magic on the B-314. He had the experience. The less the weight the better, so his items were designed for function, but were of light-

(Top left) Side view and rear view (top right) of the M-130 under construction in the Martin Aviation Hangar. (Below left) Large photo of the M-156 in the Martin Aviation Hangar. The M-156 was a larger and more advanced aircraft, and Glenn Martin had hoped it would become the successor to the M-130. Pan American decided to purchase its next aircraft – the B-156 – from Boeing. The M-156 has the Pan American logo on the front of the aircraft, but the only M-156 ever produced was purchased by the USSR. Note the small prototype of the aircraft, built for test purposes. Film footage exists of the model being pulled through the waters of Chesapeake Bay, Maryland, at the back of a fast-moving motorboat. Martin Aviation Historical Archives

Martin M-156 in flight. It was hoped that the B-156 would win the competition for the next Pan Am Clipper, but it lost out to the B-314. Only one M-156 was constructed and completed. It was sold to the USSR.
Martin Aviation Historical Archives

weight materials. He recognized that function was most important in an aircraft with limited space.

Weight was kept down by the use of duralumin on the furniture frames and plastic rather than glass on the portholes. Plastic was very much a part of the Art Deco revolution and was employed in items from windows to radios and jewelry. The new lightweight carpet material, which controlled noise levels in the various compartments, was employed throughout the entire aircraft. Even the cushions were considered. They were made of Australian horsehair mixed with latex.

The color, or hues, inside the aircraft were very important, since many of the flights were long, and items easy on the eyes were required. Howard Ketcham, a New York City color expert, was hired. The cabin had to reflect light and yet match the other items that had been designed by Bel Geddes. If the colors were too drab and dreary, the passengers

Late 1930s ad for the Martin Aircraft Company. Author's Collection

Two photos of the interiors of the S-40 and S-42 sitting and sleeping compartments.

Igor Sikorsky Historical Archives

would feel as if in a closed space. The interior required the opposite feeling, one of openness. If the colors were too bright, one's eyes would begin to hurt on a long flight. Scientific studies were conducted on different colors and hues to find the correct combinations, and Pan American decided on a Skyline Green, Miami Sand Beige, and a semi-deep shade that was named "Pan American Blue."

On other aircraft, the windows had standard blinds, but not the B-314. Since it would be carrying the rich and famous, a more appealing window blind was required. Once again, a New York City firm was chosen: Claude D. Carver Company, located on 48th Street in Manhattan. The finished design was one of an accordion-pleated shade on rollers. It was made of washable "Tontine" and was dyed to match Ketcham's colors.

The standard compartments, or staterooms, slept six passengers during the night flight: four on the starboard side in two uppers and two lowers in cross sections to each other, and two per port side in one upper and one lower.

Like a Pullman train car, it took the stewards almost 30 minutes to change the stateroom into the sleeping rooms. The full-length privacy curtains were colored "Pan American Blue," with stitched numbers, and the airline symbol made of leather encircled each Pullman-type bed. The beds on the B-314 were larger than the Pullman beds. More room was afforded the passengers of the flying boat.

The lounge chairs were decorated with stars that made each appear to glisten. The lounge was the social gathering spot, where passengers could talk, play games, or just sit and stare out the window at the clouds or the sights below.

The lounge furniture was made to be convertible from the 11-person daytime seating arrangement into the formal 14-person dining room. It was the 24-hour gathering space. Prior to dinner, passengers could enjoy cocktails in their staterooms. Little tables were pulled out to accommodate the cocktails and hors d'oeuvres and selected drinks. When a drink was required later, there were two water fountains on board the aircraft.

The ladies' powder room was in the Art Deco style and contained a sink with hot and cold running water, two stools, and a mirror. The dressing table had a beige "Micarta"

Sleeping compartment of the Sikorsky Clippers. Double bunks and sitting area.
Igor Sikorsky Historical Archives

top with two turquoise leather-covered swivel stools. As in the men's room, four Art Deco light fixtures and two square plate mirrors were attached to the bulkheads. The receptacles for towels, tissue, and other items were also in the Art Deco style.

In the aft left corner of the powder room was a door lined with black walnut that closed off the small toilet room. The canned water for the two toilets and urinal came from used washbasin water. When the toilets were flushed, an individual cylinder filled each tank with water and flushed clear all the waste material. The waste material was dumped overboard to dissipate in the air outside the aircraft.

The aircraft contained a Bridal Suite that was often termed the "deluxe compartment." It was the lower deck's last stern cabin. The suite contained a three-cushion davenport that made up into an upper and lower berth arrangement. At each end, between the outer bulkheads, were built-in black walnut sidetables that had a lower-level shelf for magazines and books. A small love seat added the final touch to the compartment. A coffee table covered in black walnut sat in the suite. The "deluxe compartment" also had a small dressing and writing table covered with leather, a beige stool, two lights, and a mirror. A tabletop concealed a washbasin. A wardrobe was filled with hangers. At the start of World War II, this room would be filled with important military figures on their way to a conference or meeting at a distant location.

Every passenger on a Pan Am Clipper was a first-class passenger. Food preparation was a critical part of the experience of flying on a Clipper. Scene of steward serving dinner to six passengers on the Martin 130 somewhere over the Pacific Ocean. University of Miami, Richter Library, Pan Am Collection

Since the galley was a mere four feet by four feet, it required engineering to find space for the necessary items. The drip coffeemaker was positioned on the galley wall. There was a built-in, 10-inch-by-12-inch aluminum sink. Once again, economy of space reigned, and the sink was constructed of easy-to-clean material.

Below the sink was a 16-gauge aluminum icebox. To the right of the galley entrance was the combination stove and steamer for the preparation of food. The new aluminum cabinet had been designed to contain all the food necessary for one hot meal. The unit could be removed for restocking at the airport. Other special equipment included thermos jugs that had special lips and lids to prevent spills. A two-tiered dish rack had capacity for 200 fine china plates, two glass-and-cup racks, one saucer rack, eight drawers, and a slop bin for waste.

There were three steward lockers to keep passenger passports and other valuables. Another storage cabinet held ten pairs of sterling salt and pepper shakers, 350 Gorham sterling-silver flatware pieces in the "Moderen" pattern, and a silver-plated tea set. Every detail had been determined for the weight of the items and their function. The serving items numbered more than a thousand and weighed 235 pounds, while the food weighed in at 256 pounds.

Food preparation was very important, since every passenger was a first-class passenger. The galley had been designed by Norman Bel Geddes and featured overhead lighting for better visibility. The counters were covered with vinylite plastic, which made cleaning easier. Easy-to-clean linoleum replaced carpet in the galley, which made it easy to spot any food that had fallen on the floor.

The grandest and largest of the Pan American Clippers was the Boeing 314. It was not known at the time, but the Boeing 314 would mark the end of the flying boat era in American aviation. The B-314 will be remembered in aviation history for flying around the world, the first aircraft to establish regular airmail and passenger service across the Atlantic. The Boeing 314 was the last piece in Juan Trippe's goal for Pan American to provide transatlantic service to Europe. The Atlantic Ocean was the last to be tackled due to the difficult weather conditions. The B-314 *Dixie Clipper* became the first (and only) aircraft to carry a U.S. President abroad and assist him in celebrating his sixty-first birthday party while returning from a secret war-strategy meeting with Churchill, De Gaulle, and Stalin in Casablanca.

Clare Boothe Luce, the famous playwright, actress, journalist, congresswoman, ambassador to Italy, and wife of Henry Luce, publisher of *Time*, *Life* and *Fortune* magazines, wrote an article for *Life* in 1941 on flying on a B-314 across the Pacific: "Fifty years from now people will look back upon a Clipper flight today as the most romantic voyage of history." On a later trip, she would be stranded in the Azores refueling depot for ten days, waiting for calmer weather and spare parts to arrive.

According to the official history of Pan American Airways, it was recognized in 1935 that larger aircraft than the Martin 130 would be required for efficient and profitable operations. As in the past, they forwarded information and specifications to the various aircraft manufacturers to submit designs for a new aircraft. The Boeing Company responded with plans for a new aircraft, the Boeing 314. The B-314 was based on an already designed aircraft, the XB-15, which had been rejected by the U.S. Air Force.

1936 ad for Sikorsky Aircraft of passengers disembarking a Pan Am Clipper declaring, "Glorious Trip." Author's Collection

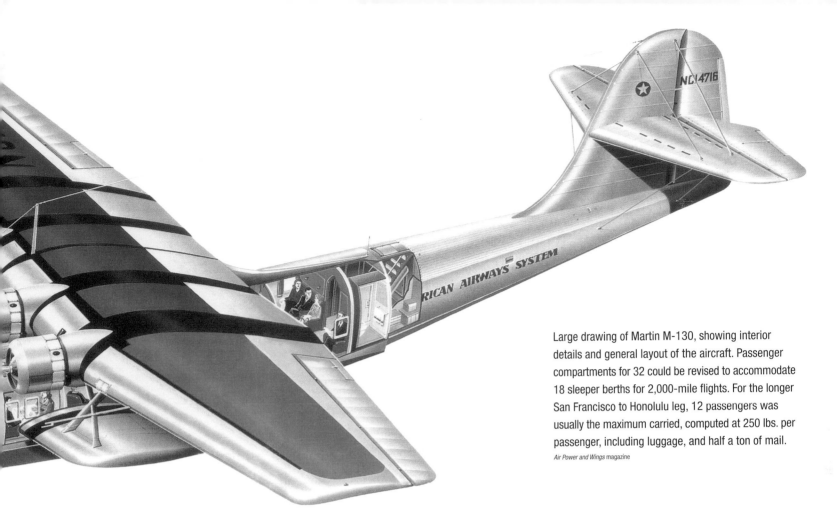

Large drawing of Martin M-130, showing interior details and general layout of the aircraft. Passenger compartments for 32 could be revised to accommodate 18 sleeper berths for 2,000-mile flights. For the longer San Francisco to Honolulu leg, 12 passengers was usually the maximum carried, computed at 250 lbs. per passenger, including luggage, and half a ton of mail.

Air Power and Wings magazine

Boeing Chief Engineer Wellwood Beall proposed to adapt the wing, nacelles, and tail of the already-designed XB-15 and convert it into an 82,500-pound aircraft, the B-314. Empty, the aircraft would weigh 40,000 pounds and would be able to carry a payload of crew, passengers, cargo, or fuel up to 42,500 pounds.

The Glenn L. Martin Company proposed a larger, modified version of the M-130, three of which were purchased by Pan American Airways. The new version, the M-156, would provide increased range and load-carrying capacity. Questions about whether the

December 1934. M-130 outside the Martin Aircraft manufacturing hangar. Aircraft is undergoing various inspections.

Martin Aviation Historical Archives

wing struts could be de-iced on the Atlantic routes became a factor. As Charles Lindbergh had emphasized to Juan Trippe after his survey flight, the Atlantic Ocean would be more difficult to span than the Pacific, due to the lack of islands to employ as landing sites and the difficult, unpredictable weather patterns of the North Atlantic.

Probably the best-designed aircraft was the Sikorsky 45. It was capable of handling a 52,000-pound useful load. The cost was more, however, and Sikorsky could not deliver the first S-45 until late 1939 or early 1940, two years later than Boeing. Trippe wanted the aircraft sooner rather than later, so Boeing won the competition.

The first contract between Boeing Aircraft of Seattle, Washington, and Pan American Airways was for six B-314s. The B-314 would be the largest flying boat until the development

One of the new Pan American Airways B-314s in the hangar under construction. (Below) The wing sections being attached on a new Pan American Clipper.

Boeing Aircraft Co., Chicago, Illinois

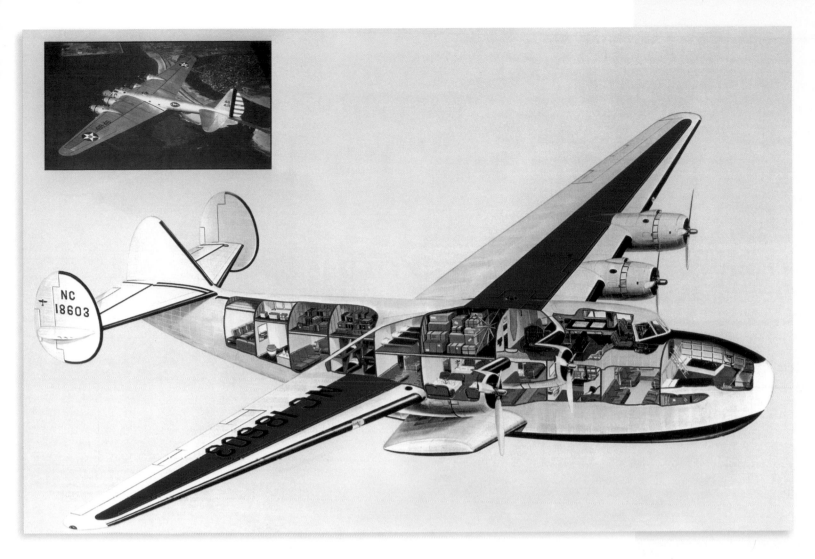

of the Martin Mars military aircraft. The contract was signed on July 21, 1936, and the first B-314 was due to be delivered on December 21, 1937.

The construction and testing of the B-314 did not advance according to plan. As passenger traffic increased on many airliners, so did the number of airplane crashes and fatalities. The public's faith in safe aircraft and travel began to be tested. The optimism of previous years was disappearing. The U.S. Government under President Franklin Roosevelt believed that government had to become more involved in the manufacture of safe aircraft and safety for the increasing flying public. In 1938, the United States Congress passed the Civil Aeronautics Act, which established a Civil Aeronautics Authority responsible for the administration of civil air operations. A Civil Aeronautics Board would authorize, approve, and regulate airline routes.

The Washington administration would have the power to review and certify each new aircraft and grant or deny a license for any type of commercial service, passenger, or cargo.

There were problems with the B-314, and the delivery dates were not met. The prototype NX-18601 was placed on the water of the Duwamish Waterway. The design of the aircraft had required 6,000 engineering drawings, 50,000 separate parts, 11.5 miles of electrical wiring, a million rivets, and 15,200 bolts. Its cantilever wing was 152 feet long.

Problems with the spark plugs produced a week's delay. On June 3, a taxiing test was aborted when it became apparent that the aircraft was too lightly loaded to withstand the sea breezes coming across the water. The sudden gust of wind lifted the wing and dipped it into the water, and Test Pilot Edmund T. Allen was forced to stop the aircraft. He tried

B-314 No. 2 being towed through the Spokane, Washington, street bridge.

Boeing Aircraft Co., Chicago, Illinois

to get the wing out of the water by gunning the four engines. When this method failed, crew members had to climb on the wing and balance the aircraft. Finally the wing was lifted from the water, but it was obvious the aircraft would require modification. As with any seagoing ship, some type of ballast would be required to keep the B-314 on an even keel.

A run across the water found that the spray from the bow of the aircraft passed cleanly underneath the sea wings and did not come over the top of the wings. This had been a problem with flying boats in the past.

A major problem was discovered in the B-314's ability to steer in flight. On the first test flight, the four powerful Wright Twin Cyclone piston engines lifted the aircraft out of the water in a mere minute. At the controls was Boeing Test Pilot Eddie Allen. When asked how the flight was progressing, Allen replied, "The plane won't turn." He continued flying a circular route and landed. Allen had kept the aircraft in the air by powering up two of the engines and powering down the other two. He was only able to fly in a horseshoe-shaped flight path. The aircraft was outfitted with a second tail in the hopes that more rudder control could be achieved. One of the tests to determine whether the problem had been solved by adding a second rudder was to open the hatch in the tail section. With the hatch wide open, Boeing Chief Engineer Beall stuck his head out, expecting to feel a massive rush of wind past his head. The wind was so little that his hair was not even mussed. A center fin was added to the twin-tail configuration and the problem was solved. Other test flights identified minor flaws that were corrected.

Trippe and Andre Priester found the B-314 to be outstanding in many critical areas:

1. Nacelle Accessibility — The rear portion of the power plant and the nacelle were made accessible in flight, as specified by Pan American's engineers for the aircraft. Many times flight engineers have feathered the propeller in flight due to power-plant

problems, and then worked and rectified the problem while flying on three engines. The nacelles were a direct inheritance from the XB-15 bomber project. The novel feature not used before or since on any U.S. military transport was the provision for in-flight maintenance. The wing was thick enough to allow a crew member to crawl to the engines and perform any required repairs or maintenance while the aircraft was in flight. The stainless steel firewall was constructed in two removable sections so that the back of the engine could be repaired while the aircraft was in flight. Each nacelle had an access door on either side for maintenance.

2. The New Engine — The B-314s had the first installation of the Wright Cyclone 14 engine. The 14 is the largest engine installed on any aircraft in commercial operation.

3. The Control Deck — A control deck was provided in the B-314, with stations and arrangements for maximum crew-operating efficiency and comfort.

4. Low Fuel Consumption — Pan American Airways was interested in the reduction of fuel consumption. The company had presented to various manufacturers the possibilities of reducing specific fuel consumption on long-range flights over water. The Cyclone 14 engines operated at the lowest specific fuel consumption of any aircraft engine in regular commercial operation at that time.

5. Hydromatic Full-Feathering Propeller — Pan American Airways fostered the design of this improvement, which combined the advantages of variable-pitch and propeller brake with less drag. Hamilton Standard hydromatic propellers were the first specified for the B-314s. The full-feathering propellers were a first on any commercial aircraft. Variable-pitch propellers had been in use for several years, but contained a flaw in the case of an engine failure. The propeller would continue to "windmill" in the air stream and damage the engine. With the full-feathering propellers, the propeller could be brought edgewise to the airframe and the propeller rotation would stop. The new system reduced the drag on the aircraft and made flying over water safer.

6. Improved Propeller Airfoil Sections — Pan American Airways was the first to employ the NACA propeller airfoil sections on air transport aircraft, installed on the B-314s in 1940.

B-314 sitting on the calm, clear blue water awaiting passengers.
Bill Thompson Collection

7. Fuel Flow Meters — Pan American sponsored the development of the first fuel meter showing rate of flow used for other-than-test purposes. The first installation of the improved design was made on the B-314s in 1939. This is now a standard instrument adopted by the airlines for all long-range air transport aircraft.

8. High-Octane Fuel — 100 octane fuel was first used in regular service on the B-314s in 1939.

9. Fireproofing — The first serious effort was made to fireproof all materials used for cabin finishing, such as upholstery, cabin wall-lining, and insulation.

10. Emergency Equipment — The B-314 set new standards for the safety of the passengers and crew members. Every standard passenger compartment had two emergency exit panels, while the deluxe compartment had one. In total, there were 15 ways to leave the aircraft in an emergency situation. All the doors on the aircraft could be opened without structurally jeopardizing the aircraft. The only exception was the fuel tank doors. Other safety equipment included eight 10-man life rafts, four of each accessible outside of the aircraft. Every passenger seat was supplied with a lifejacket and ring-type life preservers, flares, signal lights, axes, buckets, and rope. The B-314 was the first aircraft to have fireproof upholstery.

The aircraft's radio equipment was located in three different areas, and if a power failure occurred for any reason, a gas-engine generator could restore power to the radio equipment. The B-314 was a flying boat and carried a 91-pound anchor and 150 feet of rope to tie off.

11. Hydrostabilizers — Called sponsons by the Germans, hydrostabilizers were an important feature of the aircraft. Since the B-314 was a flying boat, a system to steady the aircraft in water was required. The Martin 130 had a system of sponsons, but the B-314 contained a new and improved system. The B-314 version was divided into five compartments, two of which served as fuel tanks. The new system ensured that the aircraft was steady for the passengers and crew to board. They could step onto the sponsons and then into the aircraft without fear of being pitched into the water.

12. Structure — The structure of the B-314 was entirely of metal, except for a few areas that were fabric-covered. Two fuel tanks and mail/cargo compartments were built into each side of the wing midsection. Heavy cargo could be loaded through a hatch in the center of the wing, located at the center-of-gravity point. The aircraft was described as resembling a whale.

13. Crew Accommodation — The nonstop routes flown by the B-314 were of such length that two crews were required. A shift schedule was in place, but crew accommodations were critical to the fatigue factor of the aircrew. Normal crews consisted of a pilot, copilot, navigator, radioman, flight engineer, watch officer, and two cabin attendants, the latter three positions new to the B-314. Two full crews required 16 personnel.

The pilots had a clean panel of controls. The B-314 controls included the traditional ones and several innovations. The pilot had engine, propeller, and trim tab controls to his left, while the copilot had a duplicate set of instruments on the right. The pilot employed the throttles mostly for maneuvering on the water, while the engineer was responsible for the majority of the flight, along with propeller control, fuel flow, air conditioning, and engine cowl-flap settings.

Ad for Boeing Aircraft featuring the early prototype of the B-314. In the ad the B-314 has one tail. In test flights it was found one tail made the aircraft unmanageable. A twin tail was tried next with the same results. The triple tail that became so famous was the ultimate solution.

Author's Collection

Engineering instrument of the B-314 with the engineer at the controls. Boeing Aircraft Co., Chicago, Illinois

The navigator had a large chart table, where he sat in front of the panel that controlled the navigation instruments. The B-314 had two drift sight stations for the navigator, located in the wing roots, and a celestial observation dome. The dome was situated on the aircraft's center of gravity, to ensure that minimal movement would occur in rough weather. The master had a station at the left rear of the cabin, with a large table for data and an extra chair for meetings. As on the Clipper ships of the 1800s, the master was the captain of the aircraft, but not the pilot. The aircraft contained seven canvas bunks for crew rest, three located in the cargo area and four that folded into the walls of the bulkhead.

14. Passenger Comfort — There was only one class of passenger on the B-314s: first class. For short flights, the aircraft could carry 74 passengers, and for longer flights that required overnight flying, sleeper capacity was 34.

   The passenger deck of the aircraft was divided into 11 sections: five standard compartments that could accommodate and seat ten or sleep six, one special compartment that could seat four or sleep two, and one deluxe compartment that could seat six and sleep two. There was also a dining salon that could seat 14 passengers at five tables. Once the meals were finished, the dining furniture could be moved and stowed away very quickly. It would be replaced by lounge furniture. The remaining three sections contained the galley and men's and ladies' rooms. There were three smaller lavatories located on the aircraft, and passengers were provided with hot and cold running water. An average flight required 250 pounds of food; prior to departure and at each stop, the attendants would load fresh vegetables, fruits, and meats onto the aircraft. Since this was a first class–only aircraft, cost was no object.

15. Heat and power — To operate the B-314, heat and power were drawn from the manifolds around the engine exhaust stacks. The system delivered 360,000 BTUs

Flight deck of the B-314. Pilot and copilot controls. View from the rear gives an excellent idea of the amount of visibility available to the aircraft crew.
Boeing Aircraft Co., Chicago, Illinois

per hour and a volume of 170,000 cubic feet of air per hour. A new system of carbon dioxide detection was installed for safety purposes. The C02 system had the capability to detect any leaks of exhaust gases into any part of the aircraft. Electrical power was provided through a 12/24-volt direct current system of two 15-volt generators and two 12-volt batteries.

The great depth of the hull of the B-314 allowed separate levels for crew and passengers. The upward slope of the bottom hull and the floor levels of the aft passenger compartments were raised progressively, causing the fuselage of the aircraft to resemble a whale.

While the B-314s were under construction, Pan American maintained a staff of men at the Boeing plant experienced in the maintenance and operation of large flying boats. The staff was able to assist when problems arose in the design of the new aircraft. They held expertise in the areas of control-system location, engine accessibility, feathering systems, the use of autosyn instruments and the effect of their malfunctioning on the safety and scheduled operation of the aircraft. The Pan American staff studied the problems and worked with the Boeing staff to find solutions.

Some instruments being installed had been manufactured for the Pan American company, and this included the radio equipment. When the equipment was sent to the Boeing Seattle plant, Pan American technicians were on-site to assist in the installation of the equipment.

The plane offered passengers unequaled comfort in quarters that matched any ocean liner. There were sleeping quarters, a dining salon, and even a bridal salon. Fine linen, china, and silver greeted the passengers of a Pan American Airways B-314.

The Boeing 314 was a beautiful flying boat. The aircraft was large, comfortable, and had a fantastic reliability record. At 84,000 pounds gross weight with ten degrees of flap and little or no wind, the aircraft used 3,200 feet to take off from the water. It was a majestic sight inside the aircraft or as a spectator on the water or land. The B-314 was able to become airborne in 47 seconds. At 70,000 pounds with 20 degrees of flap and a 30 knot headwind, the B-314 was airborne in a mere eight seconds. The whirling of the advanced Hamilton Standard three-bladed propellers was magnificent to observe. The propellers were 14 feet, 9 inches in diameter. The B-314 became the workhorse of the Pan American Clipper fleet and less prone to problems than the Martin 130s.

The average cost of one complete B-314 flight unit was $668,908. The six aircraft were thus worth over $4 million. Necessary spare parts came to an additional $756,450. In comparison, one complete DC-3 flight unit cost $115,000 at the time. The actual delivery of the first aircraft (NC18602) was delayed until January 27, 1939. The B-314 was the largest aircraft ever licensed by the United States Government and the first to undergo the strenuous new procedures established in 1938. Other aircraft manufacturers and airlines awaited the outcome of the licensing process. On January 25, 1937, the B-314 was approved for a certificate. And on January 27, 1937, with test pilot Earl Ferguson and Chief Engineer Wellwood Bell as copilot, the NC18602 was flown from Lake Washington to Astoria, Oregon. The aircraft was delivered to Pan American Airways in Oregon in order to avoid the tax Washington State had brought in to meet the demands of the Depression for revenue. Captains Gray and Vaughn took delivery of the aircraft and flew the first B-314 to San Francisco. Upon its arrival, Captain Tilton immediately began flights to familiarize himself with the aircraft. The remaining five aircraft were delivered at approximately monthly intervals, the last one on June 16, 1939.

NC18601 and NC18602 were assigned for the Pacific service. The other four aircraft were assigned to the Atlantic Division. By the time that the first and second B-314s were acquired by the Pacific Division in February and March 1939, a bad weather cycle was in effect and would require a concentration along with the two remaining Martin 130s to maintain the Hong Kong schedule. The Martin 130s were approaching three and a half years of flight operation and required major maintenance, including replacement of metal, skin, tubing, and wiring. In addition, the new B-314s were experiencing new aircraft problems in the areas of engine modifications and adjustments. A list of the alterations required in the B-314s and in their engines would fill several pages. From March 1939 to July 1940, the Boeings were not able to perform their full share of the scheduled weekly trips to Hong Kong and could not perform additional service to Honolulu.

Pan American had an option with Boeing to purchase additional B-314s. The option had been exercised by October 1, 1939. Another six B-314s with spare parts and engines were equivalent to 40 DC-3s. Two days before the deadline, Pan American Airways agreed to purchase another six B-314As. Pan American's engineers believed that the first year's problems with the six B-314s had been solved and the second six should not be as difficult to operate.

The six B-341s would have many improvements:
1. The takeoff gross weight was increased from 82,500 pounds to 84,000 pounds. After reinforcements were installed, this alteration was made on the six B-314s.
2. The Wright Cyclone AC1 engines were installed. The AC1 had an improved operation.
3. Fuel capacity was increased to 5,448 gallons. Experience had demonstrated that for long forecasts during the winter months, the original fuel capacity of 4,200 gallons was insufficient. The enlarged capacity was also accomplished for the B-314s through modification.

4. The oil capacity was decreased from 300 gallons to 206 gallons, and the "hopper" oil tanks were installed in place of the original plain tanks. This alteration permitted quicker engine starting in cold weather and also permitted carrying smaller oil loads, thus improving the size of payloads.

NX18601 to become the *Honolulu Clipper* sitting on the water. The water reflects the grandeur of the aircraft.
Boeing Aircraft Co., Chicago, Illinois

The final cost of each B-314A was $800,000 per flight unit, exceeding the cost of the B-314 by approximately $131,000 per flight unit. In ordering the six new aircraft, Pan American Airways assumed a total financial commitment in excess of $5 million. There was a major problem with the six new aircraft: where should they be assigned? The plan would be to assign six to the Pacific Division and six to the Atlantic Division and retire the remaining two Martin 130s.

On December 9, 1937, Pan American Airways forwarded a request for bids to eight airplane manufacturers for the design of a new four-engine land-based aircraft. The aircraft would need a payload of 25,000 pounds, a cruising speed of 200 miles per hour at sea level, and a range of 5,000 miles. The aircraft would also require a pressurized cabin, a stateroom, and accommodation for at least 100 passengers and a crew of 16, with dressing rooms, a dining room, and a galley with adequate facilities for the preparation and storage of food. None of the aircraft manufacturers contacted could meet the specifications.

On January 10, 1940, Pan American Airways once again requested interested aircraft companies to provide information on a new aircraft. It would require a payload of 17,500 pounds, be capable of flying 5,000 statute miles in still air at any altitude between sea level and 25,200 feet when operated at minimum cruising speeds ranging from 225 miles per hour at sea level to 337 miles per hour at 25,200 feet. The aircraft would have sleeping accommodations for at least 50 passengers and crew accommodations for a crew of 12. The Pan American communication offered $50,000 to the manufacturer submitting the most satisfactory proposal for such an aircraft, incorporating guaranteed performance and weights conforming to the requirements. The request did not state whether the aircraft was to be a flying boat or land-based aircraft.

The request did indicate that the aircraft would be employed for flights to Europe and from San Francisco to Honolulu. A plan to purchase 11 long-distance land-based Lockheed Constellation aircraft was approved by the Pan American Airways Board of Directors in October 1940. The new aircraft would be assigned to the Pacific Division and replace all other aircraft in the area. The Constellations would fly two daily schedules between California and Honolulu and maintain twice-weekly service between California and Hong Kong, and California and Australasia. The Constellations were to be delivered from June to October in 1942 and June 1943.

World War II would interfere and disrupt the plans of Juan Trippe and Pan American Airways. After the attack on Pearl Harbor, Pan American relinquished its rights to its aircraft to the Army. Earlier, Pan American Airways had agreed to sell three B-314s, the NC18607, NC18608, and NC18610 to the British Purchasing Commission on August 29, 1940. The British Government required a long-range, over-water capability for rapid communications to the United States and Africa.

THE FORGOTTEN BABY CLIPPERS

The S-43s, the "Baby Clippers," were commissioned by Juan Trippe in 1934. The twin-engine, 18-passenger Baby Clipper amphibians were designed for coastal and other routes in the Caribbean and Latin America.

The S-43 began its flight testing on June 5, 1935, at the Bridgeport Sikorsky plant. The aircraft immediately set four world altitude records with zero payload, 500 kilograms, 1,000 kilograms, and 2,000 kilograms. The first S-43 Baby Clipper was ferried to Miami on April 3, 1936, by Captain Swinson. The Baby Clippers entered service in May on the Caribbean routes, landing at both sea and land airports. Unlike the larger Clippers, the Baby Clippers had landing wheels as well as pontoons.

The S-43s were employed on the smaller routes and to act as some of the first feeder planes, carrying passengers who transferred to a larger aircraft to continue their journey.

The S-43 could accommodate 25 passengers, with a crew of two or three and a range of 775 miles. S-43s were sold to Chile, China, France, Russia, and Norway. The largest purchaser was Pan American Airways.

Again SIKORSKY *pioneers*

Far up in the northwest, Pan American Airways is forging an important new link in the world's chain of air line systems. Connecting Seattle with Juneau, the new route will complete the airway map from Nome to Buenos Aires!

For its 1,000 mile survey flights over water and rugged terrain, Pan American has chosen the versatile Sikorsky S-43. Once again Sikorsky pioneers!

S I K O R S K Y

BRIDGEPORT, CONNECTICUT

ONE OF THE FOUR DIVISIONS OF UNITED AIRCRAFT CORPORATION

OCTOBER 1938

CHAPTER 3

PLOTTING THE AIR ROUTES:

Latin America, The Pacific, and the Atlantic Survey Flights for Bases for the Clippers

As Pan American Airways grew rapidly with several lucrative airmail contracts in the late 1920s, Juan Trippe recognized that further expansion, especially into passenger air service, would require an infrastructure. His long-range goal was to provide extensive mail and passenger service first to Latin America, then expand to the West Coast and across the Pacific to open the door to the Orient, and then finally reach for the ultimate goal, Europe.

Central and South America became the testing ground for Pan American's development of the vast infrastructure that was required to transform itself into an efficient airline. Juan Trippe was not only a master at administration and public relations, but also realized that becoming a worldwide airline required smaller steps to reach the ultimate goal. Aviation was still in its infancy, and it had to be demonstrated to the public that safety was of the utmost in the plan for passenger travel.

In the early 1930s, few airports had ever been constructed in the tropics, and little was known of the conditions that would be encountered. Locations had to be determined by aerial surveys and ground exploration teams. Neither was an easy task, and each involved its own set of problems, new and unique problems that had never been encountered nor conquered in the past.

Construction parties at each airport had to live off the land until an air service for additional supplies was established. Heat and humidity, not only drained the strength of the engineers and workers, but also caused problems with the operation of equipment. Transportation of material and supplies was a major part of the project. Roads had to be built, since the areas were largely barren. If river transportation was available, it made the construction easier, but this was not always the case. San Juan, Puerto Rico, illustrated the problems in building an airport: the area was bottomless mud and required laying down layers and layers of gravel and cordwood.

In designing and formulating plans for the development of services in the Caribbean and down the east coast of South America, Pan American had to develop land plane and flying boat operation. In the late 1920s, there were no land airports between San Juan and Natal in Brazil. Between San Juan and Belem, there were no roads or even a railroad available. Coastal steamer was the only travel option. Construction of an airfield was not a good financial investment, with only two or three trips a week. Pan American Airways

April 16, 1935, survey flight to Hawaii of the specially designed S-42, NR823M as a long range survey aircraft. Under the command of Pan Am Chief Pilot Captain Edwin Musick. Photo taken from the chase aircraft.
Clyde Sunderland, Pacific Aerial Surveys, HJW Geospatial Inc.

did recognize that in this instance, an excellent opportunity existed for flying boats. The route was ideal, the coastline was flat, and there were many rivers and inlets that could be employed if a flying boat had to make an emergency landing. This was not the case for land planes, as the only available landing area was filled with trees and dense vegetation.

By offering flying boat travel, Pan American was able to not only create an attractive opportunity for passenger flights but also open the door for cargo to be delivered to remote areas. Pan American was able to provide more direct access for its customers than the competition. At overnight Brazilian stops of Belem, Fortaleza, and Rio de Janeiro, shore facilities were constructed so that regular maintenance could be accomplished. By the end of 1929, Pan American Airways was involved in the operation of a growing network of airports and seaports. By 1930, there were 29 airports and 26 marine bases. Some of the marine bases were actually barges in the middle of the waterway. Passengers were transported by a smaller boat to land. If a storm was on the horizon, a barge could be towed to a closer, more sheltered part of the river or waterway. This type of arrangement would become the model for Pan American Airway operations in the Pacific in the mid-1930s.

Airports and seaports were only one part of the advancement of infrastructure that was required for the operation of both land planes and flying boats. Pan American Airways became the pioneer that other airlines looked to for answers. The next problem to be resolved was the lack of radio and meteorological facilities. Aircraft had difficulty in receiving radio communications on weather conditions due to the lack of communication equipment and the crude weather forecasting system.

Front cover of a Pan Am booklet showing an M-130 in flight. Cruises on an aircraft instead of a ship were in keeping with the Juan Trippe family tradition of connecting their mid-1800 history with the present age of flying. Author's Collection

Back cover of booklet with route map, aircraft, and crew. Some booklets presented to passengers even had a section for the crew to autograph. The passenger would have a permanent souvenir of their trip. Author's Collection

S-42 in flight over South America.

University of Miami, Richter Library, Pan Am Collection

The U.S. Government, beginning in 1927, began to spend large sums of money on the installation of radio range facilities in the United States, but the development of aircraft communications did not keep pace, and very few new airlines utilized the new systems. One positive trend, however, was in the field of weather forecasting, where the U.S. Weather Bureau had developed an excellent system of facilities across the United States to assist aviators.

No such organized systems of weather forecasting, communications, and navigation existed in Latin America. Many of the flying areas of Latin America were dangerous, due to high mountains, sparsely populated areas, and flight paths that crossed large bodies of water and jungles. It was critical that a pilot have information on what conditions awaited ahead and even the correct position of the aircraft at any given time. Thunderstorms could develop quickly in the hot, steamy tropics. Governments did not provide funds to establish weather, navigation, and communication systems due to the cost and the relatively small number of aircraft flights.

Pan American set out to find the answers to these major problems that affected the expansion of the airline in the late 1920s. Pan American Airways retained radio experts at the famous Radio Corporation of America and made engineering layouts for radio equipment. After the new aircraft arrived at Key West, Florida, 10-watt and 100-watt transmitting equipment and radio receivers were installed and tested in the summer of 1928. The extensive program resulted in many critical conclusions:

1. Conventional radio equipment was soon destroyed by the excessive humidity of the tropics. New protective methods and designs had to be developed.
2. The static conditions of the tropics are among the worst in the world, particularly from May to November, and the useful range of all equipment is substantially reduced.
3. Ocean and jungles increased the distance between ground stations and necessitated instruments of increased sensitivity.

The main conclusions resulted in the placing of radio operators on all aircraft. Radio telegraph would be employed instead of radio telephone for communications. Specifications were drawn up to submit to manufacturers of 100-watt tuned radio frequency transmitters and receivers. Pan American found the new radios still not up to its standards after testing and decided that to ensure adequate equipment, it would have to produce its own aircraft radio. The manufacture began in March 1929, and by July of the same year, every aircraft operated by Pan American was fitted with communication equipment consisting of a 10-watt master oscillator power amplifier transmitter and a regenerative receiver that performed satisfactorily. Since 1929, Pan American has always operated aircraft with adequate communication equipment.

Ground communication equipment was another critical component to the operation of a bigger and safer airline system. Pan American proceeded with the construction of a number of 200- and 300-watt transmitters. The 350-watt ET 3666 ground transmitter and the 1496 ground receiver were ordered from a manufacturer but could not be delivered to Pan American until 1930. The newly constructed company receivers failed quickly due to the humid tropical conditions.

Early in 1929, radio stations were constructed in Miami; Havana; Camagüey, Cuba; Santiago; Port-au-Prince; Ciudad Trujillo, Dominican Republic; and San Juan. Facilities were created later in the same year between Brownsville and Guatemala, Guatemala and the Canal Zone, and San Juan and Paramaribo. By the end of 1930, the Pan American Airway system had 36 radio stations in operation in Latin America.

Each radio station in Latin America was equipped for weather observation purposes from the date of installation.

Poster of the S-42, NC822M *Brazilian Clipper* in flight over Miami, Florida. Either inward or outward bound from the Dinner Key Terminal.
Greg Young Publishing

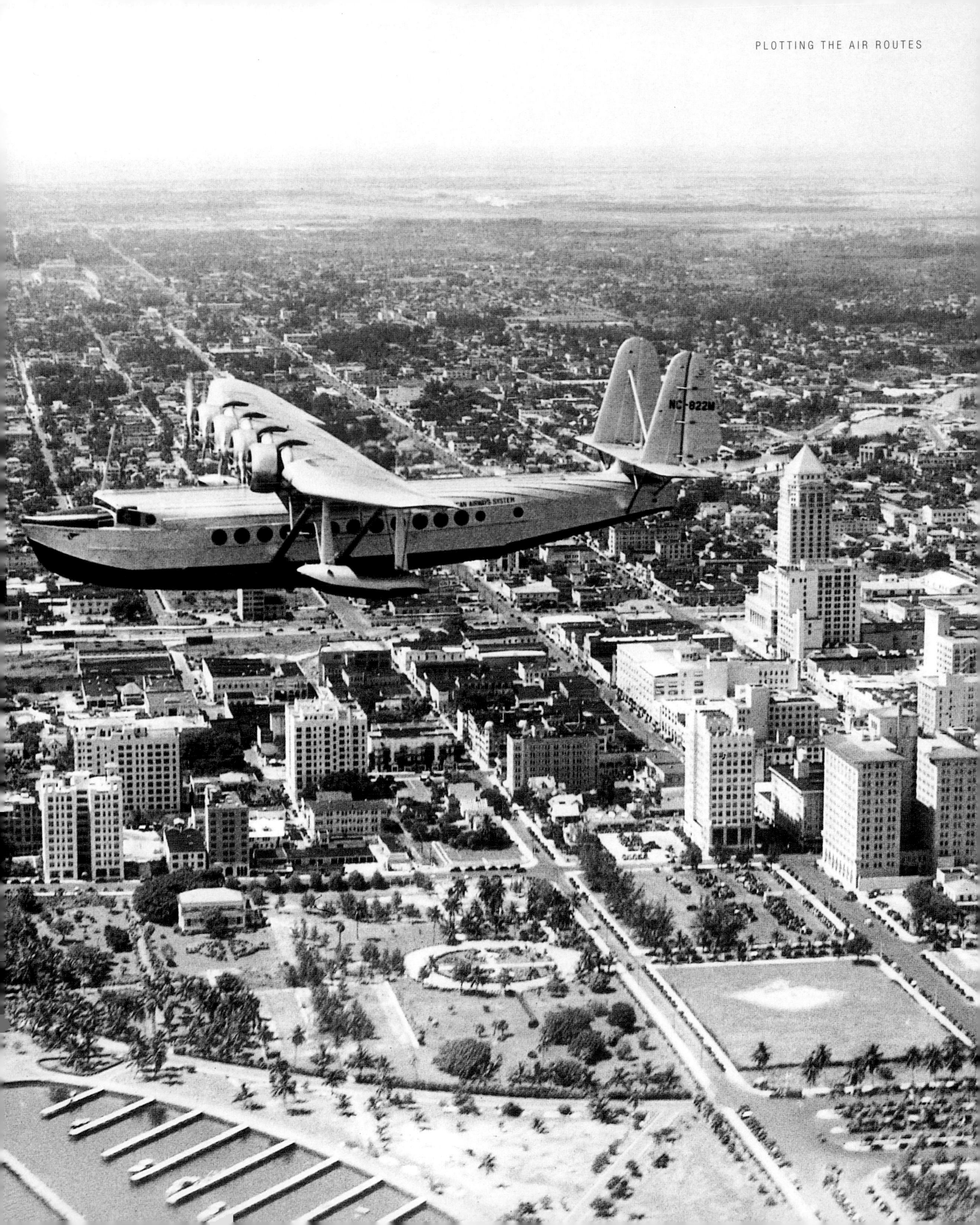
NC-822M

FOR ONLY 30
Travel Enthusiasts

"Brazilian Clipper"—America's largest and most luxurious airliner.

AROUND SOUTH AMERICA

. . . by air and ocean liner . . . 17,000 miles . . . 6 weeks . . ,
21 different countries and islands . . . $1,200 . . . all expenses

AT Miami, board the new giant "Brazilian Clipper" that broke ten world's records; America's largest and most luxurious airliner. Fly in 7 half-day jaunts clear down to Rio de Janeiro. Luxurious lounges and spacious aisles in which to stretch your legs en route. Attentive steward service. Afternoons and evenings free for sightseeing. Sleep ashore each night at world-famous hotels. Cruises accompanied by an experienced cruise director.

From Rio to Montevideo and Buenos Aires by steamer. Then take wings again in a multi-motored Pan American airliner across the towering Andes, "Roof of the World," to Chile. Finally,

"Clipper Cruises" leave N. Y. via Havana Special Sept. 11, Oct. 9, Nov. 6

start homeward-bound on a luxurious Grace Line steamer. For those who wish—an attractive air trip to Cuzco—Land of the Incas.

That, in a few words, gives you an inkling of what this newest innovation in cruises offers.

For complete details, itineraries, apply to the travel agent who sent you this magazine or any office of Thos. Cook & Sons—Wagons Lits, Inc.

PAN AMERICAN AIRWAYS SYSTEM

Reservation and Information Offices:

122 East 42nd Street, New York   Washington   Miami   Tampa
Brownsville   El Paso   Nogales   Los Angeles

In the early years, the equipment was used for surface observations and included a barograph, rain gauge, maximum and minimum thermometers, wind speed, and wind direction indicators and a psychrometer.

A ground loop direction finder was installed at Key West in 1928. Two marine ground loop direction finders were ordered from the manufacturer and installed in Miami and Port-au-Prince in 1929. The next one was installed at Cozumel, and over time, direction finders were installed throughout Latin America and continually updated. By the end of 1930, Pan American Airways Inc. had extended its routes throughout the Caribbean and almost all of South America. Flights were operating on schedules and covering over 13,000 miles of routes. Pan American Airways had flown 7,840,522 passenger miles with only a single fatality.

The management of the company believed not only that maintenance staff should be well trained, but that this should extend to each employee involved in the flight operation of the company's aircraft. As early as 1927, Pan American established a basic in-air transportation policy that included the following:

1. No aircraft may depart without a satisfactory weather report being available to the pilot and to the airport manager.
2. The airport manager at the port of destination may refuse clearance to the aircraft if conditions at that port are forecast by him to be unsatisfactory at the time of arrival.
3. No pilot can be ordered to depart if, in his judgement, conditions of weather or equipment are unsatisfactory for the flight.
4. No pilot may depart unless the airport manager agrees that both weather and equipment are satisfactory for the flight.
5. Weather conditions prevailing must be as good as or better than the minimum established for the port.
6. The load carried must not exceed that listed in the company load figures for the aircraft.
7. Engines are to be tested at the end of the runway prior to takeoff.

Gross weight on all aircraft was limited to a weight that would permit safe operation with one engine inoperative. Pan American was the first to limit the amount of flight time of pilots to a maximum number of hours per year. Regular schedules were established for the training of pilot personnel. On December 6, 1929, Pan American placed the first fully equipped instrument flight-training plane in service.

The original group of pilots recruited by Pan American had experienced the terrible conditions of World War I. The early pioneers were employed for their skills and experience in the early days of aviation. As the types of aircraft expanded and became larger and more complicated, a younger group of pilots was recruited. The 1920s and 1930s witnessed the development of many programs and technical instruction schools to assist with the professional training in the expanding new world of aviation.

One of the other strict criteria established was an iron-clad rule that developed on the first mail flight from Key West to Havana on October 28, 1927. One pilot and

1930s Pan Am booklet featuring the S-42 arriving at Havana, Cuba. Author's Collection

(Opposite) 1930s ad for Pan American Airways. A Clipper flight around South America, but one had to move fast since only 30 seats were available. Author's Collection

Passengers boarding an early pre-Clipper aircraft for the trip from Miami or Key West, Florida, to Havana, Cuba. Trimotors were the aircraft in vogue in the late 1920s. Note the U.S. Mail insignia on the nose of the aircraft. Early passenger aviation owes its existence to the transportation of the mail.

University of Miami, Richter Library, Pan Am Collection

30 million pieces of mail that had arrived by train were waiting on the dock. The weight of the mail was so heavy that the pilot, Cy Caldwell, had to leave his copilot on the dock. The rule that no passengers were allowed on a Pan American flight until it was deemed safe was thus created. No paying passengers were allowed on the Key West flight to Havana until January 26, 1928.

The new age of international travel did present other new problems, including the documentation and clearance of passengers. There were customs and immigration requirements. Pan American became a leader in assisting to overcome these major difficulties and create a smoothly operating travel system where passengers and cargo moved efficiently and quickly to the destination. Pan American arranged with most Latin American nations to allow U.S. citizens the right of transit without visa. As early as 1928, flight stewards met passengers at hotels and railroad stations and accompanied them to the airport. The stewards would check and scrutinize travel documents. Passengers were greeted at the airport by the passenger service representative, who assisted with inbound and outbound requirements and even forwarded messages. Gateway time was reduced to three minutes, and travel became an enjoyable experience.

In the late 1920s and early 1930s, 74 percent of passengers were traveling on business. Pan American Airways fostered greater communication and cooperation between the United States and Latin America. With Pan American's large system of weather stations, the company assisted in dealing with natural disasters. The vast network of radio and meteorological stations provided forecasts of approaching hurricanes, which allowed

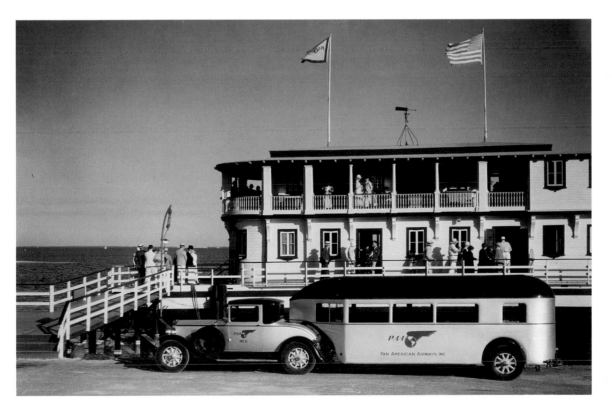

Early photo of an S-40 at the floating terminal. This predates the construction of the Dinner Key Terminal, which was dedicated on March 25, 1934. The terminal had cost $300,000 to construct and became the finest marine terminal in the world. (Below) Pan Am car and passenger trailer that operated to transport passengers to and from the floating marine terminal.

communities to prepare for the event. A good-neighbor environment was created thanks to Pan American's method of operation.

Pan American signed a contract to construct a new terminal at Dinner Key, Miami, in 1933. The new facility became the international marine base for Pan American's new flying boats. The facility was constructed at Pan American's own expense at a final cost of $300,000, which was for the terminal and did not include the cost of the land, roadways, and other services. The Dinner Key Terminal would become a major tourist attraction. Whenever a Pan American Clipper was due to depart or arrive, the area would fill with automobiles and spectators wanting to get a glimpse of the flying boats. By the end of 1934, the Latin American services encompassed 103 land airports and 56 seaports.

Establishment of radio and meteorological facilities throughout Latin American was another critical ingredient of the infrastructure system. In 1933, Pan American developed the ATM aircraft receiver, which was installed on each aircraft for its greater efficiency, reliability, and weight. The direction finders aboard the aircraft were supplemented by a system of ground station direction-finding equipment wherever this was considered to be necessary. Constant improvements were undertaken in the area of direction finders and a new and improved model of the Adcock direction finder. The Adcock had been developed by the British during World War I and was perfected and patented by Pan American in 1934. The newly patented equipment was tested and used to a limited extent in Latin America. It would find its greatest usefulness on the ocean divisions, where it would play a vital role in the inauguration of the transoceanic services, in addition to assisting aircraft of the United States Armed Forces before and during World War II.

As 1934 ended, Pan American had in operation 69 radio ground stations in Latin America. To better forecast the tropical conditions of Latin America, Pan American developed several upper-air meteorological stations to record the upper-air characteristics. In subsequent years, the system was expanded to include more sophisticated systems that would assist in determining the most advantageous flight level and course to obtain the most favorable winds and flying conditions.

The experience and the methods developed provided vast knowledge and a database that would enhance transoceanic flight operations. From the experience in Latin America, Pan American was able to train new personnel in weather forecasting and develop techniques to analyze not just monthly or daily weather patterns, but chart trends over a number of years.

Survey flights were of key importance for early aviation and the establishment of air service. According to Trippe, "The importance of tests and survey flights, as regards aircraft, instruments, and procedures was fully realized when the transpacific was placed on agenda of things to come."

An infrastructure was required, but even with the construction of more hard runways and flights across the water, Trippe recognized survey flights were still required. He would encourage a direct, hands-on approach to surveying the Latin America area for bases. Trippe would employ both Charles Lindbergh and his wife, Anne Morrow, an accomplished navigator/radio operator in her own right, for several major survey flights.

In the spring of 1929, Charles Lindbergh and Anne Morrow were married. Her father was the U.S. ambassador to Mexico. A late honeymoon was celebrated in September 1929,

Booklet advertising Pan Am Clippers and romantic destinations.

Author's Collection

when Lindbergh inaugurated the new airmail route from Miami to Dutch Guiana. Lindbergh and his new wife were accompanied on the flight by Juan and Betty Trippe. The four departed from Dinner Key, Miami, with fanfare, a cheering crowd, and roses. The trip lasted three weeks and covered over 7,000 miles.

Charles Lindbergh at the controls of the S-42 on a test flight. Igor Sikorsky Historical Archives

The trip was officially to deliver mail, but in reality it was much more. Trippe and Lindbergh were scouting for new areas to not only deliver the mail, but also introduce passenger travel. Pan American needed new routes to grow, and every stop along the journey was analyzed for marketing purposes. Discussions were held with the government leaders of each country to discuss future routes and what concessions could be provided to the new, growing Pan American Airways. Juan Trippe was the master tactician and recognized at every stop where the real power was centered. Deals were arranged for future expansion.

On one part of the trip, Lindbergh reached back to his old days of flying the mail and showing off his skills. He climbed through the hatch of the S-38 and onto the bow of the aircraft to take photographs. At 1,500 feet, he began to snap pictures of the scenery below.

The three-week trip had cemented the friendship that would last a lifetime for the Lindbergh and Trippe families. For Pan American Airways, it provided the structure to move forward into the lucrative areas of Latin America. When Lindbergh was part of the America First Movement in the 1930s, Trippe was prevented from bringing him into Pan American Airways at a higher organizational level. The American public was divided on whether to go to war over Hitler's expansion in Europe. The tone of Lindbergh's speech

Mrs. Anne Lindbergh laughing with a gentleman in Finland, one of the stopovers in their Atlantic survey flight for Pan Am. Mrs. Lindbergh appears to be wearing a Canadian Hudson's Bay coat.

University of Miami, Richter Library, Pan Am Collection

(Opposite) Side view of the Lockheed Sirius float plane. Charles Lindbergh on the wing and his wife Anne in the rear cockpit. Mrs. Lindbergh traveled as Charles', radio operator/ navigator. She came up with the idea for a canopy to reduce the weather and noise of the aircraft. (Below) Rear view of Charles and Anne and technicians attending the Sirius aircraft. Both Charles and Anne wearing the famous leather aviation cap of the period.

University of Miami, Richter Library, Pan Am Collection

indicated to President Roosevelt and others that Lindbergh was sympathetic to the Germans. After World War II, Lindbergh became a director of Pan American Airways, and while serving Pan American World Airways, he opposed the purchase of passenger jet aircraft. Lindbergh had come to believe that the environment required protection. In his later years, he moved to Hawaii and kept out of the public's eye. He was ultimately the victim of his own fame, achieving much, but also suffering a great deal: "My experience has been that the press, and this pretty much includes television and radio, confuses and cheapens everything it touches." His tombstone is inscribed with the phrase "If I take the wings of the morning, and dwell in the uttermost parts of the seas."

If Trippe was Pan American's visionary, then Lindbergh was the trailblazer. Both men enjoyed their roles. In 1931, Charles and Anne departed in their Lockheed Model 8 Sirius

1935 scene of an S-40 arriving at the Dinner Key
Terminal. Clear, bright day. Onlookers line the
observation deck of the terminal.

University of Miami, Richter Library, Pan Am Collection

float plane for a trip to map out routes to Asia. The registration number was NR211, the same number as the *Spirit of St. Louis*. The cockpit had been modified on Anne's recommendation. The aircraft had an open cockpit, and she recommended it include sliding canopies. This would assist in allowing a better environment in rough, cold weather. The flight was the first from west to east by way of the Great Circle route. It had been outfitted with special gas tanks to increase the aircraft's range. The natives called it *Tingmissartoq*: "He who flies like a big bird."

The couple departed from New York, and the journey was planned to head north into Canada and across into Alaska, Russia, Japan, and China. The Sirius landed at North Haven, Ottawa, Moose Factory, Churchill, Baker Lake, Aklavik, Point Barrow, Shishmaref, Nome, Karaginski Island, Petropavlovsk, Ketoi Island, Shana, Kunashiri Island, Nemura, Tokyo, Osaka, Fukuoka, Nanking and Hankow.

Two routes to the Orient were studied in detail by Trippe and his group of experts. Originally, it was felt that the northern route through Alaska was the most logical choice. There were problems that Lindbergh had stressed after his 1931 flight, fog and weather conditions that were less than ideal. There were also political concerns that needed to be addressed; some of the route flew over the Soviet Union and Japan. Tensions were developing with Japan over almost every major issue. The Japanese were intent upon expansion for raw materials. With relations at a low ebb, approval for routes over even Japan might not have been possible. The second option involved island hopping. Pan American could construct infrastructure and utilize hotels on the various Pacific islands controlled by the U.S. Government.

Eventually, Pan American would settle on the route to the Orient by way of the Pacific Ocean, and island bases would be constructed to allow stopovers. Trippe would determine that island hopping was the cheapest and most efficient way to reach the Orient. San Francisco would be chosen as the West Coast hub. Los Angeles was considered, but San Francisco was closer in distance to Hawaii.

The two long-distance survey flights undertaken by the Lindberghs were the first long transoceanic flights for a private airline interested in extending its routes. Work on the route survey commenced in 1932, and for three years, various flights were undertaken to chart distances and determine locations for bases and radio facilities to provide weather and navigation information, the infrastructure that would be so critical to the operation of an airline, and to provide safety for the flying public.

Trippe did not give up on the idea of a northern route in the future. He cemented the possibility by purchasing airlines in Alaska, for he still believed that one day there would be flight across the Arctic Circle.

Pan American's legal team gathered information on the implications of constructing

Mid-1930s ad with the new Pacific destination map of Pan Am, "It's a Smaller World Than Ever Now." As Pan Am increased the range of its destinations, new advertising appeared to build upon that fact. Author's Collection

THIS GLOBE OF THE EARTH—

is steel; weight 3¼ tons;
diameter 10 feet; circumference 31 feet, 5 inches.

Shows airlines of the world, in addition to chief geographical features, including ocean depths.

The globe is oriented so that its axis parallels the axis of the earth underfoot, its North Pole pointing to the North Star.

On this scale (1 inch to 64 miles) the greatest ocean depth, 34,218 feet just east of the Philippines - would be only ⅒ of an inch below the surface of this ball, showing that, compared with the bulk of the earth, the great oceans are relatively only a thin covering of water.

The deepest man has gone beneath the surface of the earth (William Beebe, who descended 2,200 feet into the ocean at Bermuda) would on this scale be scarcely through the paint - ⅟₁₅₀ of an inch down.

The highest man has ascended off the earth (Captain Albert W. Stevens, 14 miles) would be but ¼ of an inch off the surface of this globe.

The world's highest mountain (Mt. Everest in the Himalayas, 29,141 feet) would project less than ⅒ of an inch from this globe's surface.

All the people in the world, packed into a box, could on this scale be contained in a case less than ⅟₁₀₀ of an inch each way in size.

PAN AMERICAN
PAA AIRWAYS SYSTEM

The Globe of the Earth. The large globe that was situated in the center of the Dinner Key Terminal in Miami. With the closing of the terminal in the early 1950s, the globe was stored in a warehouse. Today it resides at the Miami Museum of Science, although it has been updated to include present world features.

University of Miami, Richter Library, Pan Am Collection

bases on the islands. The team certified that Midway Island, lying 1,300 miles northwest of Honolulu, was American territory. They were satisfied that Wake Island, lying 1,185 miles west of Midway and 1,508 miles east of Guam, was American territory. The charts indicated that Wake Island was a typical coral atoll. A third island was required and critical to the plan to establish island-hopping bases. Guam was chosen and was American territory. All three islands were administered by the United States Navy Department. Permits were issued to Pan American Airways to construct facilities and operate an over-the-ocean airline on March 12, 1935. As Pan American began to plan construction, the U.S. military was moving forward with its own plans to fortify the islands.

Trippe began to explore the routes along the Atlantic Ocean in 1931, with the eventual goal of flying across the Atlantic to Europe. As 1932 dawned, he worked out an agreement with the Danish Government to conduct surveys and was granted permission to land in Greenland. At the same time, he purchased the 75-year landing rights in Iceland from Transamerican Airlines Inc.

Charles Lindbergh and Anne Morrow were requested to undertake an Atlantic survey in the same manner as the northern survey of 1931. Employing the same Lockheed Sirius float plane, the couple left New York on July 9, 1933. One new modification to the aircraft was to equip it with the latest Pan American long-distance radio. The public could keep abreast of the exploits of Lucky Lindy through the newspapers, radio, and the local movie theater newsreel. The newsreel of the week of July 9 featured the opening headline, "Lindberghs Fly North on Epic Ocean Trip to Blaze New Air Route." It continued,

"North Beach, New York: taking off from the waters of Bowery Bay the Flying Colonel and his wife are seen in unusual pictures on the start of their flight to Greenland to survey a route across the North Atlantic for Pan American Airways." The first stops were Halifax, Nova Scotia; St. John's, Newfoundland; Cartwright and Hopedale, Labrador, and several stops in Greenland. In Greenland, the Lindberghs were met by the SS *Jelling*, which served as a floating base camp.

The remainder of the trip carried them to Iceland, the Faroe Islands, and Copenhagen, Denmark. From Denmark, the couple visited Sweden, Finland, the USSR, and Norway, then on to Southampton, England; Galway Bay, Ireland; Inverness, Scotland; Paris; Amsterdam; Geneva; Santander and Vigo, Spain; and Lisbon.

A possible route to the Azores was explored. The route would be from New York City to Labrador to the Azores. From the Azores, the Sirius flew to the Canary Islands, Cape Verde Islands, Gambia, Natal, and Belem at the mouth of the Amazon River in Brazil,

A section of the large crowd that turned out whenever a Clipper was scheduled to depart or arrive. The Pan Am Clippers had caught the imagination of a Depression-weary population. The crowds were interested in the aircraft and the passengers that were able to afford a flight to faraway, exotic destinations.

University of Miami, Richter Library, Pan Am Collection

M-272　FORTY PASSENGER CLIPPER SHIPS AT PAN-AMERICAN INTERNATIONAL AIRPORT, MIAMI, FLORIDA

AMERICA'S FINEST AIR PASSENGER TERMINAL

PHOTO BY W. F. GERECKE

M27　Miami Terminal of Pan-American Airways

PHOTO BY PAN-AMERICAN PHOTO SERVICE

8A-H1074

and then on to Port-au-Spain in Trinidad and Tobago, San Juan, San Pedro de Macoris in the Dominican Republic, and finally Miami. The last leg of the air journey was from Miami to Charleston to Long Island, New York. The Lindberghs had departed on July 9, 1933, and arrived home on December 19, 1933. The five-month flight had covered 30,000 miles and included stopovers in 31 countries. Of course, the purpose of the flight was not only to survey routes, but to also act as ambassadors for Pan American Airways.

Over the 1930s, many survey flights were undertaken in the Caribbean, Atlantic, and Pacific areas to establish new routes or make modifications to existing routes and aircraft. Long-range survey flights required an entirely new technique of operation.

On January 8, 1935, Pan American's premier crew began test flights over the Atlantic Ocean. The crew consisted of Captain Edwin C. Musick, the Pacific Division's Chief Test Pilot; First Officer Captain R. O. D. Sullivan; Navigation Officer Fred Noonan; Junior Flight Officer Harry Canaday; Flight Engineers Chauncey D. Wright and Victor C. Wright, and Radio Officer Wilson T. Jarboe. They began a series of 30 long-distance test flights to measure fuel consumption, navigation, instruments, sextants, autopilot, and radio.

The S-42 was modified for the trials. The interior of the aircraft was gutted to allow eight large gas tanks to be added. The extra tanks would provide enough fuel for the aircraft's range to be increased to 2,990 miles. There would be a three-hour safety margin equaling 500 miles with the addition of the eight tanks.

The original plan called for the new Martin 130, with its longer range, to undergo the testing for transpacific flights. There was a delay, and the Martin 130 missed its scheduled delivery date. So the S-42, under Captain Edwin C. Musick, was called upon.

The Pan American Clipper left Miami at 4:06 p.m. on March 22, 1935, and flew to a point past Puerto Rico, returning to Miami at 9:22 a.m. The nonstop flight covered 2,600 miles in 17 hours and 16 minutes. Other tests were undertaken, and at times the

An S-40 being loaded with mail and packages from a Railway Express truck. It is visitors day, a time when the public could tour and walk through the Clipper. Author's Collection

(Opposite top) Color postcard of the Dinner Key Terminal with two S-40s on the water. (Bottom) A long view of the Dinner Key Terminal from the air. An S-42 preparing for takeoff and in the distance the Pan American Airways hangars. Author's Collection

April 16, 1935, survey flight with Captain Edwin Musick
at the controls. Greeted in Hawaii by Colonel Young,
the Pan Am Division Manager. Musick is just appearing
at the top of the hatch preparing to depart the aircraft.
Note the bathing suits worn by the landing and
docking crew. University of Miami, Richter Library, Pan Am Collection

Captain Musick and crew in a group photo upon arrival in Hawaii. Crew from left to right: W. T. Jarboe, radio officer; Harry Canaday, junior flight officer; R. O. D. Sullivan, first officer; Captain Edwin Musick; Fred J. Noonan, navigator; Victor A. Wright, engineering officer. Standing in the second row from left to right: J. Parker Van Zandt, Pan Am station manager; Postmaster John H. Wilson; Roy A. Vitousek, Speaker of the House, Hawaii Government; Donald Ross, district manager of Standard Oil Company; Colonel Clarence M. Young, Pan Am Pacific district manager (wearing the leis); U.S. Navy Rear Admiral Harry E. Yarnell, Commandant 14th Naval District; John P. Poindexter, Governor of Hawaii; Army Major Hugh A. Drum; Colonel Daniel Van Voorhis, Chief of Staff; Fred Wright, Mayor of Honolulu; Commander E. Wayne Todd, fleet air base; John R. Galt, president Hawaii chapter Aeronautical Association; Colonel Delos Emmons, Commander 18th Composite Wing.

University of Miami, Richter Library, Pan Am Collection

smell of gasoline filled the interior of the aircraft, and the windows had to be cranked open.

After the flights from Dinner Key, Miami, the S-42 was deemed ready to undertake survey flights in the Pacific. On April 16, 1935, it departed Alameda, California, for Honolulu and made the return journey on April 23, 1935. On June 12, 1935, it departed Alameda and continued on to complete a survey of the Honolulu to Midway Island sector. The Musick-commanded S-42 returned to its San Francisco base on June 21, 1935, to depart again on August 9, 1935, for a survey of the Midway Island to Wake Island sector, returning to San Francisco on August 28, 1935. It departed once again on October 5, 1935, for a survey of the Wake Island to Guam sector and returned to its San Francisco base on October 24, 1935.

Many lessons were learned from the experience. The first was the realization that the S-42 would never be able to undertake passenger service to the new Pan American island bases. The S-42 was able to complete the surveys due to the modifications that had been performed by the Sikorsky engineers. These modifications increased the range and fuel supply, but left no room for passengers or cargo. The S-42 was not capable of even completing the San Francisco to Hawaii route. The various survey and test flights of the S-42 gave a practical demonstration of the reliability and performance, but also revealed the limitations of the aircraft.

Some of the problems encountered on the long-range survey flights of the S-42 were of a critical nature, including the transfer of fuel from cabin to wing and the need to have a transfer meter installed. Unfavorable fuel consumption had a negative impact on the center of gravity in the aircraft. There were also problems with the airspeed indicators. The S-42 had been employed extensively, not just for surveying the various new routes, but also to gain knowledge regarding many aspects of the flying boats and their behavior in various conditions.

(Right) S-42 in flight passing the unfinished San Francisco-Oakland Bay Bridge. The 1930s were a decade of excitement in the San Francisco Bay Area. The construction of the Golden Gate Bridge, the Oakland Bay Bridge, a new ferry terminal and in 1939 the Golden Gate International Exposition, with the Pan Am Clippers moving to Treasure Island and taking off from Clipper Cove. Clyde Sunderland. Pacific Aerial Surveys - HJW Geospatial Inc.

The Bee-Hive. Early 1930s copy with an S-42 racing across the water. Igor Sikorsky Historical Archives

The problems with the S-42 on the long-distance flights were communicated to the Pan American staff and Martin engineers working on the 130 in Baltimore. The information provided to the Sikorsky engineers allowed the S-42B to become a more advanced model. The S-42B would carry 24 passengers. Fuel tanks would be added and alterations made to the fuel and oil line partitions, the installation of a ventilator system for the tank compartment, and the creation of a balanced diagram and weight statement.

The tragedy was that all this would come too late to save Pan American's premier pilot, Captain Musick. On January 11, 1938, while conducting a second survey flight on the *Samoan Clipper* to open a new route to Auckland, New Zealand, he radioed that the aircraft had an oil leak problem. That radio message was the last contact with the *Samoan Clipper.*

Survey flights were one small part of the plan to cross the Pacific with large over-the-water flying boats, whether the S-42s, Martin 130s, or the Boeing 314s. Understanding the weather and climate alterations in the Pacific region and eventually the Atlantic region were critical. In the years preceding the transpacific airway, knowledge of weather over the Pacific was as limited as any other region on the globe. Almost nothing was known of the general pattern of winds and even less about the strength and behavior of frontal systems away from coastal areas. Synoptic charts of the Pacific were not available. Due to the lack of this information, concerns had been expressed that transpacific flights might not be possible. So many aviators had disappeared in the 1920s and early 1930s without a trace.

There were no weather stations, so the weather service relied on several ships that provided information on a twice-daily schedule. However, the majority of the ships reporting were located in the California to Hawaii sector. The accuracy of the weather reports were questionable, and due to the reliance on ships, almost no nightly weather information was available.

The Japanese had an effective system of land-based weather stations located on the Bonin, Caroline, and Marshall Islands, and in the Western and West Equatorial Pacific but, due to tensions with the United States, did not share any information.

Pan American Airways realized it would have to employ its own resources to ascertain the amount of upper-air weather

and create a forecasting service by implementing its own weather stations. The company recruited professional staff and established stations on Honolulu, Midway Island, Wake Island, Guam, and the Philippines. A special bureau in China was established.

Arrangements were made with the Matson Navigation Company to report on weather conditions. Pan American trained the staff in observation techniques. Once again, Pan American employed the lessons of the Caribbean and transferred weather knowledge to the Pacific region.

A more scientific method, however, had to be developed. The planned transoceanic flights would be very long, much longer than any flight in the Caribbean, and this would mean aircraft would fly through many different weather patterns. The crews would have to be able to contend with almost every type of weather.

The company carefully planned various tracks that the aircraft could fly in and through. If the weather prediction was not satisfactory for the scheduled route, then an alternate could be chosen. Every Pan American pilot would have to take a complete course in Ocean Meteorology. Ground personnel would be trained in observing the weather, and detailed records would be compiled daily.

Long barrels of gasoline are moved to another section.

University of Miami, Richter Library, Pan Am Collection

Radio facilities did not exist in the Pacific area in 1932. There were no aeronautical radio facilities, and no navigational aids existed west of Honolulu. The 3,000-mile distance from Honolulu to Guam had no radio facilities. Some of the most important cargo carried by the SS *North Haven* on its delivery of supplies to the island bases included material, equipment, and parts for installing the Pan American direction-finder system.

The long-range direction, finder system would play a vital role in the development of flying in the Pacific. Other items of radio equipment for each island base included a single-kilowatt, 10-channel point-to-point ground-air transmitter, which had been modified to meet Pan American standards. RCA receivers had been modified by Pan American engineers. Practically all of the radio equipment for the transpacific airway had been modified by Pan American engineers or manufactured by one of its subsidiaries.

Radio equipment for the new Martin 130s was specially designed and service tested by Pan American on the S-42 survey flights in the Atlantic and Pacific. During testing, the aircraft had to be in contact with ground stations at least every 15 minutes. Direction bearings were taken every half hour, and the aircraft was required to file position reports at alternative quarter hours. A special numerical code was developed by Pan American to speed up transmissions.

A deal was arranged with the Matson Navigation Company to provide dependable radio transmissions of weather reports. Pan American paid the radio operators on the Matson ships overtime to keep their radios in operation.

Experts were hired to study the issue of navigation. Flying over water would be a challenge for weather and communications, but an aircraft would have to know exactly what its position was to the destination. The solution was a system that employed the direction finder and celestial methods with dead reckoning. Celestial octants were ordered to supplant the bubble sextants then in common use. Specifications for an adequate aircraft, Pelorous, were drawn up. A newly designed drift flare suitable for the aircraft was obtained.

Landings and takeoffs in nighttime were studied. The flights from California to Hawaii and onward to the other island bases would be long. Flying boats had different problems from land aircraft, and some of the island bases had short operational areas to land on, due to the conditions on several of the islands' coral reefs. In the daytime, it was possible to see the condition of the area and the depth of the water, but the nighttime created special problems, as observation was limited.

Several of the island bases required constant dredging operations to ensure that the water depth was manageable for landing and taking off. An elaborate system of buoys and night lights was installed. In Manila, the best area for takeoffs and landings was still not suitable, due to rough waters, so the Pan American landing site had to be moved to the south end of Manila Bay. This meant that the field was 30 kilometers from the center of Manila. Transportation facilities for crews and passengers had to be constructed.

Guam did not have a suitable landing area. Operations had to be conducted in an area where swells at times interrupted schedules. Special problems arose around the issue of night flying. It was determined that no flying boat would take off or land at night in the water area surrounding Pearl Harbor, due to the amount of Navy traffic, as there was a real possibility of hitting another ship or object in the water. The flight crew would simply not have time to react. Departures from Manila were scheduled for 2 a.m., due to weather conditions between Manila and Guam. A 2 a.m. departure allowed the aircraft to reach Guam before darkness.

The crew of each flying boat was trained in night flying techniques. Although night flights were not scheduled on the San Francisco to Honolulu or Manila to Guam routes, delays may have meant the aircraft would have to land in the darkness. The crew would have to be experienced for this event.

For the over-water flights, emergency equipment was required, including lightweight pneumatic life rafts and life raft equipment, such as emergency rations, flares, and signal flags. An emergency stove and water still were designed by the company, as no lightweight or efficient equipment could be found on the market. A sea anchor was carried as standard equipment. As on a ship, the sea anchor was employed to keep the aircraft from drifting. A regular anchor was carried for mooring purposes. Emergency generators to supply electrical power were the first to be carried on an aircraft. Portable oxygen bottles and masks became standard for medical emergencies on the new class of flying boats.

Multiple flight crews were assigned, since transpacific flights could be as long as 24 hours in duration. In preparation for the first flights, the new position of Flight Steward was created by Pan American Airways. The flight stewards acted as ships clerks and butlers, taking care of passengers' needs.

May 17, 1938. *Hawaii Clipper,* NC14714 in a test flight. Aircraft has deployed a trailing antenna, so it can pick up direction signals and transmit information in morse code. Pan Am was the leader in developing the infrastructure to make flying safe. In the Pacific the United States Government employed many of their services.

Clyde Sunderland. Pacific Aerial Surveys, HJW Geospatial Inc.

CHAPTER 4

THE FIRST TRANSPACIFIC FLIGHT:
Carrying the Mail

PAN AMERICAN AIRWAYS TOOK DELIVERY of the first of its three Martin 130s on October 9, 1935. Everything was now in place for the first transpacific flight. The survey flights had been completed, the island bases constructed and the last item lacking was an aircraft that could traverse the distance from San Francisco to Hawaii. This aircraft was promptly christened the *China Clipper*, in honor of the sailing ships of the 1800s. The new promotional material for Pan American Airways featured a Clipper sailing ship on the water and a Martin 130 flying overhead. The fastest, most famous sailing ship of the nineteenth century was featured on its way to or from the Orient, and overhead flew the twentieth century flying boat that would reopen the door to the mysterious Orient.

Juan Trippe was on hand, along with his senior technical advisor, Charles Lindbergh. A ceremonial presentation was made by Lassiter C. Milburn, Chief Engineer for the Martin Company, to Juan Trippe, President of Pan American Airways. Due to illness, Glenn Martin could not be at the ceremony to turn over the first M-130 that Juan Trippe had announced would be the first of the new *China Clippers*. The aircraft was dubbed "Sweet 16," for the last two numbers of her aircraft registration, NC14716. The next aircraft, delivered in late November 1935, was the *Philippine Clipper*. The *Hawaii Clipper* was the last of the three. Sadly, each of the Martin 130s would meet a tragic fate.

May 17, 1938. *Hawaii Clipper*, NC14714 over Pt. Reyes, California, performing a fuel dumping test. This was required to meet federal regulations for jettisoning fuel to reduce weight in case of emergency landing.
Clyde Sunderland. Pacific Aerial Surveys, HJW Geospatial Inc.

The original plan was for Charles Lindbergh to be the first pilot to take the *China Clipper* across the Pacific, but this was not to happen. Even though Lindbergh had been given a retainer check to fly the first Clipper, he had returned it uncashed. There were several reasons for his reluctance. For one, he was working with Doctor Alexis Carrel of the Rockefeller Institute for Medical Research on a precision pump to assist in keeping human organs alive. Another factor was the Lindbergh couple's desire to stay out of the public's eye. The tragic kidnapping of their young son and the media circus that followed had placed a tremendous burden on their lives. The couple had been in the media eye ever since Mr. Lindbergh's famous flight across the Atlantic to Paris and the survey flights for Pan American.

M-130 *China Clipper* in the air over San Francisco. Off in the distance is the famous new prison for holding America's Most Wanted – Alcatraz.

It had even been reported that Charles Lindbergh was to conduct the survey flights across the Pacific Ocean prior to his flying the first M-130 *China Clipper* flight. The media claimed that the flight in the M-130 would be the culmination of Lindbergh's dream of flying across the Pacific.

Lindbergh set the record straight when he announced that he, Anne, and their little child, Jon, were sailing to England to get away from the media and the other hangers-on that followed the family around. Not only were they sailing to England, but they planned to take up residence there. He mailed back the last of the retainer checks to Juan Trippe and removed himself from his position as technical adviser to Pan American Airways.

The first passenger flight would not take place until 1936, but already the tickets had become hot items. With all the fanfare connected with the aircraft, the American public fell in love with the *China Clipper*. Every flying boat in the Pan American inventory would be dubbed a Clipper. Each was given their own name, and in several instances, the names were changed over the years, depending on which route the aircraft served.

The plan was to carry the U.S. mail on the first *China Clipper* flight, which would depart San Francisco and stop in Honolulu before departing for its final destination, Manila. The *China Clipper* would depart San Francisco and return from Manila on December 6, 1935, inaugurating the first transpacific mail service. Manila was chosen as the end terminal for the first flight due to the problems receiving permission from the Chinese Government to land in Hong Kong.

A week later, Captain Musick flew the *China Clipper* to Miami for further testing and to allow the crew to experience the new aircraft. The flights were shakedown cruises, as though the M-130 were a sailing ship and not an aircraft. Musick made several local flights and then flew to Puerto Rico and returned. On November 8, the *China Clipper* left Miami to make its way across the nation and prepare for the first transpacific flight on November 22. The first stop was Acapulco, Mexico, where Musick was met by Pan American Vice President George Rihl. A tour was provided to several Mexican officials, and the next day, the journey continued to California.

A final checkout and blind flight test were conducted the night before the historic event. On the afternoon of the ceremony to inaugurate airmail service across the Pacific and the first transpacific flight, over 25,000 people were on hand to see the *China Clipper* depart. Another 100,000 watched the events from across the bay. Tributes from

One of the Martin M-130s in flight over water with land in the distance. University of Miami, Richter Library, Pan Am Collection

Clipper on its land beaching platform. Aircraft had to be lifted from the water so that the underside could be checked. One of the hazards of flying boats was the possible impact of debris in the water on the fuselage of the aircraft. Prior to takeoff the PanAir boat would check the water ahead of the Clipper to ensure there were no hidden logs or objects.

U.S. Senator William G. McAdoo, California Governor Frank Merriam, and others were on hand. Greetings were exchanged among Juan Trippe, President Manuel L. Quezon of the Philippines, and Governor Joseph P. Poindexter of the Territory of Hawaii in Honolulu. Radio and newspaper journalists and newsreel teams filled the area, and aerial bursts of fireworks, whistles, and screaming sirens filled the sky.

The announcer called attention to the crew of Captain Edwin C. Musick: "Seven men in the crew, and what a crew! Five of those seven are transport pilots, three of them are registered aeronautical engineers, three of them are licensed radio officers, two of them are master mariners and two others have navigation papers. That will give you some idea of the preparation behind America's conquest of the ocean!" The original plan was for a crew of nine and two NBC journalists to be on the flight, but a heavier-than-expected mail load forced a reduction in the numbers that would make the historic flight. The crew consisted of the following:

Captain Edwin C. Musick
First Officer R. O. D. Sullivan
Second Officer George King
First Engineering Officer O. D. Wright
Second Engineering Officer V. A. Wright
Navigator Fred Noonan
First Radio Officer W. T. Jarboe

Pan Am maintenance crew in white overalls checking the aircraft and hosing it down. The hosing is to remove the corrosive salt water. Note the lifting cradle holding the aircraft.

University of Miami, Richter Library, Pan Am Collection

Most of the members of the crew were making their ninth Pacific crossing, except Second Officer George King and First Engineering Officer O. D. Wright, who were on the flight for training purposes. Second Officer T. R. Runnels and Second Junior Flight Officer Max Weber had to remain in San Francisco. The two Wrights were not brothers. The flight did not carry paying passengers. It would be 1936 before paying passenger service was instituted.

November 22 was chosen for two special reasons: It was the 100th Anniversary of the first Clipper sailing ship entering San Francisco harbor, and the United States Post Office was issuing a new 25-cent airmail stamp that featured the Clipper flying over water.

President Roosevelt sent a letter, which read as follows:

My Dear Postmaster General:

Please convey to the people of the Pacific Coast the deep interest and heart-felt congratulations of an air-minded sailor. Even at this distance I thrill to the wonder of it all.

They tell me that the inauguration of the transpacific sky mail also celebrates the 100th Anniversary of the arrival of the first Clipper ship in San Francisco. The years between the two events mark a century of progress that is without parallel, and it is our just pride that America and Americans have played no minor part in the blazing new trails. There can be no higher hope than that this heritage of courage, daring, initiative, and enterprise will be conserved and intensified.

Very sincerely yours,

Franklin D. Roosevelt.

Postmaster General James Farley added his own words to the event:

More than eight thousand miles of ocean are to be spanned by this new service which will bring Asia within five days of the United States, thus reducing the period of travel between these two continents to less than one-third of the time now required by the fastest steamships, which is seventeen days. There will be a corresponding saving

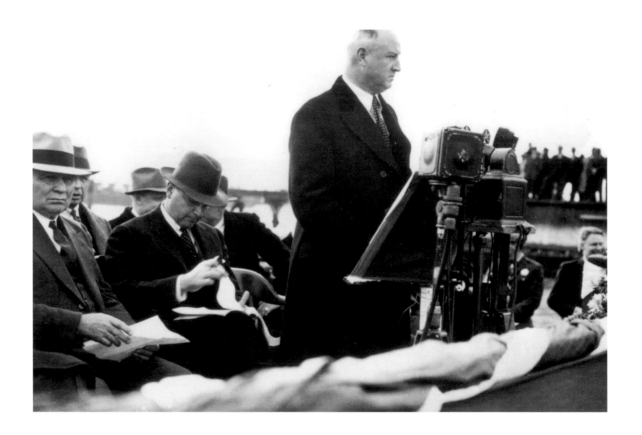

in time between the United States, the Hawaiian Islands, Guam, and the Philippines and all will benefit by this time saving. The Hawaiian Islands, now five days away by the fastest steamships, will be overnight from San Francisco.

Very soon, the super-planes flying over this route will be transporting passengers and express. A person or letter will arrive in China within six days after leaving New York. This is, indeed, an epoch-marking achievement and one which rivals the vivid imagination of a Jules Verne.

It has been the experience of the United States that when better communications and faster transportation have been established between this and other countries, better understanding has resulted and an improvement in trade and commerce has followed. Therefore, I anticipate that our friendly relations and our commerce with the countries of the Orient will be strengthened and stimulated by the transpacific air mail service.

A final command was shouted into the microphone for the radio-listening public by Postmaster Farley: "Captain Musick, you have your sailing orders. Cast off and depart for Manila in accordance therewith."

The *China Clipper* taxied and lifted off the water at 3:46 p.m. It was immediately joined by an escort of fighter planes. It was a spectacular sight, as the aircraft passed under the unfinished structure of the new Cross Bay Bridge. Climbing above the new Golden Gate Bridge, the brand new flying boat quickly flew out of daylight and into the darkness beyond. Millions of radio listeners continued to tune in to hear the latest progress report on the *China Clipper*.

As dawn broke, navigator Fred Noonan reported their position as 300 miles from Pearl Harbor. Captain Musick landed the *China Clipper* at 10:15 to a large crowd of United States Navy personnel, who stood and watched the magnificent flying boat land on the water. The flight had taken 21 hours and 4 minutes.

The *New York Times* of November 23 carried the headline: "China Clipper Off, First Mail Trip Across the Pacific." It continued: "Giant Aircraft Dips Over the New Oakland Bridge Cables as 20,000 Cheer. It Carries 100,000 Letters. Farley Reads President Roosevelt's Congratulations — Island Rulers Talk on Radio." For the duration of the flight to Manila, the newspapers would carry daily accounts of the *China Clipper's* progress across the Pacific.

Several articles were written by Captain Musick. In the article "Musick's Story of Flight: Midway-Wake Stretch Most Difficult of Trip," the Clipper Master remarks that "yesterday's 1,200-mile jump was the shortest but most difficult span in the entire serial bridge and called for one of the most exacting feats of navigation on record — striking on the nose of a tiny point smaller than a pinhead on the vast map of the Pacific Ocean."

The *China Clipper* left Pearl Harbor at 6:35 a.m. on November 24, carrying 14 passengers as replacements for staff personnel at Midway Island and Wake Island, 1,633 pounds of mail, and supplies, including fresh fruit and vegetables, for the island bases. The operation of each ocean-going Clipper ship required the expert services of 42 men on the ground and six aboard.

The Clipper departed Guam on November 29 at 6:12 a.m. and arrived in Manila at 3:33 p.m., three minutes ahead of schedule. Captain Musick presented President Manuel Quezon of the Philippines a letter from President Franklin Roosevelt. President Quezon then declared a holiday in honor of the arrival of the first Clipper aircraft.

1st day cover carried on the famous first flight of the *China Clipper*. The United States stamps feature a Clipper aircraft for airmail delivery.
Author's Collection

(Opposite top) United States Postmaster General Farley wishing Godspeed to Captain Edwin Musick and the *China Clipper* on their flight to Hawaii on November 22, 1935. With much fanfare the aircraft departed.
San Francisco Airport Museums. Gift of Pan American World Airways Archive

(Bottom) The *China Clipper* on her way over the unfinished Golden Gate Bridge.
Clyde Sunderland. Pacific Aerial Surveys, HJW Geospatial Inc.

China Clipper on the water near Catalina Island, California. Its passenger was the famous aviator and owner of Martin Aviation, Glenn Martin. It would be the only time that a Clipper would land at Catalina Island. The famous Pavilion is in the background.

Martin Aviation Historical Archives

(Left) *China Clipper*, which flew for ten years and was the last surviving M-130 of the three constructed, is seen in this painting by famous aviation artist John R. Doughty Jr. on its last leg to Paradise, flying past Diamond Head, Hawaii. The painting commemorates that first historic flight and is entitled *Musick's Trippe to Paradise*.

j.doughty@highironillustrations.com

The entire trip to Manila had covered 8,210 miles and took 59 hours and 48 minutes in air time. The *China Clipper* arrived back at Pearl Harbor on December 4 and departed on the next day to California. The entire round trip was 16,240 miles and was completed in 123 hours and 12 minutes, less than the estimated time of 130 hours. The average speed of the aircraft was 133.2 miles per hour, and the *China Clipper* set 19 world records. There had not been any delays due to weather conditions.

The flight to the Philippines had been divided into five sections: San Francisco to Honolulu, 2,410 miles; Honolulu to Midway Island, 1,380 miles; Midway Island to Wake Island, 1,260 miles; Wake Island to Guam, 1,450 miles; and Guam to Manila, 1,550 miles.

Plans were underway for the first passenger flight. The SS *North Haven* was loaded with supplies and sent on its second expedition. The manifests included such items as solar water heaters, 50 pairs of pillows, terrace furniture, staff uniforms, bridge tables, and beach umbrellas. Once again, the ship contained tons of rich soil for the gardens at Midway Island and Wake Island to provide a growing base for special grass. Juan Trippe wanted to provide a pleasant atmosphere around the Pan American hotels on the islands for the passengers. They would move from the luxury of the aircraft to the luxury of the island hotel.

Passengers found complete and attractive hotels amongst landscapes complete with lawns and shrubs. The hotels had 24 double rooms of generous dimensions, surrounded by well-screened verandas. Each room was equipped with a shower bath and electric lights. The Commissary Department had organized a staff of port stewards, chefs, and attendants who maintained a standard of service worthy of metropolitan hotels.

The first passenger flight was for October 21, 1936. The honor of the first passenger flight did not go to the *China Clipper*, but her sister ship, the *Hawaii Clipper*. The

China Clipper arriving at Manila Bay on its historic first flight. Crew member tying off the aircraft from the top hatch. Line attached to the landing pin in the front nose of the aircraft. Side hatch open with crew member peering out. Two other crew members peering out the top. San Francisco Airport Museums. Gift of the Pan Am Association

Captain Musick and crew arriving in the Philippines to a great welcome on November
29, 1935. Some 300,000 people lined the shore to watch the *China Clipper* arrive.

San Francisco Airport Museums, Gift of the Pan Am Association

Passengers on the Juan Trippe flight to Hawaii one week prior to the start of regular service. The focus was on important businessmen: Wallace Alexander, chairman of the board of Matson Shipping Lines; Baldwin; Paul Patterson, publisher of the *Baltimore Sun*; Cornelius N. Whitney, chairman of the board of Pan American Airways; Roy Howard, chairman of the Scripps-Howard newspaper chain; William Roth, chairman and president of the Matson Shipping Lines; Senator William McAdoo; Amon G. Carter, publisher of the *Fort Worth Star Telegram*; and Juan Trippe.

University of Miami, Richter Library, Pan Am Collection

passenger list included Mr. and Mrs. C. V. Whitney (Chairman of Pan American), Mr. R. F. Bradley (Standard Oil of California), Mr. Wolbur May (Los Angeles), Mr. Thomas Fortune Ryan III, Colonel Charles Bartley (Chicago), Mr. Alfred Bennett (Hightstown, New Jersey), Mrs. Zetta Averill (Aberdeen, Washington), and Mrs. Clara Adams (Stroudsburg, Pennsylvania). The flight arrived in Manila on October 27, 1935, without any problems.

The *Hawaii Clipper* would meet a mysterious and tragic fate. On July 28, 1938, the aircraft disappeared without a trace somewhere between Guam and Manila. In its last radio contact, it reported its position as 300 miles off the coast of the Philippines and 560 miles from Manila. The flight had six passengers, mail, and express aboard. The passengers were Mr. E. E. Wyman, former assistant to Juan Trippe; Mr. K. A. Kennedy, Traffic Manager, Pan American Pacific-Alaska Division; Dr. Fred A. Meir, of Washington, DC, and Dr. Earl B. McKinley, of George Washington University. The crew members were Captain Leo Terletzky; First Officer M. A. Walker; Second Officer George Davis; Third Officer J. M. Sauceda; Flight Engineer J. W. Jewelt; Flight Engineer Brooks T. Taturn and Stewards William McCarty and Ivan H. Parker Jr.

A search was carried out by 16 surface vessels and ten aircraft. An area of 160,000 square miles was covered, but no wreckage or trace of the *Hawaii Clipper* was ever found. One theory alleged that the aircraft was hijacked by Japanese agents that forced the aircraft to fly to one of the Japanese-held islands in the area. The crew and passengers were killed and the aircraft scrapped or hidden away. It was not uncommon in the 1930s, though, for aircraft to vanish without a trace. Due to the vast expanse of the Pacific and sparsely populated islands, many planes disappeared, including the famous Lockheed Electra of Amelia Earhart.

Loading the mail on the brand new B-314 at dockside. Notice the engine covers to protect from dust and, most importantly, damp and moisture.

Boeing Aircraft Co., Chicago, Illinois

With the Latin American Division operating efficiently and the Pacific routes now open, Juan Trippe turned his attention to the Atlantic routes. On the night of February 23, 1939, the first Atlantic Division Boeing 314 NC18603 was ferried from San Francisco to Baltimore by Captain Harold Gray. The Atlantic Division's main base became the marine terminal at Baltimore's Logan Airport, which had a ramp that was connected to a floating dock where the B-314 was able to dock and moor. The French Government approved Pan American flights to Marseille on January 20.

The NC18603 was flown by Harold Gray and Charles Vaughn to Anacostia, Maryland, on March 3 for christening by Eleanor Roosevelt. Juan Trippe looked on as the *Yankee Clipper* was christened with a bottle containing water from the seven seas. March 11 saw Captain Gray take the *Yankee Clipper* on an 11,000-mile survey flight to Europe.

The flight time to Horta was 17 hours and 30 minutes, with an average speed of 160 miles per hour. The aircraft remained in Horta for three days so base personnel could become acquainted with the handling and docking of the giant flying boat. The Clipper eventually flew to Marseille. Captain Gray expressed his dissatisfaction with the takeoff performance of the B-314. The *Yankee Clipper* arrived at Southampton on April 4.

On May 18, 1939, Pan American was awarded a northern route via Newfoundland to Foynes, Ireland, and on to Southampton, England. The first scheduled flight of the Atlantic service opened on May 20 with Captain LaPorte in the pilot's seat. The *Yankee Clipper* departed Port Washington, New York, for its destination of Marseille, carrying only mail. On the first flights, there were usually so many first day covers that the crew had to assist the postal officials in canceling the stamps. The large volume of mail even prevented the stewards from being able to wash dishes on the aircraft. Due to the weight limitations, the dishes were taken ashore and washed by the stewards in the Customs Building.

In May, Pan American signed a lease with the City of New York for space at LaGuardia Airport for a new marine base of operations. A hangar and terminal were constructed

Advertisement for Glenn L. Martin Aircraft Company focused on his historic flight from California to Catalina Island in 1912. The flight's distance was 33 miles. At the time he remarked, "Some day you'll see men flying across the Pacific, just as they now travel by ship." Juan Trippe honored the feat by flying Martin on the company-manufactured *China Clipper* to Catalina Island.

Author's Collection

Thirty-Three Miles Trans-Pacific...in 1912

It seemed strange, back in 1912, to think of a man in a "flying machine" going aloft and heading straight out over the Pacific Ocean—even though his destination was Catalina Island, only 33 miles distant. But stranger still was the prophesy of the man who successfully completed this history-making flight—Glenn L. Martin.

"Some day," he said, "you'll see men flying clear across the Pacific . . . just as they now travel by ship." Even the successful Catalina flight, and the fact that Martin both designed and built the plane he flew, couldn't make his statement seem more than a dream.

Years later, that prophesy was fulfilled by the man who made it. The famous Martin Clipper airliners, built under his direction, made the first passenger crossing and now ply regularly across the Pacific. Their arrival and departure now are such commonplace events that newspapers list them as they do steamship schedules.

Even before 1912, Glenn L. Martin had startled the world by his prophesies and their practical fulfillment. In later years, his unusual combination of vision and practicality contributed a really formidable list of "firsts" in practically every field of aviation. Today, intensified and developed, it underlies the thinking and planning of The Glenn L. Martin Company.

What now are the plans of The Glenn L. Martin Company? They concern, as they did in 1912, the future of trans-oceanic flying. What are the practical developments? Already a huge trans-oceanic airliner of the future has taken shape on Martin drawing-boards—waiting only for trans-oceanic aviation to grow to the point where it can efficiently use such a huge ship.

By the time that ship is built—there will be other and still better airliners on the drawing-boards to supply the needs and demands of trans-oceanic flying in its next stage of development.

THE GLENN L. MARTIN COMPANY,
BALTIMORE, MD., U.S.A.

Ready for the Future of Trans-Oceanic Flying . . .

MARTIN
Aircraft

TRADE MARK

Builders of Dependable Aircraft Since 1909

A Practical Martin Development for the future: the Martin Stratosphere Liner, now ready to build. Gross weight, upward of 65 tons. Wing span, more than 200 feet. Speed, New York to London, 12 hours in sub-stratosphere. When aviation reaches the need for such huge aircraft—Martin can and will build them.

THE PAN AMERICAN FLYING BOAT "YANKEE CLIPPER."

at a cost of $40 million. It was an exciting time, as the facility was located just north of the 1939/40 New York World's Fair, The World of Tomorrow. Sadly, the Pan American northern route would operate for only three short months as the outbreak of World War II on September 3, 1939, would put an end to the flights. Today, only two metal rods remain of what once was the Pan American hangar.

June 28, 1939, witnessed the launch of the first scheduled passenger service to Marseille and Southampton. Like the launch of the *China Clipper* on November 22, 1935, thousands turned out to cheer the *Dixie Clipper* on its way. The flight carried 22 passengers, including Pan American Chairman C. V. Whitney, Mrs. Whitney, and Mrs. Trippe. The *Dixie Clipper* arrived in Lisbon on the next day after a stop at Horta. The trip covered 3,447 miles and took 23 hours and 53 minutes.

Mrs. Trippe conveyed the excitement of the passengers: "We sighted Lisbon at 6:15 a.m. local time, almost exactly 24 hours from Port Washington.

Columbus couldn't have been much more excited than we were to see land, but the difference was his relief, and ours was exaltation at so fast a trip, and we had landed in Europe."

The one-way fares to London or Marseille were $375, to Lisbon $309, and to Bermuda $70. With the outbreak of World War II, the northern route would be canceled, but Pan American would continue to operate the Atlantic crossing by the central route or via Brazil and West Africa. At the end of World War II, Pan American Airways, had moved on to transoceanic travel, but with the use of land planes that did not require water landing fields.

Yankee Clipper arriving after crossing the Atlantic Ocean and opening air travel from New York to Europe. To signify the milestone, the aircraft flies an American flag on one side of the aircraft and a Union Jack on the other. Author's Collection

China Clipper on the water in Manila on its historic first flight. United States military aircraft in a salute formation in the distance. University of Miami, Richter Library, Pan Am Collection

JUNE 28, 1939 FLIGHT

Following are lists of the passengers and crew on the historic June 28, 1939, flight from Port Washington, New York, to Horta, Lisbon, and Marseille.

The 22 passengers formed a very interesting group, which included the rich, famous and others who would eventually become famous.

Glenn Martin arriving at Catalina Island disembarking from the *China Clipper*.

Martin Aviation Historical Archives

1. W. J. Eck, Assistant to the Vice President of Southern Railway, Washington, DC.
2. Captain Torkild Rieber, Chairman of the Board of the Texas Corporation, New York City.
3. Colonel William Donovan, Attorney, Buffalo, New York. Colonel Donovan had been the Republican candidate for the New York State Governorship in 1932. During World War II, he would create and head the Office of Strategic Services, the forerunner of the Central Intelligence Agency. He would eventually become the first Director of the CIA.
4. Roger Lapham, President, American Hawaiian Steamship Company, San Francisco, California.
5. Mrs. Clara Adams, Maspeth, New York.
6. Mrs. Sherman Haight, New York City.
7. J. H. Norweb, General Motors Acceptance Corporation, New York City.
8. Louis Gimble Jr., of the famous New York City department store.
9. H. L. Stuart Halsey, Chicago, Illinois.
10. Ben Smith, New York City.
11. Russell Sabor, Midland Laboratories Affiliated, Minneapolis, Minnesota.
12. Mark W. Cresap, Chairman of the Board and President, Hart Schaffner & Marx, the famous men's clothing manufacturer, Chicago, Illinois.
13. Julius Rapoport, Allentown, Pennsylvania.
14. James McVittie, Union League Club of Chicago, Chicago, Illinois.
15. C. V. Whitney, Chairman of the Board, Pan American Airways, New York City.
16. Mrs. C. V. Whitney
17. Graham Grosvenor, New York City.
18. Mrs. Graham Grosvenor
19. E. O. McDonnell, New York City.
20. Mrs. E. O. McDonnell
21. Mrs. Elizabeth S. Trippe, wife of Juan Trippe, East Hampton, Long Island.
22. John M. Franklin, President, United States Lines, New York City.

Crew: Captain R. O. D. Sullivan
Flight Officer Gilbert B. Blackmore
Flight Officer Robert D. Fordyce
Flight Officer Benjamin B. Harrell
Engineering Officer John A. Fiske
Assistant Engineering Officer Melvin C. Anderson
Radio Officer Harold G. Lambert
Radio Officer Harry L. Drake
Steward Bruno Candotti
Steward John Salmini
Assistant Flight Engineer Officer Stephen H. Kitchell

PATROL

10911
6-8-37

CHAPTER 5

CONSTRUCTING THE BASES

Dinner Key, in the Coconut Grove section of Miami, would become the main flying boat terminal for Pan American Airways. Dinner Key sits on Biscayne Bay, and plans were made to construct a facility that would have the capability to handle 35 aircraft. Mayor H. C. Reeder broke ground for the new airport on February 22, 1931. Dinner Key would have the capability to handle land aircraft, but its main interest was for the flying boats of Pan American Airways.

The waters were to be dredged to a depth of six feet, since the expected Sikorsky S-40s were to be one of the main users of the airport. The new facility would assist in the further expansion of what was already the largest airline in the world. Juan Trippe foresaw that the new Sikorsky flying boats and other aircraft would expand services even further. The construction cost was $300,000.

The interior of the terminal had a giant world globe ten feet in diameter. It was accurately made to a scale of $1/64"$ to the nautical mile. The circumference was 31.5 feet and it weighed 6,500 pounds. The globe was installed in the middle of the terminal and it had been properly aligned to the axis of the earth at the Miami location. An electric motor rotated the globe every two minutes. Passengers and guests could see every destination of a Pan American Airways flight on this globe. The globe now resides in the center entrance hall to the Miami Museum of Science and Technology. Whenever a Clipper was due to arrive or depart, the surrounding area would be filled with interested spectators. Others fortunate enough to get to the field early would seek a spot on the large promenade.

Dinner Key established a new signal light system in 1935. The new range lights enabled pilots to taxi flying boats directly along the water channel leading into the four loading docks, thus avoiding the dangerous shoal areas, which had proven deadly to various types of flying boats in the past. When pilots advised the tower by radio that the terminal was in sight, a bell sounded to alert ground personnel to prepare for docking and quarantine officials to take their posts.

Dinner Key was sold to the City of Miami in 1952 for $1 million and became part of Miami City Hall.

(Left) Two Pan Am ground crew waiting for the Clipper to arrive. The Midway Island sign indicates the great distance to Honolulu. Personnel were rotated on a six-month schedule to keep morale high. Not a great deal to do on a small island. Films and library books were flown in on the Clippers, but still a lonely tour.
University of Miami, Richter Library, Pan Am Collection

Technician checking one of the aircraft's many tanks.
University of Miami, Richter Library, Pan Am Collection

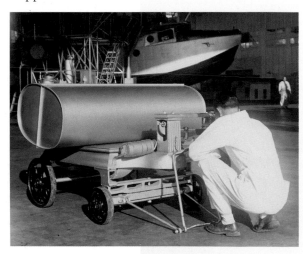

The Pan American Airways system was built upon careful planning and experience. If a problem occurred, the goal was to find the solution and build upon the knowledge base. In the 1920s and 1930s, so much of aviation was unknown.

Before attempting to build flying boat bases in the Pacific, Pan American gained experience in what was called the "Caribbean Laboratory." By 1930, the airline had built a solid, dependable business model in the Caribbean. In dedicating the transpacific service at Alameda, California, on November 22, 1935, President Trippe gave the following address: "The first long-distance, over-water route flown anywhere in the world was the 600-mile journey across the Caribbean from Kingston, Jamaica, to Barranquilla, Colombia. For five years Pan American has flown this route; it has been our laboratory of preparation for the service instituted today. There our technical staff has developed our ocean direction-finding and navigation apparatus, and there our flight captains and their crews have qualified for over-ocean service. So complete and effective was this accumulated experience that when our first experimental flight across the Pacific was undertaken six months ago, the Pan American Clipper cruised without incident for the 2,400-mile course and set down in Honolulu one minute late."

On June 20, 1935, Pan American Airways entered into an agreement with Matson Navigation Company and Inter-Island Steam Navigation Company, with the three companies agreeing to the establishment of transpacific services. Matson Navigation Company would be responsible for providing various meteorological services and transportation of baggage of air passengers on Matson boats. Inter-Island Steam Navigation Company was appointed Pan American's general agent in Hawaii, and Matson in Australasia. Matson and Inter-Island were each given the option to acquire 13,750 shares of Pan American stock at $37 per share. Both exercised their options the next year.

Pan American Airways chartered the SS *North Haven* early in 1935. The 15,000-ton Maersk Line ship had been contracted to transport supplies, equipment and personnel to the new island bases. The ship arrived in San Francisco on March 22. Pan American hired construction workers and other skilled tradesmen for the journey to Midway Island, Wake Island, and Guam to build the new transpacific support bases that the Clippers would require from square one.

On board were 74 construction workers, 44 Pan American airline technicians, a doctor, 300,000 gallons of aviation fuel, power generators, weather and radio stations, hotel supplies, refrigeration equipment, tractors, launches, maintenance and aircraft servicing equipment, and prefabricated housing units.

Docking and unloading plans had to be devised. Cargo for Manila was loaded first, Guam second, followed by Wake Island, Midway Island, and, lastly, Honolulu. On board were Captain Grooch, Pan American's Chief Administrative Officer; John Steel, Technical Assistant; C. H. Russell, Construction Supervisor; and Leroy Odell, Pan American's Chief Airport Engineer. Even columnist Junius Wood from the *Chicago Daily News* was along to

(Left) 1940 Marine Air Terminal, LaGuardia Field, in the Art Deco design of the period. From the desk to the passenger benches. The large mural is painted by James Brooks, a New York artist who became known later for Abstract Expressionist paintings. In the style of the 1930s, the mural depicts men, women, and machines in the Social Realist style of art.
University of Miami, Richter Library, Pan Am Collection

The official signing of the contract that would allow Pan American Airways Inc. to move its operation from Alameda to the new facilities that would be constructed at Treasure Island, San Francisco, in conjunction with the 1939/40 Golden Gate International Exposition. The three signing parties are holding their hands over an M-130 Clipper to mark the historic event.
University of Miami, Richter Library, Pan Am Collection

S-40 next to the floating dock terminal prior to Dinner Key. Seminoles in their canoes alongside the flying boat. Pan Am maintenance crew members next to dock and on the aircraft. Large crowd watching.

University of Miami, Richter Library, Pan Am Collection

provide dispatches of the journey to the paper's readers on the marvelous adventure that was being undertaken. Wood was an expert on aviation subjects and had witnessed the inauguration of Pan American service in 1929 to Argentina.

The SS *North Haven* left Pier 22 in San Francisco on March 27, filled with a quarter of a million gallons of fuel, enough food to last for several months, and enough material to construct two complete villages and five air bases. Months of planning intended to cover every possible angle. On board were stills to provide fresh water from the sea, equipment to hold down support cables as protection against typhoon-velocity winds, and oversize desert tires to compensate for the sandy soil that would be encountered. The new radio equipment for the stations was critical, as the schedule and its time line were very tight. The equipment would have to be in place quickly, so that survey flights could be conducted. Even before the SS *North Haven* reached Midway Island in April, survey flights to Honolulu had been undertaken under the direction of Captain Edwin C. Musick and his crew.

The expedition did encounter many problems and hardships. The coral reefs surrounding Midway Island required that the ship be unloaded several miles from shore. Weather conditions were difficult for equipment.

On tiny Wake Island, the problems were even more numerous and difficult. Cargo was required to be lightered from ship to shore and then transported over an improvised railway to the lagoon. Upon reaching the lagoon, the cargo had to be loaded once again and towed across to Peale Island. The lagoon then had to be cleaned of hundreds of thousands of coral heads. The problem was made even more difficult by the fact that the operation could only be undertaken by divers. In five short months, the entire five-ton supply of dynamite brought to Wake Island had been exhausted.

The blasting was necessary to create a landing site in the water for the expected Clipper aircraft. If not detonated properly, the underside of the fuselage could be breached or damaged. Wells were blasted and dug, but no water could be found on Wake Island. The distillation plant that had been carried on the SS *North Haven* was found to be inadequate for the job. One solution was to construct open water towers to catch the rainfall when it came. Of course, the major problem with catching the water in open towers was that when the hot sun returned, other systems had to be in place to prevent large-scale evaporation.

The immensity of the construction of the island stopovers and the rapid transformation of a desolate island into a base is a measure of the tenacity of the Pan American construction workers and staff. Each was dedicated to completing a job as quickly as possible. This experience would serve the Pan American company well in the coming long years of World War II. It was a leader in not just the construction of airfields and related infrastructures, such as power stations, refrigeration, runways, and control towers, but also in developing ready-made, well-trained, and professional staff.

John Borger, an Assistant Airport Engineer, worked on Wake Island from the first days until the completion of the project. He kept an almost daily log of progress and the problems encountered and solved in building a desert island airfield and luxury hotel for the passengers. Following is an excerpt of several pages of his log. Some spelling and punctuation have been standardized.

April 13, 1935
Three men injured during day. Doctor ashore. Towing bitt of PanAir launch pulled out in heavy swell. Barge tied up at channel buoy. Midway launch fully repaired at 8 p.m. approximately. Directions received for unloading on the 14th. Told to go ahead and get things ashore, regardless of selection.

April 14, Sunday
All men up at 4:30 a.m. Barges alongside at 6:15; had difficulty bringing alongside due to shortage of barge ropes. First two barges loaded with generators, electrical equipment and boats, sleds, emergency foods. Off slightly before 10 a.m. Second two barges loaded with part cement, mixer, miscellaneous lumber and tents, tarps, tools. Off at 11:15a.m. Third two barges arrived at 1:15, off at 2:35. Loaded with mudsills, posts, beds and gravel, lumber, etc. Fourth two barges arrived at 4 p.m., off at 5:40. Loaded with Wake tractor, gasoline, diesel oil, and food for shore crew, miscellaneous from after hatch. Russell,

Part of the Wilkes Island railroad. A small railroad had to be built to bring and move supplies and equipment as the material arrived by ship. Food and hundreds of drums containing aviation fuel required unloading.
University of Miami, Richter Library, Pan Am Collection

117

Grooch, Cleaves, Porter, and Steele along with first barges; all went back ashore at first opportunity. Most of the stevedores and sailors retained ashore; as result had to work at first with untrained crew. Sent number of men ashore. Got rid of crowd of hangers on, for which we had no work. Things going much more smoothly. Sending goods ashore too fast for shore crew to handle. Refueled PanAir. This launch to be used for passenger purposes only. Ward and Young ashore with food for men; back at 1:15. Borger ashore with PanAir at 3:45, back at 5:40. Short survey. Almost all executives except Mittag, Taylor, Lueder back aboard ship.

April 15, Monday
Still good weather for unloading. Ship to barge unloading progressing rapidly, but barge to shore unloading delayed. Men have been fishing steadily since arrival. Outside of shark, only fish caught have been Lua. Beach barges further up the beach. Extremely high tide caused moving of load of food further up from the water. Even Captain Borkland working to save food. Building panels, lumber, pipe wet. Pipe half filled with sand. Windmill started. Foundations not complete — poor mix. Refrigerator building well under way to completion. Refrigerator well under way. All food in future to be cooked in camp. To be shipped from NH in bulk. Night work again, relieved by Taylor.

Pirate girl employed to advertise the 1939/40 Golden Gate International Exposition at the newly created Treasure Island in San Francisco Bay. Treasure Island was constructed of landfill from the Sacramento area. Someone mentioned that the landfill could contain gold, hence Treasure Island. University of Miami, Richter Library, Pan Am Collection

April 20, Saturday
Camp progress established. Reveille at 5 a.m. Breakfast at 5:30, dinner 12, supper 6:30 p.m. Mess tent completed. Mosquito netting side drops from tarp roof. Three long tables each, seating 24. Set ready, men pass by kitchen table, receive food on plate, rest in mess hall. Three small wells for washing water sunk (water brackish). Gasoline drums sunk in to keep sand from flowing back. Broke well point in driving for water. Well points also proved impracticable, so started to dig 6' x 6' well instead. Single still place. Cannot supply sufficient water for camp personnel. Fresh water for cable compound. Weather clear, two barge tows again. Kept unloading barges pretty fast — ten loads over from ship in day. With two cats in action again, cleaned up beach a little more. If have unloading crew for sleds in camp are able to get sleds back on beach much faster. Main trouble yesterday was

that tractor crew had to unload sleds themselves. Next to last load in had load of gravel. Very slow in unloading, so delayed beach crew in getting to camp until 8 p.m. Went over to ship with load of brass hats. All well aboard. Selected movies for Sunday night showing.

April 21, Sunday

Easter — up at 6 a.m. Men to work till noon only. Only six barge loads for day. Last load in at 1:30, unloaded by 2:30, with help of men from ship. Beach crew up to camp for very tough fried chicken dinner. Then down again to complete unloading. Foundations for windmill completed. Mix this time with 2:2:4 instead of 1:2:4. Fishing party; also expeditionary force to Eastern Island in launch PanAir. Caught only large fish 16" Lua. Lots of fun and kidding. McKenzie caught small 8" fish unnamed variety; trolling also. Mr. Steele found first of big glass balls on Eastern Island. First movies on Midway in history in evening. Betty Boop cartoon, comedy, "Big Broadcast" on program. Complete with sound; very excellent. Almost entire cable station crew are our guests.

M-130 *Hawaii Clipper* NC14714 over Treasure Island on May 17, 1938. Two hangars and the crescent-shaped Administration/ Passenger Terminal are under construction and would be finished in time for the opening of the International Golden Gate Exposition on February 5, 1939. Visitors would come to visit the Exposition and watch the takeoffs and landings of the new fleet of Pan American Clippers. As at the Dinner Key Terminal, crowds would line the waterfront to watch the famous departing and arriving. Pan American operated a special, large automobile to bring passengers to the Treasure Island Terminal. Clyde Sunderland, Pacific Aerial Surveys, HJW Geospatial Inc.

April 22, Monday

Sea best yet; almost dead calm. Unloading as usual. Mostly building materials coming over now. After beaches almost cleaned out. Storm blew up at noon exactly, wind blowing from due North. Lagoon roughest yet. When storm hit, men eating lunch on beach. Load of cement at shore hastily covered, hurry call sent to camp for all hands. Two more barges away in time. Cement barge pulled as high as possible on shore by tractor, ten unload rapidly as possible. Launch PanAir, tied to anchored scow, driven ashore, freed with minimum by Kuhn and Ferris. Other barges successfully landed by having launch head into wind (fortunately directly offshore) drop back — two men with tow ropes attached to tractor. When tractor rope attached, launch line let go. Full speed ahead. Both barges beached in fine order. Small scowl containing case oil unloaded in about ten minutes. Large barge building, materials, generator panel board. All unloaded OK. Nothing damaged. Onshore wind; expected high tide, so had to move everything back from beach. Moved up beach about 500 feet. Cleared whole beach, except oil, poles, and heavier materials. Two new anchors put down. Midway and Wake launches had much difficulty in properly mooring. Mr. Grooch took charge; left Mr. McKenzie in charge after clearing. Rain started after nightfall. Ruined watch working in salt water. Beach made shipshape for night. Only one barge anchored; others beached. One tractor anchored to Wake barge as deadman. Ramp adrift, but held to deadman. Two-man watch left on beach for night.

April 23, Tuesday

Rain and wind again. Very nasty. With two tractors and unloading crew camp cleared up entire beach, except for some gravel and oil. Ration of hot grog served to all hands. Double ration for beach crew and men digging well. Men carried hot coffee around all morning. Work on construction progressing well. Transmitter building floor in. Concentrated load of two transmitters too great for design. Necessitates placing another two of supports. No contact with ship throughout day. Weather clearing afternoon.

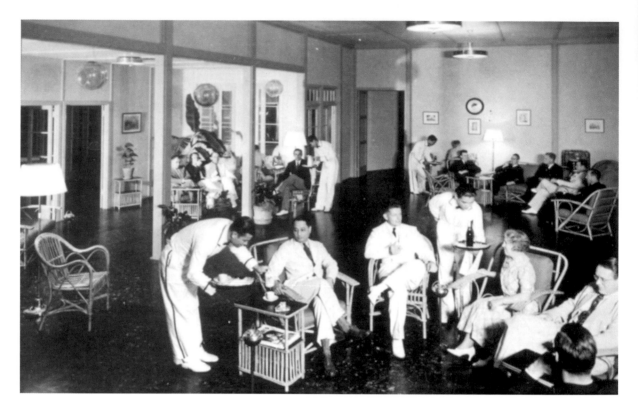

Interior of sitting area, Pan Am island hotel. A system of hotels was constructed on the island stopovers to provide comfort for the passengers as they waited for the next day's departure. During World War II, the United States military would employ this concept of island hopping to reach the ultimate destination.

University of Miami, Richter Library, Pan Am Collection

April 24, Wednesday

Weather clear; still high swell in lagoon. Work received from Mate that loading would be OK. Went out on Midway at 9 with Mr. Grooch aboard. Cleaned up, got cigarettes and movies for showing at night. Lunch on board, then back to shore. Very little time spent on beach. Material coming in very uniformly — best to leave beach crew alone, no interference. Spending more time inspecting construction. Movies again at night. Complete program again. Cable personnel present; all enjoyed.

April 25, Thursday

Weather clear, unloading conditions excellent. Nine barge loads today, finishing up building panels and other building materials. Should finish these tomorrow — leaving only oil and gasoline remaining. Radio transmitting station transferred to H building. Still using small emergency transmitter, however. Mr. Lueder started meteorological observations today. Took upper-air observation with theodolite at noon and 6. Windmill tower practically complete — very difficult for men to assemble since blueprints were quite poor. Believe they would get along much better if they put things up in most symmetrical fashion. Started assembly first AGA stove. Kitchen floor completed. Necessary reinforce section of kitchen floor with extra joists to withstand weight of stoves. Refrigerators washed out in preparation for storing food. Night gang on beach transferring further cargo to camp. Necessary repair clutch Midway tractor. Ashore for night.

April 26, Friday

Now transferring gas and oil to beacon. By night only these items left for unloading, and we should be able to finish unloading sometime Sunday. Out to ship in morning to clean up, get cigarettes and movies for evening. Stayed aboard until afternoon, then back to shore. Now that major part of unloading has been completed, there is not very much for

McKenzie and self to do. Both constantly inspecting and trying to learn from mistakes here what not to do at Wake Island. Proposed that general storage depot be used at Wake to facilitate unloading. No time lost in distributing cargo properly at various sites — all cargo together, therefore relatively easy to locate any single item. Party under Mr. Porter surveying lagoon and channel. Seeking shorter route for launches. Checking obstacles in landing area, also checking south channel entrance. Nine barge loads again today. Handle oil quite fast. Complete movie program again tonight. Refrigerators put in operation this morning. Will check for at least 24 hours before bringing food ashore. AGA stove finished late this afternoon.

April 27, Saturday
Still unloading oil and gasoline. Gasoline drum count may be off due to faulty count on drums used for launches, etc.

Note: No complete detailed record kept between April 28th and July 4th, when I took over the duties of Assistant Airport Engineer at Wake after Mr. McKenzie's departure on the return voyage of the North Haven.

July 4, Thursday
North Haven sailed at 4:45. Big supper; beer. Men settled down to read for the evening.

July 5, Friday
Day of rest. All up at 7:30. Breakfast at 8. Moved perishable foods up from beach. Cleaned up mess hall, installed some furniture, made room into recreation room. Went fishing in the afternoon in PanAir. Messrs. Bicknell, Kenler, Stuhrman, Ziegler along. Caught a few. Stuhrman caught a shark — shot by Col. Bicknell. Mullahey and Mackota chased shark up on beach and speared it. Dinner a little late; only two servants now since others were fired. New #1 boy seems to be a good cook. Recreation room opened in evening. Wonderful to see boys settle down as if at home.

July 6, Saturday
Up at 5; regular schedule now. Meals 5:30, 12 and 6. Work from 6 to 11, 2 to 5. Sundays, holidays. George Kuhn took three others over to Wilkes to move 1,000 bags of cement off beach, restack and cover in storage yard. Took all day for job and men were plenty played out. Two men breaking up camp and cleaning up in general. Moved garbage pile from neighborhood kitchen. One airport, two operations men laying gasoline pipeline along dock. Obstruction lights on windmill repaired and placed two feet further apart. Original location too close to fan when mill shut off, broke two red globes. Started screening mess hall with mosquito netting. Made stand for theodolite. Used top old cable reel. Checked and gave Col. Bicknell true North position.

July 7, Sunday
Up at 5. No holiday today since Friday was day of rest. Three men on Wilkes rolling gasoline drums back from high water level and bringing others down to spit on lagoon side. Geo. Kuhn working on hold-down cables. Two men finishing up camp cleanup/other general cleanup. Finished tacking down canvas roof B building. Men had not quite finished on Thursday. Chaumont arrived off Wake Island (near landing place) at 2:30 p.m.

All dressed up to go aboard. Col. Bicknell, Dr. Kenler, Stuhrman, Gray, and self went aboard. Col. Bicknell conferred with officers regarding location windmills, buildings, etc. Stuhrman visited with Winters — en route Guam re. DF. Was treated to fresh milk and ice cream by First Assistant. In all, I had probably best time of all aboard. Launch crew, Magill and Mullahey: barge crew, Sadler and Neidiger. Magill did excellent job bringing barge alongside. Not a word spoken either side. Captain of Chaumont commented favorably; life jackets worn by men, coveralls as uniform. After being aboard about half hour, came ashore with four new Chinese, mail, few new supplies. On Peale again by 5. Spent night reading newspapers and magazines. No mail for me.

July 8, Monday
Whole crew plus Magill and myself over to Wilkes in morning to bring barge into lagoon — clean up waterfront. Brought large barge in fine shape, but one sampan grounded as we were trying to bring it through. Tied up for night. Landing float dismantled, Wake — launch refueled. Brought fairly decent load over Peale. In afternoon two men sawing lumber for dock, one uncrating and moving furniture. Assembling beds myself. Remainder men Wilkes cleaning up cargo there. Made lemon ice for the gang in evening for dessert. Don't seem to like my methods in kitchen. (Note: August these methods later adopted.)

July 9, Tuesday
Four men on Wilkes finishing up cargo transfer, loading barges. Brought over tractor — food and oil. Some miscellaneous. This cleans up most of cargo on Wilkes and now we ought to be able to get along without going over except for things as we need them. One man working interior trim D building. Finished most of work by evening. Two men on camp half morning. Cutting decking for dock. 2,000 board feet of 2 x 12 was ordered, instead of 2,000 linear feet. We are short 800 linear feet to complete dock. Assembling beds myself today again. Finished furnishing C except for wardrobes. All men over here in afternoon. Working on leaders to cistern from K. This is the largest roof and best from which we shall be able to catch fresh water. Seems rather evident now that more men should have been left behind, especially carpenters. Will be quite a rush to finish up everything necessary for receiving Clipper before it arrives. Must check all depths all over landing area in lagoon. Broke out books in evening. Seems to be quite a selection. Wake is getting more like home every day.

July 10, Wednesday
Work on Wilkes finished, for time being at least. One man working interior trim D building. Sink in bathroom was so placed that door would not open completely — had to alter doorway to allow for complete opening. George Kuhn assembling wardrobes in C building. Longer job than we had first suspected. Other men moving cargo from beach. All food now stored in building. Doctor very busy stacking food away. Took upper-air observation this morning. Last balloon just above 6,000 feet. Beach practically all cleaned up by evening.

July 11, Thursday
Reports today. Back to regular procedure again. Still having some goods from beach, but by noon beach was entirely clean. Finished assembling furniture for C and D building complete except for furniture, exterior paint, and a little cleaning up. Sadler working

on leaders from K. Neidiger burying cable. Pumps received on Chaumont tested out. Outboard motor set in place on pump and clamped to barge. Pump suction in lagoon. Found pump satisfactory, except that suction must be immersed. Will be difficult to start outboard down 15' in 4 x 4 well. CO and room necessary for starting outboard. Having trouble with voltage regulation. Kratz, from all accounts, did not connect regulator correctly. Having Neidiger check into this thoroughly. Starting inventory of commissary myself today. Rather a tedious job — counting needles, buttons, thread, etc. Received word from Capt. Odell that supplies ordered would be sent as soon as possible.

July 12, Friday
George Kuhn working on hold-down cables, four buildings finished. Sadler and Tatum finishing leaders from K. Tractor busy with three men in forenoon, two in afternoon, hauling furniture from K and cleaning up grounds. Benny finishing up around D — siding hot water tank, etc. Neidiger finishing ditching in electric cable. Mullahey now driving tractor. Still having trouble voltage regulator. Will not balance, especially when two generators are running. Believe vibration may have something to do with this, for ordinary regulator is designed to work in power house which is on exceedingly firm foundation. No criticism against our foundations, which I believe are excellent, but there is plenty of vibration present. Mackota suggested this morning that fresh water be used for refrigerator since trouble caused by salt seems to have brought on failure of the North Haven reefer. Immediately contacted Capt. Odell and he sent his OK. Will probably take small cistern out of ground and place it near L building, using it as a reservoir for water, returning exhaust from compressor to the tank.

July 13, Saturday
Two men on tractor still cleaning up. Camp and station in fairly good condition tonight. Col. Bicknell held inspection today at 10:30 a.m. and found things generally to his

satisfaction. Kitchen spick and span; K building looking much better now that furniture has been moved out. Zeigler moving lathe and woodworking machine into place. Uncreated and assembled most of D furniture today. Still have wardrobe and cabinet to assemble. George Kuhn still working on hold-down cables. Six buildings complete except for blocks under wire. Tatum and Sadler cleaning up on various plumbing left over since the North Haven left. Also finished leaders K. Neidiger and Benny cleaning up at B. Neidiger finished covering electric cable. Stuhrman and Mackota finally completed work on voltage regulator. Among other things, they found that the wrong phase had been grounded. Took entire upper-air observation myself, today.

July 14, Sunday
Day of rest, breakfast at 7. Read the whole morning. George Kuhn laid the linoleum in D building, assembled kitchen cabinet. Went out in the afternoon with Col. Bicknell and Zeigler in PanAir to look again over lagoon for coral heads. Found more than we wanted. Col. Bicknell dropped several marked bottles overboard to ascertain currents in lagoon. Found that mooring area had several heads with less than 4' of water. Barometer today highest we have recorded here 30.07" at 11 p.m. High clouds and overcast in evening. Looks like we may have something coming on.

July 15, Monday
Started work on dock again today. Two men drilling stringers and spiking them down to bents with ¾" x 12 dock spikes. Mullahey gathered part of our supper with the proper use of his throw net, which he kept handy, when a school of mullet swam by while he

Large machine shop on the island base. Not only were supplies in large quantities required, each island base had to have large shops to ensure that if a problem developed with the arriving Clipper, it could be repaired. Each island base was a miniature city and repair facility.

was at work. Two men still finishing up on exterior of B before proceeding to interior. Pulled small 2000 gal. cistern out of ground today in about ¾ of morning. Brake on tractor froze, so some time out before refilling hole. George Kuhn assembling furniture in D. Sadler working on water system. Went out in lagoon again with Messrs. Bicknell, Kuhn, Zeigler to mark out landing area with cork buoys.

July 16, Tuesday

Two men still on B building windows and louvres and cleaning up siding. George Kuhn finished up D furniture, then working on hold-down cables. Two men on dock. Almost all stringers spiked to bents. Tatum on tractor digging hole for tank and placing tank, etc. Took more time due to shrubbery restriction. Sadler on water system, leaders, etc. Helped Zeigler make up buoys to mark landing area. Overcast all day, with heavy rainfall in the morning. Rain again at night.

July 17, Wednesday

Very nasty weather today. Frequent heavy squalls. Rainfall last 24 hours 1.3", which certainly is plenty. Bothered the men working. Wanted to start work on the lagoon today, but decided to await better weather. Very difficult to see coral heads under water in cloudy weather. Two men started working on D, painting. However, after finishing half, rain forced to them to quit. Most of men working interior B. Seems best to keep men inside in bad weather. Found roof K leaking badly, rain had driven in windows and louvres. After conference Col. Bicknell, Geo. Kuhn, it was decided that flashings would be needed on windows, at least on weather side, roofs should be battened down and more and heavier paint should be ordered. Sent a long radiogram to Capt. Odell and McKenzie regarding situation. Capt. Odell wired back saying he would take matter up with McKenzie. Also said he was leaving for New York and that McKenzie was taking charge of division up to and including Guam. Also instructed me to go ahead and finish landing facilities in lagoon.

July 18, Thursday

Weather shows signs of clearing this morning. Geo. Kuhn took two men over to Wilkes to bring further cargo over, dynamite, caps, lumber, etc. Downpours began again shortly before noon and lasted for rest of afternoon. Started finishing off painting D roof myself but was prevented by downpours from accomplishing very much. Tatum and Sadler finish covering tank for refrigerator cooling water system. Tatum caulked connection between roof saddle and generator exhaust pipe — water running down onto generator. Discovered windmill had run practically dry after fresh windmill had been shut down for cleaning purposes preparatory to use with fresh water, had to turn stand pump on. Started to show signs of a cold myself, so Dr. made me go to bed early, sleep long. Probably due as much to loss of sleep as to anything else.

July 19, Friday

At last signs of a little cessation in the rainfall. Looks like we may be coming into a rainy season, though. Got up a little after 8, after a terrific shower, 2.6" rain in a little over five minutes. Does look like better weather, though. Started work in the lagoon today. Rigged drag aft salmon scow and dragged northwestern end lagoon. Coral situation looks pretty bad. Two men dynamiting one on scow, launchman on launch. May have

An S-42 receiving a major maintenance checkup. Ground crew checking the four engines, fuselage, tail, interior of the aircraft. Operating in salt water created many problems in the operation of a flying boat.

University of Miami, Richter Library, Pan Am Collection

to clear away runway only if proves too difficult to clear whole area by first of month. Two men on dock, Geo. Kuhn building decking on salmon scow for walkway float. Starting to spike down dock clearing. Windmill running OK again. Trouble caused by sand in foot valves. Sadler working windmills and water system. Discovered valve to cistern damaged by tractor. Will have to replace. Didn't do much of anything today. Felt a little rocky.

July 20, Saturday

Really down to work on the lagoon today. Up to tonight 22 heads have been dynamited, and there are plenty more to come. Two men, Tatum and Mullahey, doing the blasting, while Neidiger and Magill drag the lagoon with a length of rail tied six feet below waterline on salmon scow towed by the PanAir launch. Neidiger, on the scow, drops a cork float every time the drag strikes a projection. Of course this method is not infallible, since it is very difficult to make sure that every square food has been covered, but it is the surest

method available. Two men spiking down decking on dock. A long and tedious job, for there are no common spikes left, and we are forced to use dock spikes which were sent from Manila (Lord knows why, we didn't order them). It is therefore necessary to drill each plank before using 5/8" square spikes. George Kuhn decking over salmon scow to be used for landing float, also on marker buoys. Sadler still working on leaders, etc. Fresh water windmill pumping fresh water for the first time today. Pumped out G and L tanks without difficulty. Col. Bicknell and Dr. Kenler entertained at housewarming tonight. A grand time was had by all.

July 21, Sunday
Up at 6:30, breakfast at seven. With crew of three and George Kuhn, laid oil drum marker buoys on landing area boundaries in lagoon. Also checked location of several coral heads and found a few more. They're plenty thick, and there are far more than any of us suspected at first. Later in afternoon located all buoys and a few salient points on Wilkes and Peale with transit. Will plot these locations with view to possibly transmitting same to Alameda via system of coordinates. Col. Bicknell initiating tide watch today to record tide. Stood watch from 10 to 2.

July 22, Monday
Still working in lagoon and on dock. Eleven coral heads blown today, making total of 33. Not dragging. Dock coming along slowly, but in good fashion. Plotted results of yesterday's transit work regarding buoys and found maximum run to be in neighborhood of 4,000 feet. Some points seemed to be in error, so decided to repeat using 1,000-foot baseline instead of 300 feet. Did this in afternoon. Plotted results again at night — drawing B1-3W and found that maximum run is 5,000 feet from West to East. Results apparently more accurate this time. Finished painting D roof. High barometer again, may have bad weather in a few days.

July 23, Tuesday
Stood 2 to 6 a.m. watch on tide gauge. Was elevated to position of launchman today. Running launch while towing drag on lagoon. Only six heads blown out today. Total now 39. Sea too rough this afternoon for men to work from small boat. All decking available spiked down to dock. Three-foot catwalk laid for remaining length — 100 feet. Salmon scow completely decked over for use as landing float. A bit grouchy tonight — too tired probably. Every time I get a little too tired, I tend to become easily disturbed, so must watch that.

July 24, Wednesday
Out on lagoon again this morning. Weather somewhat threatening though. Towed pit barge across to Wilkes for load of cement. Finished dragging second section of landing area. This brings total to about 1/6 of entire area. Drag seems to work fairly successfully, although we are very liable miss some spots. Very difficult on water to determine exact course for each run so that entire area being dragged will be covered. Eight heads blasted. Barge not completely loaded with cement by noon. Brought crew back to Peale. Storm came up shortly afternoon. Has been raining ever since. Very heavy rainfall. Had to go out in rain to rescue barges. Drag barge had been hung up on coral head, had to be brought in. Cement barge brought over from Wilkes — tied up at buoy. Plenty wet.

July 25, Thursday

Still nasty weather. Tatum and Mullahey started work in the lagoon near dock. Blew three heads (total 50) then were forced to quit. Cold and wet weather. Yesterday's rainfall 1.37". Men inside B building working partitions, interior. Linoleum laid in bathroom. Roads cleared by operations men on tractor. Clearing of whole place in general, dragging off and burning brush, etc. Place looks marginally better. Short linoleum for F building. Did not order enough for both kitchens.

July 26, Friday

Same procedure as has been going on for last few days. Men working on dock spent morning and part of afternoon gathering barge load of gravel preparatory to pour concrete bases for piles. Began pouring dry mix late in afternoon and completed four bases. Twelve more coral heads (total 62). George Kuhn working on gangplank. Dr. Kenler kindly volunteered to act as barge crew on drag barge. Very wet late in afternoon while out on lagoon.

July 27, Saturday

Concrete crew have completed pouring 2/3 of pile bases. Cross section bent. Method used in pouring: barge loaded with gravel and mixer tied up alongside dock. Barge with cement tied up alongside first barge. Concrete poured dry down chute into oil drum. Some difficulty encountered in pouring without losing too much of the dry mix. Six coral heads blown today. Accidents befell lagoon crew. Line holding drag rail severed by coral cuts, launch ran out of gas, slowed up work. Probably my own fault for running out of gas, although launch had 20 gallons in tank when I checked in the morning. Had to row a mile for the gas. Gray and Dr. Kenler on drag.

July 28, Sunday

Expedition formed today to look over Wake Island. Headed by Col. Bicknell all except five joined the party. Among findings were five hydrographic current bottles. Didn't do much of anything myself today. Moved engineers' equipment from shack to A. Excellent ice cream tonight. Col. Bicknell has issued a memorandum regarding his inspection of yesterday. Although his inspection covers the entire station, including construction projects, I have not been invited to accompany him, as was the custom when Mr. McKenzie was here. I have not received any official copy of the memorandum, although it especially mentions certain items for which I consider the Airport Department responsible.

July 29, Monday

Still running launch in lagoon. Accomplished quite a bit today. Dragged one entire area and finished off another. Boys blasted fourteen coral heads (total 82). Estimate more than 1/3 of total area dragged. Finished pouring concrete bases for dock piles. Except for cleaning up around the dock, the dock is complete as far as we may go at the present time with the material available. George Kuhn still working on gangplank, making a wonderful job.

July 30, Tuesday

Decided I had to quit working on the lagoon today and go to work on my own business, so started one of several drawings to be completed before arrival of the Clipper. Score

Waiting in the terminal, passengers pass the time. Large map of North and South America on the back wall.

University of Miami, Richter Library, Pan Am Collection

now 86 coral heads. Mullahey and Tatum pulled drag all morning, dynamiting in afternoon — blasted four heads. Have completed dragging about half total landing area. Other men finished cleaning up about dock, unloaded remaining cement on barge and after this was completed went to work in B building. Geo. Kuhn brought salmon scow into position as landing float, placed gangplank into position. Moved into rooms in B tonight. Stuhrman and I in same room. Three of total six rooms completed. Re. concrete for dock: Dry mix 1:3 (sand and gravel mixed). In pouring dry mix into drum below surface much cement is lost, so resultant mix estimated at 1:4. Total of 115 bags used for 51 footings.

July 31, Wednesday

No work in lagoon this morning. Men working on dock and landing float jetting down piles. Jet consists of 12' length of 2" pipe with one end flattened attached to end for 1 ¼" hose. Centrifugal pump with outboard motor power supplies pressure. Worked quite satisfactorily. Soft sand extends 3' to 4' down, then bed well-packed gravel. Dynamited rock in way of one pile. Sank piles in about 5'. Collars put on salmon scow to hold to pile. Piles cut off 4' above low water. Two men working interior B building. One still cleaning up around entire station. Dynamite gang blasted five heads in lagoon in afternoon (total 91). Drawings are coming along fairly slow. One man rewiring refrigerator panel board half day.

August 1, Thursday

Dynamite gang dragging today. Finding very few heads, so continued dragging all day, instead of blasting in afternoon. Have completed dragging about 2/3 of total landing area. George Kuhn moored float in position. Built pivot arrangement to allow barge to swing into wind. Impractical to use pile arrangement as suggested by Mr. Grooch. Also cleaning up both barges. Two men B partitions all day. Coming along well. Man finishing up plumbing in B. One man with tractor helping in general cleanup. Finished three drawings today. Speeding up a little.

August 2, Friday

No work on lagoon today. Three men working on moorings. Replaced four carwheel anchors for holding mooring barge, jetting anchors dug below the surface of the bottom. Two men on B partitions and interior trim — should finish tomorrow. One on plumbing, one painting B roof. Drawing again today. Men changed chains to mooring anchors. George Kuhn finishing off salmon scow.

August 3, Saturday

Marine equipment finished as far as we can go, today. Except for clearing the lagoon, which should take another week, and a few odds and ends, we are ready for the Clipper now. Dynamite crew dragging all day today. Haven't been finding many heads in middle area, so are continuing dragging until get sufficient heads to spend a couple of days blasting. B partitions and interior trim except for linen closets complete today. Woodbridge fell off B roof, which he was painting — not seriously injured. Resumed work after short rest. Water in two water closets, two lavatories, one shower of B. Fresh water in E.

August 4, Sunday

Up at 6:45; breakfast at 7. After breakfast all men turned to taking down tents and moving to B building. Only one tent left standing as medical tent and one tent as temporary storage for cots and mattresses. Two A tents erected behind B — Benny and Woodbridge occupying these. Twelve men in B — two per room. Sorely in need of some place to be used as permanent dressing station, infirmary, etc. Need not be very large (10' x 12' or thereabouts). Ziegler, Kuhn, Col. Bicknell, and self went out in lagoon to check area already dragged and look over possibilities for extending area southwards. Found area as far as boat channel not too bad, but will take some time to thoroughly check. Received notice today that Clipper is scheduled to arrive Wake August 16, leaving for Guam August 19. Unless something unforeseen occurs we will be ready for her.

August 5, Monday

Dynamite gang blasting again today — got 12 heads (total 103). Two men working interior trim — B building. One man removing valve from middle of read opposite C. Working on water system. One on dock, starting railing, one carrying lumber half day. Got into a bit of a tangle with George Kuhn today regarding responsibility for entire job. Discovered he was told by McKenzie that he was to take charge of construction. Capt. Odell, in confirming list of those remaining, said "in charge of number four," number four being myself. Can't have two bosses here, and as George has much more experience, I am to let him direct all construction work, and I'll try to give him guidance along lines laid down back in the States as best I can. I don't believe there'll be any trouble whatsoever.

August 6, Tuesday

Started dragging last portion of lagoon this morning. Should finish area marked out fairly soon. Two men working on piping form pump (centrifugal with outboard) in well to windmill tank. Very little wind sufficient to turn mill for past few days, therefore necessary fill tank. Pump started at four. Backfire from motor, which is 12 feet down in well, started fire in well. No damage, two extinguishers used. Exhaust fumes prevent manual operation of motor, and considerably hampers efficiency. Pump must be run at high speed to lift water 52 feet to tank and 15 feet out of well. Will be necessary make proper exhaust for motor. George Kuhn trimming off decking and putting up rail posts on dock. Two men still on interior B. Message from McKenzie today saying my photographs had turned out OK.

August 7, Wednesday
Same old thing this morning. Dynamite crew dragging last portion of lagoon — 50-yard strip to go at noon. One man nailing up vermin pans on E and L. One man still working on water pump. Two on B porch; one electrical. One still on dock with rail posts. Storm front appeared in NW shortly after noon, strong breeze flowing from NW. Threw up quite a swell in lagoon and landing barge, which received swell abeam, started pitching quite violently. Pivot broken off. Necessary to move barge out from piles, lift gangplank. Was nearly caught under gangplank when barge started moving out from underneath. Gangplank lifted on hinges, tied down in vertical position. Spent rest of afternoon preparing for storm which did not appear, except as from in NW. Temporary hold-down cables on those building not equipped — boarding weather side gable louvres. Stuhrman has discovered water in the insulator boxes of the DF. Checking original calibration tonight with Midway and Guam.

The ill-fated *Philippine Clipper* tied off. The front mooring pin would be one of the few pieces of wreckage to survive the crash into the mountains of Northern California on January 21, 1943. Crew members are working on the engines.

University of Miami, Richter Library, Pan Am Collection

August 8, Thursday

Started blasting again this morning. Now close in near dock, where Dave Richards supposedly cleared. Drag at five-and-a-half feet depth — blasted 11 heads in morning (total 114). In afternoon dynamite crew over to Wilkes for load of lumber. Two men B porch — ceiling and siding. Finish electrical. Fresh water standpipe installed at B. Fresh water lines put into D. George Kuhn fixing up dock and marine equipment in preparation for Clipper. DF bearings taken last night came out OK. Will not be necessary to recalibrate.

August 9, Friday

More trouble today. The blasting magneto went out of action this morning and would only blow one cap, and as the gang are in an area with fairly large heads, this slowed them down tremendously. Only two heads in morning. Dragged down several heads in afternoon. After checking magneto and finding it irreparable, ordered another via Clipper. One man finishing up gasoline pipe line. Straightening out and connecting from dock to pit. One man cleaning up on dock. George Kuhn remaking pivot and contacts between barges. Blow Wednesday had smashed up others, too light. Two on B porch and siding. Operations men putting up wind cone upright. Still drawing, but not getting too much accomplished. Have to leave desk too often to make any real progress.

The journal ended there.

Part of the planning for the hotel on Wake Island included growing vegetables and produce to feed the hungry passengers and staff. Gardens would reduce the cost of transporting fresh vegetables and produce to the island bases. Growing soil was discovered to be inadequate, so tons of soil had to be shipped from Guam to create the bathtub garden of Wake Island. Pan American engineers contacted experts in hydroponics at the University of California.

Ground crew member working on the back of the refueling barge at Guam. Refueling barges on the water were in use at several island sites.

Pan American was so successful that a large feature story appeared in the *New York Times* on November 26, 1939, on the monumental hydroponics operation on Wake Island. Torrey Lyons, Chief Gardener for Pan American Airways at its mid-Pacific base at Wake Island, announced that the capacity of his water-culture gardens, in which fresh vegetables are scientifically nurtured, would shortly be quadrupled.

Prior to the hydroponic system, four redwood tanks of 280-square-foot total area yielded average weekly crops of 12 pounds of tomatoes, 8 pounds of cucumbers, and experimental lots of lima beans. Raised by hydroponics — the feeding of plants with weak solutions of mineral salts and without earth — the truck crops were used to supplement food supplies shipped to the barren island.

With the addition of a new 70-foot hydroponicum with a 980-square-foot area, Mr. Lyons foresaw tomato production rising to 30 pounds weekly and his output of other green foods assuming greater stature in the effort to feed the airline's personnel stationed at Wake Island.

The hotels and infrastructure on Midway and Wake Islands had been completed in 55 days. The secret was that the buildings and construction material had been prefabricated for easier installation. There were even large fountains constructed in front of the hotels to provide a homier atmosphere. Each room contained a beautiful bed, several dressers, fans, and always fresh flowers. The furniture was in the Art Deco style of the 1930s. Each hotel provided the stopover guest with hot and cold running water and a shower in every room. The dining rooms featured the finest linens and china.

Pan American Airways became a leader in the construction of airfields and infrastructure facilities in difficult situations. Juan Trippe came to believe that 90 percent of aviation is on the ground. The experiences gained in building island bases would become more evident after the attack on Pearl Harbor, Hawaii, on December 7, 1941. President Franklin Roosevelt would request that Pan American Airways take a leadership and training role in the new war that had been unleashed in the Pacific, Europe, and the Middle East.

Upon arriving at an island destination, every member of the crew, no matter what their job, was thrown into unloading the SS *New Haven*. This was the first order of business and the most critical. The second task was to establish the radio and direction finder installations. After 15 days, a designated group for permanent construction was put into constructing the airfield. As each group finished their job, the SS *North Haven* sailed to the next island on the list.

The entire task was completed in the amazing time of 55 days. The Pan American Airway island-hopping system was complete. Each island in the chain had different requirements, and different solutions were required. Refueling barges containing 4,000-gallon fuel tanks were employed at Midway Island and Guam. At Honolulu and Wake Island, crews installed seaplane landing pontoons, duplicated from Pan American's Caribbean design and experience. A seaplane could pull along side a shore-connected dock that contained permanent fuel, fresh water connections, electrical contacts for power poles, and lighting for nighttime operation. When a seaplane was not docked, the platform was turned into a workstation.

Pan American Airways had designed special seaplane tenders. The low, sturdy boats were fendered, so that the boat would not damage the hulls of the aircraft. They were also powered for towing fully equipped foamite fire-fighting units. Each small boat was equipped with special generators and batteries to operate radio, telephones, and search-lights. The ships had a range of 500 miles for rescue missions. Complete first aid and crash equipment were carried on board.

The dedication of the Marine Air Terminal, LaGuardia Field, March 31, 1940. Pan Am's new home for the *Atlantic Clippers*.
University of Miami, Richter Library, Pan Am Collection

Another Pan American innovation installed at the Manila base was a nose hangar. The seaplane could pull up and fit its nose into the special hangar. New systems of landing lights and techniques for nighttime landings were put in place, and crews were constantly undergoing training. The Pan American system was the first to employ parachute flares for nighttime landings.

A small airfield used for private aircraft in Queens, Long Island, was turned into the major flying boat base for the Atlantic Clippers. It was owned by Curtiss-Wright and named the North Beach Airport. Juan Trippe used the facility when he piloted his own small aircraft to East Hampton. An announcement was made that the field was to be sold for a housing development, so Juan went to the Appropriation Committee of the City of New York and gave a lecture on how aviation was developing so quickly that New York would soon require another airport to serve the needs of the traveling public. His testimony appeared to turn the tide, and the City of New York purchased the parcel of swampland. Bulldozers and heavy construction equipment were brought in, and by 1940, the Marine Air Terminal was completed. Pan American moved its flying boat operation from Port Washington to the new Marine Air Terminal at LaGuardia Airport.

The interior of the Marine Air Terminal was, like the Treasure Island Terminal, in the Art Deco style.

Art Deco was very appropriate here because the style appreciated modern machinery and the work that men did with their skills and machines. Over the archway in the building, a mural by James Brooks features the Pan American B-314 in flight. Other images include Pan American employees and other workers. The mural was created in the Social Realist style, which portrays working men and women. Other murals featured the construction of bridges, highways, roads, and giant electric dams.

An aerial view of the official opening of the Marine Air Terminal, LaGuardia Field, New York. In the distance a Pan Am Clipper on the water. During World War II, the terminal would service U.S. military flying boats as well as the Clippers. University of Miami, Richter Library, Pan Am Collection

SANDFORD B. KAUFFMAN

Sandford B. Kauffman, who held a number of different positions for Pan American, remembers building the base in Botwood:

The first thing I had to do was to set up a base of operations in Newfoundland, at a place called Botwood on the north side of the island. It was a godforsaken place. Once I got to Newfoundland, I caught a narrow-gauge train that was supposed to go from St. John's to the other side of the island. We were about halfway there when the train stopped in the middle of nowhere, and all the passengers were told to get off. I sat in the station for a long time. Finally someone told me that I could get a lift from the mailman. He came along at about eight o'clock in an old ramshackle car, and he drove me down to Botwood.

When I got to Botwood, there was no place to stay. So I didn't have any place to sleep. However, there was one general store in town, which carried everything, including furniture. One of the show windows had a bed in it, and I made a deal with the manager of the store to let me sleep there. I slept in the window with shades drawn for several nights until finally something opened up at the inn. It was in a bed in which severalrailroad engineers slept. One was on the night duty and slept in the daytime. I could use the bed at night.

CHAPTER 6

THE MYSTERIOUS DISAPPEARANCES OF AMELIA EARHART, FRED NOONAN, AND CAPTAIN EDWIN C. MUSICK

Amelia Earhart's Vega aircraft in Newfoundland prior to her historic solo flight across the Atlantic Ocean. Memorial University of Newfoundland, Centre for Newfoundland Studies, Robert Tait Collection

(Left) Amelia Earhart in her flight suit. Author's Collection

AMELIA EARHART, FRED NOONAN, AND CAPTAIN EDWIN C. MUSICK all had connections to Pan American Airways, and each would meet a tragic, unsolved death. Amelia Earhart employed the services of Pan American on her travels on many occasions. As the navigator on the first Pan American *China Clipper* that flew to Manila on November 22, 1935, Fred Noonan had received a great amount of publicity. The circumstances that caused him to leave his employment with Pan American Airways have never been fully explained. No documents can be found to indicate his reason for leaving. Was it to find more lucrative employment? He was recognized as being one of the best navigators of the period. Other rumors indicate that he had a drinking problem and was fired or forced to leave for being unreliable. It was reported that prior to a flight, Captain Musick would usually ask, "Has anyone seen Fred?" There is no doubt that Fred Noonan was a mysterious man in many ways. He was born in Cook County, Illinois, on April 4, 1893; his mother died when he was four years old, and the census report three years later indicated he was living alone in a boarding home. He left school in 1905 and began to work on ships as a seaman.

He continued his maritime career until 1930, when he received a "limited commercial pilot's license." He then worked as an instructor in Miami and later turned up as the airport manager for Pan American Airways in Port-au-Prince, Haiti. While employed at Pan American, he mapped out routes in the Pacific and flew to Midway Island, Wake Island, Guam, the Philippines, and Hong Kong. By 1937, his skills as an expert navigator had earned him an excellent reputation. Some felt his departure from Pan American resulted from the feeling that he would not be able move any higher. There are many theories and not one conclusive reason for Fred Noonan leaving Pan American Airways.

Amelia Earhart planned to fly around the world. On March 17, 1937, she left Alameda on a route that would take her to Hawaii. For several days, she and Fred Noonan had met with Pan American officials to discuss the flight and make arrangements for stops along the way. Pan American had the most efficient island bases and most

experienced service crew. Earhart's flight had been planned for months. She noted, "When you plan an automobile journey through New England, or, say to Yellowstone, the needed maps can be had any filling station. But with a flight around the world, much of it off the beaten paths of established air transport, there are complexities. It took many weeks to get all the maps and charts we wanted. Once secured, the courses to be followed were laid out in detail on them, mostly by Commander Clarence Williams of Los Angeles, who had helped me plot previous flights."

Earhart would have three passengers on this trip: Paul Mantz, hitching a ride to Honolulu; Fred Noonan, serving as navigator; and Harry Manning, who would leave the crew after the accident at Hawaii forced Earhart and Noonan to return to Alameda. On the evening of Earhart's departure, a first was recorded: the first time that three aircraft were in flight over the Pacific Ocean in one night.

Captain Dahlstrom in the *Hawaii Clipper* was 150 miles ahead, on a regular flight to Manila. An hour out from Alameda, Earhart sighted the Pan American Clipper, silhouetted against a large bank of cumulus clouds, and flew close enough to snap a picture. This was the first time Earhart had seen another plane at sea, and she later learned it was the first time that Pan American aircraft had sighted one another. Her Lockheed 10E Electra left Musick's Pan American Clipper behind. She recorded in her logbook that she had taken two photographs of the Pan American aircraft.

Pan American radios, drift sight, and other navigational equipment had been installed in the Earhart Electra, and the Pan American Airways ground stations were to provide communications and other services as required on her journey. Fred Noonan was and would continue to be a controversial figure in aviation circles in the mid-1930s. Like his departure from Pan American, his official relationship with Captain Edwin is still one of heated debate.

One school of thinking held that Noonan was a man with a drinking problem who was the greatest navigator of the period and put into place many of the navigation advances that Pan American Airways pioneered. The blame for the disappearance of Earhart on the flight is placed on her shortcomings as a pilot and possible flaws in the design of the Lockheed Electra. Even if Amelia Earhart and Fred Noonan are found one day, the questions of the flight will never be answered.

Later that year, on July 2, Earhart and Noonan would disappear on their round-the-world flight. One of the United States Navy ships that would search for the two missing fliers was the USS *Avocet*, a seaplane tender that had been assigned to the area on May 5, 1937. Her home port had been Pearl

March 17, 1937. Amelia Earhart in flight above the San Francisco Bay Area in her Lockheed Electra en route to Honolulu.

Clyde Sunderland. Pacific Aerial Surveys - HJW Geospatial Inc.

The ill-fated S-42 of Captain Edwin Musick, in which he and the entire crew would disappear. It is believed that the aircraft exploded in midair, very little trace ever found of the aircraft or crew. Igor Sikorsky Historical Archives

Harbor. The USS *Avocet* would not find any trace of the missing aviators or their aircraft.

Early in 1938, the USS *Avocet* would become involved in the search for another famous aviator, the individual who had become the face of Pan American Airways: Captain Edwin Musick. For several months, Captain Musick had been surveying the area around New Zealand and Pago Pago in preparation for the expansion of routes. By 1937, the Atlantic surveys were complete, and attention wa s focused toward the new Pacific routes. The S-42B NC16734 was ferried to Honolulu on December 2 and refitted as the *Samoan Clipper*. Captain Edwin C. Musick formed a new crew to make one more survey flight of the area around Auckland, New Zealand.

On board the aircraft was Chief Inspector E. L. Yuravich of the Department of Commerce. If he approved the operation, scheduled airmail service would begin with the return flight. Everything went according to plan, and Musick returned to the United States with the first pieces of mail on December 29.

Musick made a fateful decision, one that would turn tragic and cost him his life. Originally, Captain Sellers was to command the next scheduled flight to New Zealand, but Musick decided to make one last check on the Pago Pago landing area. He had serious concerns about the landing areas and approaches on this leg of the journey. The *Samoan Clipper* lifted off from Pago Pago at 5:37 a.m. on January 11, 1938. The weather was reported to be clear, the wind calm, water surface in the takeoff area smooth with no problems. The aircraft was carrying 1,150 gallons of fuel in the wing tanks, 1,150 gallons in the hull tanks, and weighed 41,936 pounds upon takeoff.

Radio communication was established with Pan American radio station KABS. At 6:37 a.m., an hour after takeoff, a radio message announced that an oil leak had appeared in engine four. The *Samoan Clipper* would return to Pago Pago to have the problem rectified. It was uncertain when the oil leak had occurred. The Pago Pago radio operator believed it was at 6:08 a.m., 31 minutes after takeoff.

A radio message at 7:20 indicated that engine four had been braked to a stop, and aviation fuel was being dumped to lighten the weight of the aircraft for landing. At 8:26, Pago Pago radioed weather and landing instructions to the aircraft.

Musick last reported that he was continuing to dump fuel and would not be in contact until the procedure had been completed. No further radio message arrived, and the Pago Pago radio operator continued to call with no response. Musick's last reported position was NW of Tutuila, at 14 degrees 08 South Latitude and 170 degrees 51 West Longitude. The last message received advised, "We are going to dump gas — We cannot use the radio during the dumping — Stand by."

The USS *Avocet* that had assisted in the fruitless search for Amelia Earhart had also been posted to Pago Pago on October 25 to search for another famous aviator. The seaplane tender sighted an oil slick and some small pieces of wreckage. The captain lowered his motor launch to take a closer look. No sign of any survivors or bodies was found. The USS *Avocet* returned to Pago Pago with only a few small pieces of the *Samoan Clipper*.

The board of inquiry found that the *Samoan Clipper* had received a full check the night before her flight, and the aircraft did not have any history of problems with oil leaks. During a previous inspection in Honolulu, the studs at the front of the oil sump on engine four had been found to be broken. Holes had been drilled, and new larger bolts had been fitted into the holes.

A witness reported observing the *Samoan Clipper* turning north with fuel being dumped from both wings to the west of Pago Pago at 8:35 a.m. The aircraft then appeared to descend abruptly, with fuel still being jettisoned from both wings. The witness stated that as the aircraft hit the water, a flash of light was observed and the sound of an explosion heard. After the explosion, black smoke rose from the area. Other ships on the scene had also retrieved a few interior pieces, most from the compartment adjacent to the fuselage fuel tanks. Few other parts of the structure were recovered. Pieces that were in the area to the rear of the fuel tanks were considerably burned, while those from the areas ahead of the tanks had evidence of heat but did not appear to have the effects of exposure to flame.

It was determined that Musick was attempting to make an emergency landing when fuel vapors ignited. The heated engine exhaust or the vapors may have entered the wing. The fire may have spread under the hull fuel tanks and penetrated the floor of the navigator's compartment. Investigators concluded in their report that the probable cause of this accident was a fire that led to an explosion.

Crew of the USS *Avocet* that searched for Amelia Earhart, Fred Noonan, and the S-42 *Samoan Clipper* of Pan Am's Chief Pilot Edwin Musick. Life ring in front of crew. Old four-stack destroyer can be seen in the distance.

Naval Historical Foundation/Historical Services, Washington DC

Pan American Airways had suffered a major blow. The world had come to recognize the face of Captain Edwin C. Musick. His fame was worldwide in a time when aviators and their exploits were followed closely by the public.

Fred Ralph, a Pan American colleague, recalled, "I was first officer with Uncle Ed from Hong Kong to Honolulu on his last flight in the Martin 130. He left our crew there, to take the S-42B to New Zealand. It was the last time I saw him." Musick was described by fellow Pan American crew members as a cautious and very low-key man who always appeared to look serious. His death was a great loss for Pan American Airways; his experience and knowledge were missed.

In his brief life, Captain Edwin Musick was awarded many honors for his aviation skills. In April 1936, he traveled to New York City to receive the Harmon Trophy, which cited Musick as the "World's outstanding Aviator of 1935." This prestigious trophy was awarded for his pioneering Pacific survey flights and the transpacific service. Only two other Americans had received the award: Wiley Post and Charles Lindbergh. In his usual modest manner, he accepted the award with the comment, "There must be some mistake."

A few days after accepting the award, he was back at work plotting and planning new routes across the Pacific. As he arrived at Pearl Harbor, he was escorted by 20 military aircraft from Wheeler Field and a welcoming crowd of over 3,000 people.

Posthumous tributes continued for Captain Musick and the crew of the Clipper. On January 11, 1941, the Auckland Harbor Board dedicated and named a new radio station Musick Memorial Marine Radio Station at Bucklands Point. The station's communication responsibilities were transferred in 1977 to the new Auckland International Airport. A bronze plaque and photos of Musick and the S-42 are on permanent display at the Musick Memorial Radio Station. On display at Auckland's International Airport is the annual award presented within the United States and Commonwealth nations to promote safety in the air.

Flight tests on the S-42 were conducted by Miami Chief Pilot Bob Fatt, Copilot Williard Biggers and Engineer Frank Hankins. Colored water was employed to simulate the dumping of fuel. The tests indicated a problem with the dump chutes, and they were modified. The chutes were extended aft to assure expulsion of jettisoned fuel into areas clear of the aircraft. Even with the modification, crews never appeared to have the same confidence in the S-42 series as prior to the tragic accident.

The USS *Avocet* continued to keep dates with history. On December 7, 1941, she was moored south of the battleship USS *California* at Pearl Harbor, Hawaii. Stationed near the Naval Air Station dock, the crew opened fire on the attacking Japanese aircraft with their single .50 caliber machine gun. The crew shot down a Japanese Kate torpedo bomber after it had launched a torpedo at the USS *California*. The aircraft burst into flames and crashed near the Naval Hospital. Later in the day, the USS *Avocet* attempted to keep the warship *Nevada* afloat.

The ship's luck would run out after World War II, when the USS *Avocet* was declared surplus and sent to the scrap yard.

Igor Sikorsky and Pan Am Captain Edwin Musick discussing aviation on the dock with an S-42 floating in the water.

Igor Sikorsky Historical Archives

The USS *Avocet* on December 7, 1941, docked at Pearl Harbor. A Japanese aircraft shot down by the gun crew of the USS *Avocet* has crashed and is burning in the distance. The USS *Avocet* had one .50 cal. machine gun and was able to shoot down one of the attacking Japanese aircraft.

Naval Historical Foundation/Historical Services, Washington DC

CHAPTER 7

THE MYSTERY OF THE HAWAII CLIPPER

As the United States and Japan moved onto an unavoidable collision course for war in the Pacific, Pan American Airways became a target for aggression. The Japanese believed that the Clippers were a political outreach of the United States Government in the Pacific and that the airline spied on their military buildup throughout the area. The Japanese were further outraged at Pan American's island bases built across the Pacific in Hawaii, Midway Island, Wake Island, Guam, the Philippines, Macao, and then to the mainland of China.

Suspicion existed in the halls of the United States Congress as well. The attack on the USS gunboat *The Panay* in China in 1937 was perceived as a message to the United States Government and Pan American Airways to remain clear of the Chinese mainland. On July 28, 1938, the Pan American *Hawaii Clipper*, one of the three Martin 130s, disappeared without a trace. The *Hawaii Clipper* was carrying six passengers and nine crew members and was en route from Guam to Manila. The Guam island base was located very close to the Japanese Marianas bases.

The navigator of the *Hawaii Clipper* had reported his position as two hours from the Philippine coast at 12:11 p.m. He signaled that he would await a current weather report from the Panay Island station, just south of Manila. The communications and flight appeared to be moving normally with no reported problems. The weather station attempted to raise the Clipper at 12:12 p.m. to pass along the weather information and received no response. Several other messages were sent to the *Hawaii Clipper* without any reply.

There was some concern, but not panic, as the M-130, with powerful Pratt & Whitney 950-horsepower engines could remain aloft with only two engines functioning. The aircraft carried two main radios and a third auxiliary set had been added recently. The M-130, like every Pan American Clipper, had been equipped with life rafts, provisions,

(Left) M-130 *Hawaii Clipper* racing across the water, gathering speed for takeoff. Martin Aviation Historical Archives

(Below) M-130 *Hawaii Clipper* moored in the water. Crew member looking out from the front hatch. Martin Aviation Historical Archives

HAWAII BY FLYING CLIPPER

PAN AMERICAN AIRWAYS SYSTEM

Vintage Pan American Airways advertising of the Clipper with passengers departing to be greeted by Hula girls and have leis put around their neck. It was ads that focused on the exotic and romantic that allowed Pan Am to sell tickets. Each Clipper was named to increase the romance and branding of the airline. Poster by Frank Mackintosh, Swann Galleries, New York City

weapons, and fishing equipment. There were more than enough supplies to assist the passengers and crew into a survival mode if required. Since the Pan American Clippers flew such great distances over water, the company had always provided for the safety of everyone on board.

Unfortunately, after weeks of searching by aircraft and surface craft, not a trace of the aircraft was found. No debris, not even an oil slick was found to indicate where the aircraft had crashed or whether anyone had survived.

An electrical storm was considered as a cause for the disappearance, but a message from the aircraft should have been sent out. If there was a structural failure, pieces of wreckage would have been found. Some suspicion focused on a bomb on board, but again there should have been some wreckage and even a distress signal. The Panay Island station had lost contact with the aircraft in the course of one minute, a very short time. If the aircraft had been attacked by a Japanese aircraft or forced down, William McCarthy, the radio operator, should have been able to send some sort of distress signal.

A hijacking in flight is another theory that has been considered since that hot July day in 1938. Three million dollars in U.S. currency was on board the aircraft. It was being transported to China by wealthy Chinese restaurateur Wah Sun Choy. He was the chairman of the Chinese War Relief Committee. The money had been raised in the United States and was to be turned over to the Chinese Government in Chungking.

Hawaii Clipper in flight, possibley a test flight, since the terrain appears to be along the Baltimore coast. Pan Am logo can be seen on the nose of the aircraft. Later as war clouds grew darker, a large American flag would be painted on the nose of each Clipper aircraft to provide recognition.

Martin Aviation Historical Archives

Guam was 100 miles from the Japanese island of Tinian: Did Japanese agents stow away on the aircraft and force it to fly into a Japanese-held possession in the Carolines or to Palau? Could this be the reason that no wreckage of the *Hawaii Clipper* had been sighted? There were stories over the years that the Japanese had performed many acts of sabotage against Pan American Clippers. Then again, with the size of the Pacific Ocean and few places to land, many aircraft had disappeared in the early days of aviation in the same areas. The real reasons may never be learned.

The disappearance of the *Hawaii Clipper*, like the fates of Amelia Earhardt, Fred Noonan, and Edwin C. Musick, remains a mystery of the 1930s. The United States and Japan were constructing island bases throughout the 1920s and 1930s to protect their spheres of influence, and the tensions between the two nations would eventually reach a deadly flashpoint at Pearl Harbor on December 7, 1941.

Pan American Airways, already involved in the conflict long before December 7, would witness the destruction of many of its island facilities and the loss of many of its personnel.

(Left) *Hawaii Clipper* floating at rest in the water.
Martin Aviation Historical Archives

WORLD WAR II AND THE CLIPPER'S EXPLOITS

Even before the United States entered World War II, Juan Trippe was involved in providing material and personnel to the British Government at the request of the President of the United States. Unlike Charles Lindbergh, who was an isolationist, Trippe believed that political signs pointed to a Second World War. He also believed that Pan American Airways had a role to play in the coming hostilities.

President Franklin Roosevelt and the British Government were interested in the expertise that Trippe could bring to the operation of aircraft, including transports. As Trippe had always said, 90 percent of aviation is on the ground. Juan Trippe traveled to London in June 1941 under the guise of being the featured speaker at the Wright Brothers Lecture. Juan spoke on the issue of civilian aviation and was well received. He offered to assist in the upgrade of the Trans-African Imperial route. Pan American Airways had experience in the organization of a large worldwide airline corporation and, importantly, a large number of skilled workers, including not just pilots or navigators, but also ground staff, the lifeblood of any airline.

After dinner, Juan Trippe and General Hap Arnold were watching the searchlights and anti-aircraft fire on the Dorchester as German planes were bombing a part of London. An aide to Prime Minister Winston Churchill appeared on the roof and announced that the Prime Minister would like to meet with Mr. Trippe. It was late, but Mr. Churchill's routine involved sitting up late into the night with a drink and his famous cigar.

It was approximately 11 p.m. when Trippe reached 10 Downing Street. Churchill had received details of the speech that Trippe had delivered earlier in the evening. He wanted to know more about the Trans-Africa route, so in front of a roaring fire, Juan had a second dinner with Prime Minister Churchill.

Trippe explained to Churchill that he could create and operate a route over land in the same manner that he had created an aerial route over the ocean. A line was drawn from the West African coast to Liberia to the British supply depots on the Gold Coast. It then moved northeast through the deserts of Sudan and Egypt. The route covered 10,000 miles, but Trippe believed it was achievable. Pan American had the experience from developing

B-314 taxiing on the water on San Francisco Bay. Pan American employee watching from the PanAir boat.

Clyde Sunderland. Pacific Aerial Surveys, HJW Geospatial Inc.

the over-ocean aerial system, not just across the Pacific, but also into Central and South America.

Prime Minister Churchill was interested due to the fact that a northern route was established. Hudson bombers were flown from Burbank, California, to Newfoundland and then across the Atlantic to assist in the war effort. This operation was called the Ferry Command and was staffed with American, Canadian, and British pilots. The aerial lifeline had demonstrated it could succeed where the dangerous shipment of military equipment was in danger of being sunk by U-boats.

In July 1941, Trippe signed five contracts to legally commence the plan to upgrade the British assets in the Middle East and East Asia. The only concern of the involved parties was the United States Neutrality Act, but with President Roosevelt directing the legal issues, it would not be a problem. The United States Congress had recently passed the Lend-Lease Act. The various contracts to create Pan American Airways-Africa Ltd. would be written in such a way to prevent the parent company, Pan American Airways, from violating any of the provisions of the Neutrality Act.

By mid-August of 1941, five contracts had been signed. Three contracts were signed with the United States Government by American Airways and its subsidiaries, and two contracts, one signed by Pan American Airway-Africa Ltd. and one by Pan American Air Ferries Inc., with His Majesty's Government.

Various provisions provided for air transport service between the United States and West Africa. Facilities were to be established in Miami, San Juan, Port-au-Spain, Belem, and Natal, Brazil, and at least one point on the west coast of Africa. Pan American Airways agreed to operate a transport service between Miami and the west coast of Africa. The United States Government would purchase a Boeing flying boat NC18612 for the Atlantic. Pan American Airways would take two S-42Bs and transfer them to Manila. Pan American agreed to operate a ferry service to deliver aircraft to Russia or a point in the Middle East. A statement issued by the White House discussed some of the role that Pan American aviation would play, but it stressed that no aircraft would be flown over hostile territory. Despite the press release, official documents were marked secret and filed away by Pan American in locked desks.

The first contract was signed on August 12, 1941, and amended on September 6, 1941. The contract was between the War Department and Pan American Airways company. Pan American would be paid $2,800,000 under the terms of the deal. Major provisions specified that the passenger priority service would be controlled not by Pan American Airways, but by the United States War Department. Pan American would provide air transport between the United States and West Africa and establish new facilities in Miami, San Juan, Port-au-Spain, Belem, and Natal, Brazil, and at least one point on the west coast of Africa. The United States Government purchased B-314 NC18612 and Pan American would transfer the aircraft from its Pacific Division to the Atlantic Division. Two S-42s would be transferred to the Pacific Division to replace it. The U.S. military would have the right to use all new ground-based facilities that would be constructed according to the agreement.

Group of civilians and military officers at Shediac, New Brunswick. Prior to and during World War II, Pan Am and its fleet of Clippers and transports ferried men and material across the Atlantic Ocean.

University of Miami, Richter Library, Pan Am Collection

The second contract concerned transport service between African points. Signed by Pan American Airways, the United States War Department and Pan American Airways-Africa Ltd. on August 12, 1941, and amended on December 13, 1941, the agreement specified that Pan American Airways would be paid $7,613,945 over the life of the contract. Pan American would provide an air transport service over a trans-African route, which would cover Tehran and points in the Union of Soviet Socialist Republics. Other points covered would include Khartoum, Basra, and Port Sudan. The contract would also involve the building of new facilities and personnel. The United States Government agreed to furnish 24 Douglas DC-3s to Pan American Airways-Africa.

The third contract covered the ferrying of aircraft to African points. The contract was signed by Pan American Airways Inc., Pan American Air Ferries Inc., Pan American Airways-Africa Ltd. and the United States War Department on August 12, 1941, and later amended on December 13, 1941. Pan American Airways would receive $10,186,055.

Pan Am ad from the *Saturday Evening Post* issue of November 22, 1941. Pan Am was instrumental in developing a Southern Ferry Command to North Africa. The critical military parts and supplies assisted in the defeat of German Field Marshal Erwin Rommel's Afrika Korps at the famous Battle of El Alamein. Author's Collection

Aircraft would be ferried from new facilities constructed in Miami, Florida, to destinations on the west coast of Africa, and then on to various other destinations, including Port Sudan, and on to Asia. Pan American Airways-Africa would provide gasoline, oil, labor, and other technical services as needed.

The fourth contract did not have an official title. It was signed on August 12, 1941, by Pan American Airways-Africa Ltd. and His Majesty's British Government. Pan American would be paid £30,000 and the British Government had agreed to ensure all taxes and duties were paid in order to ensure access to the facilities and routes that the Pan American-Africa Ltd. aircraft and personnel would be using.

The fifth contract was also unnamed and signed on August 12, 1941, by Pan American Air Ferries Inc. and His Majesty's British Government. No monetary amount was stated on the contract, and the terms were identical to the fourth contract to provide access for Pan American Airways-Africa Ltd. aircraft and personnel to construct and assemble facilities on British territory.

Pan American's African Division designed and built many installations in Africa. Construction teams of 400 skilled carpenters, electricians, bridgemen, steel foremen, diesel mechanics, glaziers, painters, plumbers, embarkation clerks, tractor operators, refrigeration experts, and iron workers were organized.

Pan American, in conjunction with the U.S. and British Governments, established a regular schedule to employ the Martin 130s on shuttle runs to Africa and Asia. The Clippers were stripped of their rich interiors and turned into large four-engine transport aircraft. An 18-day schedule was developed to make efficient use of aircraft.

The aircraft on the Africa to Asia route would leave New York for Natal and from Natal make five round-trips to other parts of Africa. Each M-130 would then return to New York after flying 197 hours. This would leave approximately three hours for maintenance. Each Clipper required a full maintenance check for every 200 hours of flying time.

Yale football players were many of the first volunteers to go to Africa to start the construction of the airfields for Pan American. Whenever new management or other employees needed to be hired, Juan Trippe always returned to his old alma mater.

Since much of the African terrain was desert, new methods had to be found to allow for the landing of large aircraft. Juan Trippe knew that the Mayor of New York City, Fiorello LaGuardia, had plans to destroy the Sixth Avenue elevated subway line. Trippe approached him about securing the metal from the various support beams. The material was then sent on to the United States Steel Corporation, which refined the beams into long narrow strips at their plant in Bayonne, New Jersey. The new iron strips were shipped to Africa to hold down the chicken wire that would become the new runways in the sand.

Frank Gledhill, a friend of Trippe's from his Yale days, was put in charge of the project, which was completed in 60 days. The Africa-Orient air route was in operation from Miami to India and the southern route was established and operated in the same manner as the Ferry Command in the North. Pan American crews flew aircraft from Miami across the Atlantic to Africa and hitched rides back to Miami to start another flight across. The famous Captain Harold Gray made nine flights in nine days.

The Battle of El Alamein, the turning point in the war in Africa, was won by the large amount of support General Montgomery was able to receive from the Trans-Africa supply line, which included tires, spare parts, men, equipment, and spark plugs for vehicles and aircraft. On return flights, the aircraft would ferry critical items required for the war effort in the United States and Pacific.

Mail room scene of four men sorting packages and supplies for the war effort.

University of Miami, Richter Library, Pan Am Collection

British Clipper racing across the water during World War II. Note large Union Jack on the fuselage below the cockpit window.

British Airways Plc/British Airways Museum

A coincidence in the management of the Lend-Lease Program was that Mrs. Betty Trippe's brother, Ed Stettinius, was the Secretary of State in the Franklin Roosevelt Administration. Under this new program, 50 World War I Navy destroyers had been given to the British Navy. In return, the United States had received a 100-year lease on a base in Bermuda and other bases in the Caribbean. These bases would become very important in the war effort and in the growth of Pan American Airways.

One last issue was discussed by Pan American Airways and the British Government. In August 1940, the British Government requested the purchase of three of the B-314s awaiting delivery. The British Government was finding it very difficult to fly officials back and forth across the Atlantic Ocean, although the original request stated that the B-314s were needed to provide transportation between the United Kingdom and Africa. The permission of Pan American Airways was not the only requirement, as the U.S. Government would have to agree to the sale of the aircraft.

The U.S. Government did approve the sale of two B-314s, and on August 22, 1940, the sale was made with an option to take delivery of a third B-314. The third would become part of the deal if Pan American Airways had to close down its Lisbon, Portugal, service. Each B-314 was sold for $1,035,400. Part of the agreement added 12 spare

Wright Cyclone GR-2600-A2A engines at a cost of $16,753 each and six Hamilton propellers totaling $21,750. Pan Am agreed to train the BOAC crews and fly the aircraft from Astoria, San Francisco, to New York City, where delivery would take place.

The B-314s were towed out of the water at LaGuardia on a Pan American-owned dolly and placed in the base's hangar. For 33 days, the B-314s underwent new registration numbers and camouflage painting. The black paint on the aircraft's hull was removed and replaced with a silver lacquered coating that was later darkened. The operation was performed since the British Government had concerns that the aircraft that were not concealed as much as possible would be an easier target for enemy aircraft or anti-aircraft gunfire from ships.

The regal color of the B-314 was altered, with the name *Bristol* painted in medium blue letters outlined in white on the aircraft's bow panels. The new British registration number, G-AGBZ, appeared on the wing bottoms of the aircraft, and a British flag was added to both sides of the forward hull section just below the bridge window panels.

The official announcement read: "We are pleased to announce that Pan American Airways has agreed to the transfer to Great Britain of three of their six new transoceanic flying boats which are now nearing completion in the Seattle plant of the Boeing Aircraft Company. The British Government are gratified that the United States has granted consent and approval for our purchase of these aircraft which are to be used to maintain essential lines of Empire communication. We also appreciate Pan American Airways' agreeing to the transfer of these new aircraft, notwithstanding the pressing needs of their own services."

The second B-314 sold to BOAC was given a flight on April 19, 1941, by Pan American Captain Harold Gray. He arrived in Baltimore, Maryland, four days later. As with the first B-314, the United States registration numbers were stripped. She became the British aircraft *Berwick*.

The mission for the three B-314s during the war years was to transport important officials to Africa and other destinations. The aircraft flew unarmed and unescorted through enemy skies; the only weapons on board were .38 pistols stored on the flight deck.

As tensions continued to build in the Pacific, the U.S. Government called on Pan American Airways for information on movements in areas controlled by the Japanese. While the United States was building bases on Midway and other islands, the Japanese had been constructing similar projects. The lack of an adequate and rapid communication link between Oahu, Midway Island, Samoa, and Dutch Harbor plagued the operation of the mid-Pacific radio direction-finding network. The military had complained to Washington that the poor apparatus and lack of suitable control facilities made the direction-finding network a weak link in the case of attack. It was so inadequate that Washington had made arrangements with Pan American Airways to take over their network of stations in the event of a war with Japan.

Pan American Airways crews did provide intelligence information to the U.S. Government, since its Clippers flew very close to Japanese territory on some legs of flight.

"Vital to Victory"—Pan Am ad and the history of the airline and its present wartime service. A common theme of Pan Am ads prior to the war, during, and after was the world globe and the increasing number of Pan Am routes. Author's Collection

British Clipper moored at Lagos, Nigeria.
Fishermen looking on.

British Airways Plc/British Airways Museum

British Clipper with boat launch pulled up alongside. Front hatch open and the Union Jack plain to see. British Airways Plc/British Airways Museum

One of the Clippers that Pan Am allowed to be sold to the British Government. On the ramp at the Boeing plant, Seattle, Washington.

Boeing Aircraft Co., Chicago, Illinois

CLIPPER TRAINING

Beginning prior to the start of World War II and continuing once the Americans entered the war, Pan American Airways operated training schools for British, Canadian, and other Commonwealth military fliers. The British and Commonwealth trainees were guaranteed spots in various specialized training programs at the University of Miami in Coral Gables, Florida. One program was in the training and instruction of aerial navigation and meteorology, an area Pan American Airways led. The normal training cycle for most trainees was 15 weeks.

A. FLYING TRAINING

1. Familiarization — 2 hours
2. Two three-hour day missions — 6 hours
3. One two-hour day mission (swinging ship for compass deviation) — 2 hours
4. Three five-hour day missions — 15 hours
5. Five five-hour night missions – 25 hours

TOTAL FLIGHT HOURS — 50

B. THEORETICAL INSTRUCTIONS

1. Plane and mercator flying — 6 hours
2. Charts, mercator chart construction, pilot and map reading — 10 hours
3. DF correction angle and radio fixes — 12 hours
4. Altimeter and airspeed meter, the United States Army method of calibrating airspeed meters — 4 hours
5. Triangle of velocities, flight procedures, theoretical DR missions — 54 hours
6. Time in navigation and the hour angle — 16 hours
7. Definitions of celestial navigation terms, plotting on plane of meridian — 8 hours
8. Aircraft familiarization — lifeboat and lifesaving equipment drill — 4 hours
9. Aerial octant — 2 hours
10. Horizon system and correcting altitudes — 2 hours
11. Latitude by Polaris — 6 hours
12. Theory of celestial navigation and procedure — 38 hours
13. Preparation of mission and critique — 30 hours
14. Compass magnetism-deviation by celestial Azimuths — air swinging by celestial and terrestrial bearings — astro compass — 16 hours
15. Alignment of drift meter and pelorus — 2 hours
16. Star altitude curves and the astrograph — 10 hours
17. Latitude by meridian altitude — 8 hours
18. Review — 48 hours
19. Examination — 32 hours

TOTAL — 308 hours

C. METEOROLOGY

60 hours

D. MISCELLANEOUS

1. Star identification — 18 hours
2. Briefing prior to and after flight — 12 hours
3. Supervised home study — 10 hours

GRAND TOTAL TRAINING — 458 hours

Marching cadets in training by Pan Am personnel during World War II at the Dinner Key, Miami, Florida, installation. Pan Am was a key resource for training pilots, navigators, weather personnel before and during World War II. Pan Am had the trained, experienced experts.

University of Miami, Richter Library, Pan Am Collection

(Left) WAVES in training at Hunter College, New York City, on tour of the Pan Am pilot training facility. Each WAVE was afforded the opportunity to sit inside and fly the Links trainer.

University of Miami, Richter Library, Pan Am Collection

(Below) Pan Am personnel at Shediac, New Brunswick.

University of Miami, Richter Library, Pan Am Collection

The four Clipper classrooms had flown 2,079,000 miles with a perfect safety record when World War II ended. During the four years of the operation of the program, the four seaplanes soared through the South Florida skies for the equivalent of 83 trips around the world.

The 5,000 cadets that graduated from the training section that had been established in August 1940 charted the courses of night flights southward to Cuba and eastward to the Bahamas. The coursework focused on practical aerial navigation problems. Each trip averaged 450 miles.

The total flights represented 20,796,000 student flight miles and 95,000 flight crew man-hours. The graduates of the Pan American Airways program blazed a path of glory around the world as they guided aircraft in all the theaters of war. The graduates received over 2,500 medals for their exploits during World War II.

When World War II ended, a new group of professionals had been trained and, more importantly, had acquired experience in very difficult conditions. This new group, like the group at the end of World War I, would move aviation into the next major expansion of commercial aviation.

War clouds grew darker and darker in November 1941. A coded message from Tokyo informed envoys Kurusu and Nomura in Washington, DC, that "relations between Japan and the United States have reached the edge — this is our last effort. We will wait until November 29. After that things are automatically going to happen." On November 26, six Japanese carriers, escorts, and, supply ships silently slipped out of the Kurile Islands, north of Japan.

A second cable on November 28 advised: "In two or three days, negotiations will be de facto ruptured. Should Nomura yet perform a miracle in Washington, the attack force could be recalled up to December 5."

The U.S. destroyer *Ward* sank a small Japanese submarine on December 7, and at 7:02 a.m. blimps were spotted by a new radar station, but the duty officer felt it was "probably just a pigeon with a metal band around its legs." On several occasions, the Army Air Corps aircraft had scrambled when the *Honolulu Clipper* was approaching, which the Army Air Corps did on an irregular basis as practice for aircraft and crews. On this morning, nothing was sent aloft and life continued on.

At 7:55 a.m., the first code was issued: "Climb Mt. Niitaka." Three hundred and fifty-three Japanese aircraft attacked Battleship Row, Hickham Field, and other targets. By the time the attack was over, eight battleships, three light cruisers, and 188 aircraft were destroyed and 2,400 people killed. The Japanese lost 29 aircraft, five midget submarines, and one fleet submarine.

Pan American Airways would not only go to war along with the United States military on that day, but would also suffer its own losses. The first American civilian aircraft destroyed at the start of World War II in the Pacific was the *Hong Kong Clipper*. The aircraft, commanded by Captain Ralph, had arrived for its stopover on December 7. Captain Ralph had just received the message that Manila had been bombed, but before he could take any action, Japanese aircraft appeared. Ralph and his crew had just reached the dock and were a few yards away when the bombs began to fall. Everyone made for shelter and turned to see the *Hong Kong Clipper* take a direct hit. The attacking Japanese aircraft made short work of the Clipper. Only a short few weeks later, the Japanese would capture the entire island of Hong Kong, the gateway to the mainland of China. A more fortunate aircraft for the time being was the Martin 130 *Philippine Clipper*.

As tension with Japan grew and war appeared on the horizon, each Pan Am Clipper captain was given sealed orders to be opened if war was declared. In the case of Captain Harry Lanier Turner, Commander of the Boeing 314 *Anzac Clipper*, the briefing may have taken so long as to delay the departure of his aircraft and its passengers for close to 40 minutes. Those would become the "miracle 40 minutes" that would prevent the *Anzac Clipper* from being destroyed at Pearl Harbor on December 7.

According to one version, the *Anzac Clipper*, commanded by Captain Turner with crew and 17 passengers, left Treasure Island, San Francisco, California, an hour late due to a mechanical problem, delaying their arrival in Honolulu until 8:30 a.m. Due to fuel limitations, Captain Turner did not attempt to increase the airspeed to make up for the delay in leaving. The second story concerns entirely different circumstances that would make the Clipper late just enough to avoid the Japanese attack on Pearl Harbor and prevent the destruction of the aircraft by not just Japanese aircraft, but also friendly fire from the air and ground.

Captain Turner was one the first Pan American pilots to fly the transpacific runs. He had joined the company in 1929 at Miami and moved to the West Coast. He was an experienced pilot and was given the command of the million-dollar investment that was the B-314, the largest and most luxurious aircraft of its day.

(Top opposite) Clipper moored on the water outside the terminal at Shediac, New Brunswick. Many famous dignitaries that were forced to flee their countries landed at Shediac. (Bottom left) King Peter of Yugoslavia and aide recently arrived on the Clipper discussing important issues. (Bottom right) Rest and Relaxation in the surf at Shediac, New Brunswick. Pan Am employees in the cold Atlantic Ocean.

University of Miami, Richter Library, Pan Am Collection

Chelsea Cigarette ad from World War II with a Pan Am Clipper flying in moonlight over a tropical beach as palm trees sway in the gentle breeze. Author's Collection

His recollection of the events of December 6 indicated that he had stopped to drop in and listen to some of his daughter's first piano recital. He had phoned the dispatch at Treasure Island and received permission to make a brief stopover. On the way from Oakland, where he and his family resided, traffic delayed him by about ten minutes. Because it had been suspected for many months that war with Japan was imminent, he was given a briefing and sealed orders prior to departure. The orders were to be opened only if an attack was underway and the United States was at war with the Japanese. Since the two Japanese envoys were in Washington for one last attempt to reach an agreement, the briefing was much longer. Sunday, December 7, was to be the day that the Japanese met and presented an ultimatum to the U.S. Government. Turner's aircraft had been scheduled to depart Treasure Island at 5 p.m. Instead, the *Anzac Clipper* did not lift off until 5:40.

The flight was uneventful that evening, with the Clipper cruising along at 92 knots. The crossing to Honolulu usually took 14 to 16 hours. There was always the point of no return on the flight to Honolulu, the line that, once crossed, meant turning back was impossible due to the amount of remaining fuel. On this night, though, the flying weather was excellent and the aircraft was operating at its peak.

Everything was fine until about 8 a.m. Honolulu time. First Radio Officer W. H. Bell was listening to music from the Honolulu station as the aircraft was closing in on its destination. Sunday was great for listening to music, as the radio stations catered to the sailors and military personnel who were in the process of getting up to spend a lazy Sunday morning. Captain Turner had left the flight deck for breakfast. The flight deck had room for two pilots, a flight engineer, and the radio operator, with room left for a workspace for the captain. Turner worked his way down the spiral stairway that was located next to Bell's radio station. Most of the 17 passengers were up and moving around and some

The crew of the *Hong Kong Clipper* and Joe Crosson, the Canadian station manager of the Alaska Division. S. E. Robbins, Jerry Jones, Murray Stewart, Gene Meyrig, Jack Egan, Dave Williams, Larry Biske, Opel Johnson, Harry LaPorte, Andy Anderson. Inaugural flight Juneau to Seattle, June 20, 1940. The use of a Clipper on the Alaska route was short lived.

University of Miami, Richter Library, Pan Am Collection

getting ready for the descent of the aircraft to its final destination. No sooner had Captain Turner poured his coffee when Bell came charging down the stairway. He blurted out that Pearl Harbor was under attack by the Imperial Naval Forces of Japan. Turner retraced his steps and put on the radio phones to see if this was really true and happening.

Captain Turner realized that the original report from Bell was true. In fact, Pearl Harbor was under attack, and gunfire and explosions could be heard. The B-314 was 40 minutes from landing at Pearl Harbor, 40 minutes that saved the aircraft. He reviewed the situation and made the decision to change course and fly to Hilo and land in its protected harbor. The next step was to explain to the passengers the change in the flight plan and the events that were unfolding at Pearl Harbor. The copilot headed for any space where the clouds could hide the *Anzac Clipper*. The Boeing 314 was a large aircraft, and the main goal was to protect and hide it as much as possible. The flight to Hilo took approximately two hours. The area below appeared as though nothing was happening on the rest of the islands. It looked green and tranquil and the white beaches were deserted. Captain Turner brought the aircraft down slowly and the crew scanned the water below for any obstruction that the aircraft might hit on landing. This was uncharted territory, and the one destructive element in landing a Clipper is any obstruction in the water. He landed the aircraft very cautiously, but remained concerned that there could still be Japanese in the area. He also considered the fact that if residents of Hilo knew what was occurring at Pearl Harbor, they could believe his aircraft was Japanese. The B-314 was a large target.

Alaska Governor Ernest Grueing and guest on the press flight prior to the commencement of regular service.
University of Miami, Richter Library, Pan Am Collection

When the aircraft landed and was tied off, it was met by a launch, which contained FBI, military, and other agents. Once the army in the launch was assured the aircraft was an actual Pan American Clipper, the process of taking the passengers from the aircraft to the land was undertaken. Captain Turner asked to use a telephone and placed a call to the Pan American control tower at Pearl Harbor. His protocol was to ascertain the level of destruction and the plans for his aircraft, if any. Luckily, the procedure was for the Pan American station manager to be in the control tower at the time of each landing. In the telephone conversation, he provided details of what destruction could be seen at the present time. He became very graphic in the details of which ships were sunk or burning and what the condition of the airfield was. This conversation did not last long, as someone must have recognized that sensitive information was being transmitted over a phone line that the Japanese could be listening in on. Captain Turner was to return to Treasure Island on December 8. It would take the entire day to refuel and check over the Clipper for the long flight back to its home base. The other problem was that the B-314 was exposed and could be attacked by another wave of Japanese aircraft or even aircraft returning from the attack on Pearl Harbor. He and the crew pushed it into the lush foliage. Captain Turner remembered that in his early barnstorm-flying days he would take buttermilk and lampblack, mix them together, and make a wonderful concoction that coated an aircraft. In the old days, it was used to write advertising messages on the aircraft that could easily be washed off. Turner and the crew found five gallons of buttermilk

"Wings of Democracy"–Pan Am and its 10th Anniversary of airline service in China. During the war Pan Am ads still ran but were given a wartime patriotic feel. Some would promise the return of regular service as soon as victory was achieved. Author's Collection

World War II ad for Rohr aviation parts and assemblies. One method of delivery to difficult areas was the long-range Pan Am Clipper fleet. Author's Collection

and the lampblack and made a crude camouflage for the Clipper. The aircraft lost its bright metallic lustre and was transformed into a dull black object.

During the night, aircraft could be heard overhead. The question was whether the aircraft were U.S. military or Japanese observation aircraft. The dull black hid the aircraft very nicely. On the morning of December 8, the *Anzac Clipper* was ready for the return trip. None of the 17 passengers wished to return to San Francisco. Two were important political figures: the Shah of Iran and U Saw, the Premier of Burma. U Saw's decision was not surprising, since he had been suspected of collaborating with the Japanese.

Loaded aboard the aircraft were three full barrels of leftover aviation fuel. Captain Turner and the crew uncovered the aircraft and began to taxi into the harbor. The Clipper lifted up gracefully and began the 2,400-mile journey back to Treasure Island. The blackened, camouflaged aircraft maintained radio silence for the entire journey. It was not known whether the Japanese fleet was still in the area or had withdrawn. Information was very limited. Bell did monitor conversations on the radio and heard several conversations of Japanese submarines in the water off the California coast. The crew attempted to scan the water for any signs of submarines traveling on the surface or periscopes breaking the surface, but nothing was observed. The *Anzac Clipper* arrived at the Pan American base at Treasure Island on December 9; the round-trip had taken 72 hours.

A debriefing was held for about four hours upon arrival at Treasure Island. The military and Pan American officials wanted any information on the last 72 hours. Captain Turner and his crew were the first civilians to return to the mainland from the attacked area. Two days later, all were taken into active duty as a transportation squadron. Clipper flights began the day after the attack on Pearl Harbor. Experts in underwater salvage and other necessary skills to raise, repair, and rebuild were on their way to Pearl

Harbor on Pan American Clippers. The Clippers were now part of the war effort and under the control of the military. The Pan American Clippers would have their paint removed and replaced with 290 pounds of drab blue-gray.

The *Pacific Clipper*, a B-314 captained by Robert Ford, was in the Pacific on that fateful day and was ordered to return to the United States. The aircraft left Auckland, New Zealand, and headed in the opposite direction. The normal path would have been to leave Auckland and fly eastwards to Honolulu. This was not possible, so the *Pacific Clipper* undertook a journey that would be one for the record books.

The westward route carried the Clipper across Australia, Southern Asia, Saudi Arabia, and Africa. Finally, the last leg took it across the South Atlantic to Brazil and then home to New York City. The journey demonstrated the professional capability of Captain Bob Ford and his crew and their ingenuity in finding spare parts, fuel, and other critical material that made the flight successful. These routes would be flown over and over again in the years of World War II. Captain Turner flew Admiral Nimitz to Pearl Harbor on Christmas Day. Admiral Nimitz was to relieve Admiral Kimmel as Commander-in-Chief of the Pacific Fleet. For the remainder of the war in the Pacific, Captain Turner spent the majority of his duty flying Admiral Nimitz to various high-level meetings where strategy for the eventual invasion of the Japanese homeland were plotted.

Many months before the Japanese attack, Wake Island was a beehive of activity. In February 1941, 1,200 civilian employees arrived on the island. Under the direction of Nathan Teters, their job was to construct a 5,000-foot airfield on the island for the United States Marine Corps' fighter planes and B-17 bombers. Large fuel tanks were being constructed underground to protect from aerial and sea bombardment. Peale Island and Wilkes Island were being linked by a road system to Wake Island. The ability to move men and material quickly was the goal of the project. A new seaplane ramp was being constructed next to the Pan American Hotel on Peale Island. The Pan American Clipper employed a channel between the two smaller islands (Peale and Wilkes) for its landing and departure zone.

The United States Military had recommended the expansion of the island defenses of Wake Island as early as 1938. The work was underway, but whether it would be completed in time was the unanswered question. On December 4, 1941, a dozen Marine F4F-3 fighters under the command of Major Paul Putnam had arrived from the United States aircraft carrier *Enterprise* and landed on the small airstrip on Wake Island. On December 8, 1941, the *Philippine Clipper* left Wake Island on a scheduled flight to Guam. The plane contained eight crew members and five passengers. No sooner was the Clipper airborne than word came over the radio about the attack on Pearl Harbor. The airport manager on Wake Island, John Cook, contacted the *Philippine Clipper* and told her to return to Wake Island.

By 7:30 a.m., the aircraft was moored at her floating dock, which was located at the

"Rubber raft with shoulder pads"—Good Year Tire ad of a rubber supply boat pulling up to unload cargo from a Pan Am Clipper. Purpose of the ad was to demonstrate how the rubber boat will not only take on the cargo, but will not damage the fuselage of the aircraft.

Author's Collection

end of a very long pier. A ground crew removed all the cargo, refueled the Clipper, and started to walk along the pier to the shore for lunch. No one had any real idea of what had happened at Pearl Harbor and whether any other targets had been hit. Confusion reigned supreme.

Pan American Captain John Hamilton met with Commander Cunningham of the United States Navy and Major James Devereux of the United States Marine Corps about plans for the *Philippine Clipper*. The aircraft had been lucky due to a day's delay in turnaround at San Francisco. She was late in leaving; otherwise, the *Philippine Clipper* would have been caught at Guam. The military commanders requested a reconnaissance flight of the Pan American Clipper before the aircraft departed back to Midway Island and Hawaii at 11:30 a.m.; a long flight of aircraft appeared heading toward Wake Island. Even though the report had been forwarded that Pearl Harbor had been attacked, the personnel on the island believed it was just a flight of U.S. aircraft, as Wake Island was expecting more reinforcements, including aircraft.

The reality became obvious when bombs began to fall and aircraft emblazoned with the Rising Sun flew low and strafed the entire base. Everyone began to run for shelter. At least one man on the pier dove into the water in the hopes of staying out of the line of fire. Others took shelter wherever possible, one even hiding inside a dredging pipe. He was unlucky, as a bullet entered the pipe and hit his leg.

The base, the hotel, and the storehouse were all left in ruins. It was a miracle that there were only two fatalities and several seriously wounded, including two Pan American Airways personnel.

The *Philippine Clipper*, sitting in its mooring, made a prime target. The pier caught fire and at least 20 machine-gun bullets hit the Clipper. The hotel and power station received direct hits. It was a miracle the Clipper was not severely damaged. Once the Japanese aircraft flew off into the horizon, Jack Egan, the Chief Mechanic, entered the plane and started the engines.

A decision was made quickly to load the entire Pan American station crew, along with the eight crewmen and five passengers, and start immediately for Midway Island.

Captain Hamilton knew there was no time to be lost. As soon as the door shut, he gave the M-130 full throttle and it roared across the lagoon, but the heavily laden aircraft could not break loose. He taxied and attempted to make waves in the lagoon. The aircraft failed on the second try, but the third time was the charm and the *Philippine Clipper* gained enough speed to lift up off the water and set a course for Midway Island. Fearful of detection by the Japanese, Captain Hamilton piloted the Clipper so low that it was at times almost skimming the waves.

The Clipper was safe traveling at a low altitude, but night was approaching and the visibility would be reduced. Hamilton had to take the aircraft to a higher altitude. The passengers were cold due to the altitude and the fact that almost everyone had left Wake Island with short-sleeve shirts, and some were shirtless.

A message to Midway was sent by way of Pearl Harbor. At Pearl Harbor, the message was relayed by submarine cable. The Japanese had attacked Midway Island, so it was not difficult to find; most of the facilities were burning. As the aircraft grew closer, the radio operator began sending blind transmissions, repeating the number "1135" every few minutes. The receiver of the message on Midway Island realized the number was the estimated time of arrival.

(Left) Martin 130 *China Clipper*, NC14716 high over Oakland, California. Below several U.S. Navy four-stack destroyers sit at dock.
University of Miami, Richter Library, Pan Am Collection

World War II booklet of maps. Sold to the public so that every family could follow the progress of the war and learn where the battles were being fought.
Author's Collection

The *Philippine Clipper* reached Midway Island almost 24 hours after leaving Wake Island. When the aircraft arrived at Hawaii, a damage assessment counted 26 bullet holes on the aircraft. The *Philippine Clipper* was lucky, even though one large hole was found next to the flight engineer's station. The bullet had just missed the critical area where the structural brace to the wing was located. The lucky ones on the aircraft did not know the terrible fate that awaited those left behind to face the Japanese onslaught on Wake Island.

Those who survived the attack would become prisoners, and very few would survive the war. Many were killed on a Japanese ship that was torpedoed by a U.S. submarine unaware of the prisoners on board. Besides the crew and employees, the only other item to depart Wake Island on December 8 was the American flag that flew over the Pan American Administration Building. The tattered and torn flag was given to Mr. William Van Dusen, Pan American's Director of Public Relations.

On December 23, 1941, Wake Island fell to the invading Japanese. Right out of a scene from a Hollywood movie of World War II, Japanese Admiral Kajioka, in white uniform, medals pinned to his chest, and carrying a long dress sword, waded ashore to accept the surrender. One of his aides offered Marine Corps Major James Devereux a cigarette and informed him that he had attended the famous Golden Gate International Exposition on Treasure Island in 1939.

At 7:30 a.m. on January 21, 1943, the luck of the *Philippine Clipper* would run out. Painted in the drab blue-gray, the aircraft had been purchased by the U.S. Government for $1 million. The crew remained Pan American, but the aircraft was under control of the military and ferried VIPs on important missions.

Philippine Clipper with large American flag on fuselage. Crew member peering out of the side hatch. University of Miami, Richter Library, Pan Am Collection

B-314 tied up at the dock
of the Canton base.
University of Miami, Richter Library, Pan Am Collection

Severe storms had been raging along the California coast, and the rain and high winds did not appear to relent for another several days. Mrs. Edna Wallach of Bell Valley, near Ukiah and Boonville, Northern California, heard the sound of a large aircraft come over her house. The engines sounded normal, but looking up, she saw a large aircraft fly over in the midst of the storm. Mrs. Wallach was knowledgeable about aircraft, since she was a certified airplane-spotter.

She could see the lights on the outside fuselage and lights on the interior. It was not possible to report the aircraft and the sound of it hitting the mountain, since the storms had taken down the phone lines. She finally was able to give her information to Piggy Hogan, a member of the road crew, who turned it over to James Busch, District Attorney of Mendocino County, Northern California.

It was still several days before the military began a search for Flight 62100 from Pearl Harbor. In 1938, Pan American Airways signed a 20-year lease for a new base at Treasure Island. The base, with its four hangars and Administration Building, officially opened on February 5, 1939. This was in conjunction with the Golden Gate International Exposition being held on the island. Clipper Cove, where the Clippers were displayed, was a big hit of the Exposition, as people flocked to view the large flying boats.

Flight 62100 was attempting to land at Treasure Island, but due to the poor weather conditions was diverted to another landing site. The last contact with the control tower was at 7:15 a.m., when the captain of the *Philippine Clipper* was told that the weather would not improve for some time, so he had to make a decision on an alternate landing site. San Diego was recommended as the alternate site, but they would wait to be advised.

Flight 62100, piloted by Pan American Captain Robert Elzey, departed Pearl Harbor on January 20, 1943, with a crew of nine along with ten military officers. Admiral English was the Pacific Submarine Commander, and eight of the other passengers were senior

M-130 *Philippine Clipper* nose in. Aircraft moored and tied off with its front mooring pin showing the ropes holding it in place. Man above on wing appears to be working on one of the four engines. University of Miami, Richter Library, Pan Am Collection

members of his staff. The last passenger, Nurse Lieutenant J. G. Edna Morrow, was returning home to die of terminal cancer.

Admiral English was flying to Mare Island Naval Shipyard in San Francisco. The other senior members of the staff were carrying various plans and proposals. The purpose of the meeting was to discuss the Japanese improvements in the ability to detect and sink submarines and problems with their own Mark IV torpedo. The data indicated that the Mark IV either missed the target, did not detonate, or its torpedoes dropped down in the water and went under the enemy target. The Mark IV had been in service since the 1920s and had in reality only been tested twice, once successfully. Since the two tests in the mid-1920s, it had never been tested again.

The other secret reason for the flight was a briefcase Admiral English was carrying, filled with Top Secret documents. The documents concerned photos and information on various Japanese-held islands. The meeting was intended to discuss the information and to continue the journey to Washington, DC, to plan strategy for the remainder of the war in the Pacific. American submarines had been exploring and infiltrating many Japanese-held islands to observe shipping patterns and movements. The surveillance submarines had launched small groups of sailors at night to gather sand from the beaches and to observe any physical areas that would prohibit the landing of troops or even flying boats. These were the photographs, charts, and microfilm that were aboard the *Philippine Clipper* when she slammed into the mountainous area of Northern California.

It would appear from the direction that the *Philippine Clipper* was flying that the aircraft was attempting to make a landing on Clear Lake, near Ukiah and Boonville. Clear Lake, nestled in the mountains and resembling a scene from a Swiss postcard, had been employed in the past as an alternate landing site for the large Clipper flying boats.

The headline from the *San Francisco Chronicle* of January 25, 1943, announced, "Lost Air Transport Reported — Fire reported on ridge near Clear Lake." It continued to note that ground crews and military personnel were scouring the mountain for wreckage.

On February 1, 1943, the *Chronicle* screamed, "US Navy Plane Found — All 19 Are Killed In Crash Near Ukiah." The *Philippine Clipper* had over 22 hours' worth of fuel and it was estimated that over 1,000 gallons was left in the gas tanks upon impact. It was also estimated that the wind was reaching 70 miles an hour in the Ukiah/Boonville area at the time of the crash, and the aircraft was traveling at 190 miles an hour. Everyone was still strapped in their seats, and it appeared that there was no warning of the fate that awaited the crew and passengers at 7:30 a.m.

The search for the aircraft was one of the most extensive ever undertaken by the U.S. military. The search for survivors was of concern, although the chances of anyone surviving, let alone until the time they would be found, were almost zero. The military was most concerned about the documents that Admiral English and his staff were carrying for their meetings.

A U.S. Navy PBM flying boat returning from a routine patrol saw a glint in the mountains, and the wreckage of the *Philippine Clipper* was found on January 30, nine days after the last contact.

The area was very rugged, and it was difficult to reach the wreckage and bodies. The crash site was about six miles from the closest local road, so bulldozers and blasting equipment were brought to the site to slowly make a road into the area. It was a slow process, and all 19 bodies had been either burned beyond recognition or were covered with large pieces of wreckage. One of the last victims to be found was George Angus, the Second Radio Officer. Unlike the others, his remains had not been badly burned, but he had been crushed beneath one of the engines. One member of the search team recognized his face. When the site was finally accessible, horses were required to bring the dead from the crash site to the closest road for removal to a morgue.

"Global Skyway - is here today." Airfield with hangar and fuel truck. In the tropics, a large Clipper flies overhead.
Author's Collection

The area was filled with military personnel and Pan American Airways officials who were there not only to search for the cause of the crash, but also to see if any of the engines, propellers or other equipment could be salvaged for the other Clippers. United States Postal Officers arrived to search for the many mail bags that the aircraft had on board. Most of the mail bags had been badly burned in the fire that consumed the aircraft, but the postal officers were relieved to see that the locks were still intact. No other persons had opened the bags.

The investigators believed that Pan American Captain Elzey may have noticed his impossible situation seconds before the crash. As he was coming down to reach Clear Lake, his wing tips appeared to have brushed the scrub pine of the mountain area. A few seconds

(Top) Rugged mountains that surround the Boonville/Ukiah area of Northern California where the *Philippine Clipper* slammed into the mountains on January 21, 1943, at 7:30 a.m. Author's Collection

(Below) Bodies of the *Philippine Clipper* crew and passengers were carried down the mountain to the newly cut road by horse and mule.

Mendocino City Historical Archives, Ukiah, California

later, the 26-ton *Philippine Clipper* would slam into the rocky ridge and slope. Due to the severe storms, the crash went unnoticed, and eventually the rain smothered the flames.

All of the bodies had been removed, save one. The searchers did not want to remain with one body on the mountain over night, but not enough body bags had been brought to the site, and animals threatened the integrity of the crash site. So as bodies reached the highway, the body bags were removed and sent back to the site for the next group.

It was decided that the last body would be wrapped in a piece of tarpaulin and stood on the floor of the jeep between the front and rear seat. There was no rope to secure it, and upon beginning the descent down a steep incline, the jeep hit a bump and the corpse catapulted forward, unwrapping as it came. The driver and passenger had neither gloves nor covering to pick up and move the body again. Once the highway was reached and the body turned over, the two immediately returned to Oakland and burned all their clothes.

Once it appeared that everything the military was searching for had been found, dynamite and bulldozers were brought to the crash scene. The dynamite was used to blast the surrounding mountain and rock, and then the bulldozers finished covering over the wreckage.

In San Francisco, the United States Civil Aeronautics Board of Inquiry convened an investigation into the crash of Flight 62100 on February 8, 1943. The board completed its inquiry by February 9, 1943, and issued its full report on June 18, 1943. One of the main witnesses at the inquiry was aircraft-spotter Edna Wallach. She testified to the sounds of that morning and the noise that she heard a short time later.

The final report found that Captain Elzey was at fault in the crash, even though he was an excellent pilot with impeccable qualifications, including a degree in aeronautical engineering. Prior to joining Pan American Airways, he had been trained as a Navy pilot, undergoing flight training at Pensacola, Florida. He had been a senior pilot with Pan American Airways, logging in more than 4,900 hours of flying time. The report did not consider the weather conditions that were more severe than Captain Elzey had been advised. The board concluded that he had failed to determine his position accurately before making his descent. Also left out of the report was any mention that he had requested to use radar to determine his position, but was denied on the grounds that radar was only employed to search for enemy aircraft.

Even today, a great deal of mystery surrounds the flight. Who decided to take the aircraft from Hawaii to San Francisco? Since the aircraft were operated by the government during the war, did the Pan American Airways crew have the final word or the military? Why did the aircraft even leave when storms were raging in Northern California, and who decided to head for Clear Lake rather than the alternate field at San Diego? With the demise of the *Philippine Clipper*, the only remaining M-130 was the *China Clipper*.

While the tragedy of the secret mission of the *Philippine Clipper* was unfolding, a second Pan American secret mission was underway and would achieve results that would set the course for the remainder of the Allied strategy in World War II. The groundwork for the second mission had been put into place on that first dark Christmas of 1941. President Franklin Roosevelt had campaigned in 1940 to keep the United States out of the war in Europe. In reality, he was steering the United States in a different direction. Lend-Lease programs were providing supplies to the Allies, and the secret agreements had been signed to provide technical training and supplies to Great Britain. The Neutrality

(Above) Part of engine cylinder of the *Philippine Clipper*. One of the few surviving pieces of wreckage. Author's Collection

Wreckage of the M-130 *Philippine Clipper*. Soldier searching for documents and the mail bags.
Mendocino City Historical Archives, Ukiah, California

British Prime Minister Winston Churchill at the controls of a British Clipper smoking his famous trademark, a large cigar.
British Airways Plc/British Airways Museum

Patrol was operating in the Atlantic and Pacific Oceans under the stated policy of protecting neutral shipping from attack. The reality was very different: the Neutrality Patrol aircraft and destroyers were actively protecting shipping loaded with war goods en route to Great Britain. Lockheed aircraft were leaving the Burbank, California, plant and flying to Newfoundland and across the Atlantic with Canadian and British Ferry Command pilots.

On those first dark days of December 1941, Winston Churchill had flown to Washington, DC, to spend the Christmas holidays with Franklin Roosevelt and to plot the early strategy of the war that now involved Germany, Italy, and Japan. The secret meeting was code-named "Arcadia" and was a follow-up to their first meeting code-named "Riviera" and held in Argentia, Newfoundland, from August 9 to 12, 1940. "Riviera" instituted the transfer of surplus United States World War I destroyers to the British and Caribbean bases.

Churchill immediately moved into the White House and began giving orders as if at home: "I don't like talking outside of my quarters, I must have a sherry in my room before breakfast, a couple of glasses of scotch and soda before lunch and French champagne and 90-year-old brandy before I go to sleep at night. I hate whistling in the corridors. For breakfast I want eggs, bacon, or ham and toast, and two kinds of cold meats with English mustard and two kinds of fruit, plus a tumbler of sherry."

On Christmas Eve, Roosevelt and Churchill lighted the National Community Christmas Tree on the South Portico of the White House. The men gave a joint radio address to their nations.

The dark days for the Allies continued until the summer of 1942. The U.S. Navy destroyed the force of Japanese aircraft carriers at the Battle of Midway. The Marines invaded Guadalcanal and, after months of naval and land fighting, gained control of the area. Guadalcanal and the aircraft from Henderson Field began the long climb up the ladder to the eventual attack on the Japanese homeland. During the summer, the British Army under General Montgomery was successful in blunting Rommel's Afrika Corps at the Battle of El Alamein. A large amount of the equipment that had been rushed in to counter Rommel's attack and turn the tide had been provided by the Southern Ferry Command route that had been established at the London meeting between Juan Trippe and Winston Churchill. Building on these successes, the Allies invaded North Africa on November 8, 1942, and began the drive to push Rommel and the Afrika Corps out of North Africa and create the staging bases to invade Italy.

Major War Bond Rally with many of the guests on the platform having flown into the hangar rally on a Pan Am Clipper.

University of Miami, Richter Library, Pan Am Collection

By December 1942, President Roosevelt began to believe that the turning point had been reached, but that the war would continue for several years until the ultimate victory. He became weary of sending aides and senior staff to meet with other generals and leaders to discuss strategy and the road ahead. That December, a memo was send to indicate that Roosevelt wanted to meet with Churchill, Soviet Leader Joseph Stalin and the Leader of the Free French Forces, General Charles de Gaulle, at Casablanca, Morocco. An inspection of the Allied forces would be undertaken as part of the visit. Plans for transporting the President and his party by land and air were drawn up. Early in January 1943, Pan American's Atlantic General Manager, John C. Leslie, had received a call from Washington, DC, requesting that two Clippers be in Miami on January 11. Each aircraft was to be equipped to undertake a "special mission." The name of the special passenger was not mentioned and the Pan American administrators were used to carrying special passengers and cargo in the first two years of the war. British Prime Minister Winston Churchill, Queen Wilhelmina of the Netherlands, King George of Greece, Admiral Nimitz of the United States Navy, General Marshall of the United States Army, and numerous high level diplomats and senior officials were among the special passengers served by Pan American airlines.

President Franklin Roosevelt (white hat) and part of his traveling party in a motor launch alongside the *Dixie Clipper.* Scene at the first stop, Trinidad, en route to Casablanca meeting.

United States Navy Archives

The Pan American personnel were civilian employees, but since the start of World War II and the government takeover of the aircraft, they were in the military reserve for thousands of missions. John C. Leslie had received the request and immediately assumed his rank as Lieutenant Commander in the United States Naval Reserve. Arrangements were organized and the aircraft and crews assigned. Both captains, Captain Cone of the *Dixie Clipper* and Captain Vinal of the *Atlantic Clipper*, took on their ranks in the United States Naval Reserve, as did the other crew members.

The only special request was for a double mattress for one berth. The orders were forwarded to the staff in the hangar at LaGuardia Field, New York. Work began immediately on the two B-314s assigned to carry out the mission — the *Atlantic Clipper* and the *Dixie Clipper*. Routine checks were completed on each aircraft, with an extra mattress provided as requested, as well as extra supplies of linens, a few more upholstered chairs, and approximately 216 pounds of new dull gray camouflage paint.

January 9, 1943, Saturday

In the national capital, not even the White House staff was aware that the mission would be the most unprecedented of presidential trips. In a time of war, the Commander-in-Chief was leaving the United States and would fly across the Atlantic Ocean to a meeting with the other wartime leaders. The meeting was unique, since it was taking place so close to the actual hostilities in North Africa. It was shortly before ten o'clock in the evening when President Roosevelt and his party secretly left the White House and headed to Washington's Union Station.

The special train that was to carry the President and his party to Miami had been prepared and awaited the all clear to pull out of the train station. Mr. Dewey Long had arranged the details. Baggage, food, and other supplies had been stowed aboard one hour before the scheduled departure. The crew was carefully selected in line with wartime security measures. With the exception of the train engineer and fireman, no other railroad company employees were on the train. Five Filipino messmen from the Presidential Yacht, the USS *Potomac*, had throughout the day made up the berths and other equipment on the train. There would be 30 passengers on the trip, and food for the party was supplied through the commissary section of the President's private dining car. Tray service was provided for all who were not actually dining with the President in his private car. If there was one aspect that defied security, it was the size of the train. It was smaller than a normal passenger train and contained the President's car, one compartment car, one Pullman sleeper, one club/baggage car and the special United States Army radio communications car.

January 10, 1943, Sunday

The trip through the southern countryside was smooth during the night. The problem in the morning became that five messmen were not enough to take care of the needs of the President and the party. A letter was sent to Lieutenant Kevers that three additional messmen were to be at the Jacksonville Naval Air Station for the return trip to Washington, DC, on January 20. The messmen provided trays of scrambled eggs, bacon, toast, jam, and coffee for all the passengers. A luncheon of chicken chow mein, boiled rice, peas, bread, butter, and iced tea was served. The evening meal was broiled steak, French-fried potatoes, asparagus, and baking powder biscuits, topped off with strawberries, cream, and coffee. There was a charge of 50 cents for each meal.

When the train stopped at Savannah, Georgia, a set of scales was brought on board. The four Secret Service agents carefully weighed and tagged each piece of luggage. Accurate information was essential to estimate the weight that the *Atlantic Clipper* and *Dixie Clipper* would be taking aboard. There was 3,100 pounds of personnel, 2,200 pounds of luggage and 900 pounds of bottled water. Red-tagged luggage was to go on the *Dixie Clipper* and green-tagged on the *Atlantic Clipper* and five cases of bottled water on each aircraft.

January 11, 1943, Monday

President Roosevelt's train arrived at Military Junction, Miami, at 1:30 in the morning. Baggage and water for both planes and all personnel for the *Atlantic Clipper* were unloaded into Army trucks and cars and dispatched to the Pan American Airways base. The train remained at Military Junction until shortly after 5 a.m. and then proceeded to Miami. The President and those who were to travel in the *Dixie Clipper* detrained at 5:45 a.m. at 27th Avenue and Dixie Highway. The motorcade immediately departed for the Pan American Airways base.

The *Dixie Clipper* and *Atlantic Clipper* were owned and operated by Pan American, but were under charter to the U.S. Navy during the war. Both aircraft would be commanded by Masters of Ocean Flying (the highest commercial pilot rating in the world). Captain Howard M. Cone and a crew of ten would man the *Dixie Clipper*. Captain Richard Vinal and a crew of ten would man the *Atlantic Clipper*.

The crew of both aircraft would wear the uniform of the United States Naval Reserve, since they were flying a military aircraft on a military mission. Both captains and crew

Sylvania Electric Products Inc. "Midget lightships to guide the giant Clippers home!" One of the major developments at the New York World's Fair of 1939/40 was the introduction of fluorescent lighting systems. Pan American Airways was always at the forefront of any scientific innovation that would benefit the airline. During World War II on the island bases, the implementation of bright fluorescent lighting allowed the Clippers to take off and land even on moonless nights.

Author's Collection

Formal luncheon (left to right, back row): Secret Service Agent Charles W. Fredericks, USN Captain John L. McCrea, Secret Service Agent Elmer Hipsley, Lt. (TIC) George A. Fox, Admiral Ross T. McIntire, and Pan Am Captain (pilot) Howard M. Cone Jr. in U.S. Navy Reserve uniform. (Front row from left to right) Secret Service Agent Guy Spaman, Admiral William D. Leahy, President Franklin Roosevelt. United States Navy Archives

were told to be ready to leave New York on January 7. Late that afternoon, the two large, newly recamouflaged flying boats taxied and lifted up from the waters of New York City's Bowery Bay and began the seven-and-a-half hour flight to Miami, Florida. Upon arrival in Miami, the maintenance crews gave both Clippers another inspection and check. New orders were given that informed the two crews that the next destination was Port-au-Spain, Trinidad, and the very special passenger was a gentleman named "Mr. Jones." Each Clipper, when fueled to capacity, had a cruising range of 3,800 miles. However, when carrying a maximum payload, the cruising range was reduced to 2,100 nautical miles. Each Clipper was equipped to carry 4,600 gallons of gasoline, which weighed 14 tons.

Approximately 20 minutes before takeoff, the motorcade pulled up to the dock and the various passengers began to disembark. Captain Cone, standing in the lounge of the *Dixie Clipper*, could not believe his eyes when he realized that passenger Mr. Jones was actually the President of the United States. The President was wheeled down the ramp in his wheelchair and lifted over the ramp and gently placed down in the lounge. Captain Cone snapped a salute and stated, "Mr. President, I'm glad to have you aboard, sir."

AIRCRAFT CREW AND GOVERNMENT PERSONNEL ABOARD THE DIXIE CLIPPER AND ATLANTIC CLIPPER

PLANE 1, *DIXIE CLIPPER*: AIRCRAFT CREW

Captain Howard M. Cone
First Officer Frank J. Crawford
Second Officer William F. Hughes
Third Officer James L. Steen
Fourth Officer Richard L. Bohner
Flight Engineer D. Raymond Comish
Assistant Flight Engineer Martin E. Basehore
Radio Officer Arthur R. Moore
Assistant Radio Officer Gail A. Bisbee
Steward Albert A. Tuinman
Steward Edward J. Garcia

PLANE 1, *DIXIE CLIPPER*: GOVERNMENT PERSONNEL

(The President and party)
President Franklin Roosevelt
Mr. Harry Hopkins
Admiral W. D. Leahy, United States Navy
Rear Admiral Ross T. McIntire
Captain John L. McCrea, Physician,
    United States Navy
Guy H. Spaman, Secret Service Agent
Elmer R. Hipsley, Secret Service Agent
Charles W. Fredericks, Secret Service Agent
Arthur Prettyman, Valet

PLANE 2, *ATLANTIC CLIPPER*: AIRCRAFT CREW

Captain Richard Vinal
First Officer Timothy B. Sheehan
Second Officer Robert N. Ellenberger
Third Officer John Ray Morrison
Fourth Officer William C. McAmis
Flight Engineer Donald R. Fowler
Assistant Flight Engineer William F. Daminger
Radio Officer Stanley W. Call
Assistant Radio Officer Robert E. Guest
Steward Gustave Garreau
Steward Philip A. Casprini

PLANE 2, *ATLANTIC CLIPPER*: GOVERNMENT PERSONNEL

Colonel W. A. Beasley, Signal Corps,
    United States Army
Captain George Durno, ATC,
    United States Army
Lieutenant George Fox, United States Navy
F. J. Terry, Chief Ship's Clerk,
    United States Navy
Mr. J. M. Beary, Secret Service Agent
Mr. J. A. Marshall, Secret Service Agent
A. C. Black, Chief Photographer's Mate,
    United States Navy
First Sergeant Hoch,
    United States Marine Corps

Four Secret Service Agents on the *Dixie Clipper*. (Foreground left to right) Hipsley, Spaman. (Next to the bulkhead of the aircraft) Fredericks and James M. Beary. United States Navy Archives

The *Atlantic Clipper* was the communications aircraft and would receive and transmit any important messages or information to the President.

The *Dixie Clipper*, carrying President Roosevelt and piloted by Lieutenant Cone of the United States Naval Reserve, moved away from the dock and proceeded to the takeoff area, where it taxied and gently soared into the sky shortly after 6 a.m., bound for Trinidad on a journey of 1,410 miles to the southwest. It was reported that President Roosevelt, approaching his 61st birthday, was as excited as a young child as the *Dixie Clipper* taxied, revived its four large engines and moved across the water and into the air. He looked out the window at the lights of Miami.

The *Atlantic Clipper* followed the *Dixie Clipper* at 6:34 a.m. It took the aircraft a mere 30 seconds to lift up from Biscayne Bay and into the still darkness of the cool Florida morning. The *Atlantic Clipper* trailed the *Dixie Clipper* by about 35 miles to the rear.

Shortly after takeoff, the course was set at 135 degrees, and after gaining altitude for 40 minutes, the aircraft leveled off at 9,000 feet. Sunrise was observed at 7:50, and ten minutes later the course was altered to 124 degrees. As the Clipper leveled off at 7,000 feet over the Great Bahama Bank, Captain Cone spoke to First Officer Crawford: "Let's not forget that his is just a normal operation." Crawford replied, "That's right. But this will be something to tell our grandchildren."

Captain Cone turned the controls over to First Officer Crawford and went down to the main deck. There he saw President Roosevelt dressed in a loose sweater and open collar poring over the navigation charts. After all, FDR had been Assistant Secretary of the Navy and was an old hand at sailing and employing the charts. Looking out the window, he pointed to the spots where he had been deep sea fishing. He inquired whether the route would take the Clipper over the old citadel built by Haiti's Henri Christophe, the second largest masonry structure in the Western Hemisphere. Captain Cone took the *Dixie Clipper* for a tour of the eastern portion of the Island of Hispaniola, on which Haiti is situated. He circled Christophe's Citadel to provide the President with an aerial view of the historic fortress, which President Roosevelt had visited in 1917 while serving as Assistant Secretary of the Navy in the Woodrow Wilson Administration. FDR identified points of interest in the manner that a taxi driver would provide local history lessons to his passengers.

At 3:45 p.m., both Clippers began their descent, and Trinidad was sighted 25 minutes later. They entered La Boca Grande of the Gulf of Paria at 4:15 p.m. The *Dixie Clipper* touched down on the waters off the newly constructed Naval Air Station in Trinidad at 4:24 p.m. The weather for the ten hour, four minute trip had been mostly favorable, with only light scattered clouds and no bad weather. The first leg of the flight to the Casablanca Conference covered 1,633 miles.

Upon landing at Trinidad, the President and his party left in launches for the dock at the Naval Operating Base and, upon disembarking, transferred to automobiles for a beautiful 15-minute drive to the Navy-operated hotel at Macqueripe.

Every arrangement had been made for the special visit, and the comfort of the President and his party was of the utmost concern. The Secret Service advance party and the local Navy officials had completed their work very well. The patio of the hotel provided a breathtaking view of the bay and a nice sea breeze to cool everyone. The President was able to relax for a brief time before dinner was served. Over cocktails, the President chatted with Admiral J. B. Oldendorf and Major Henry C. Pratt. These two officers met the President at the boat landing and joined the party for the drive to the hotel. Rear Admiral Oldendorf and Major General Pratt were guests of the President that evening at dinner, served on the second-floor veranda, just outside the President's suite. Admiral Leahy, Rear Admiral McIntire, Captain McCrea, and Mr. Harry Hopkins were the other guests at the dinner.

The decision was made that the *Atlantic Clipper* would depart for Belem, Brazil, at 4:30 a.m. the next morning. The passengers and baggage left the Macqueripe Hotel at 11:30 p.m. and made their way to the aircraft. It had been decided that the easiest course of action was to sleep on board the aircraft for the early morning takeoff. The President's plane, the *Dixie Clipper*, would not depart until 6:00 a.m. The members of the aircraft remained at the hotel that night.

Pan Am employee checking the undercarriage of the large berthing trailer that was employed to lift the Clipper out of the water. The Clipper and its trailer were then pulled onto the land for maintenance. Since salt water is very corrosive, it was critical to see if any salt damage was occurring to the underside of the aircraft.

University of Miami, Richter Library, Pan Am Collection

183

Admiral Leahy had been suffering what the doctor described as a heavy, hard chest cold for several days, and the trip had not improved the condition. On the advice of Admiral McIntire, the first bad news of the mission to Casablanca was delivered. Admiral Leahy would have to remain behind and be picked up on the return trip.

The *Atlantic Clipper* did not take off as early as planned, but did leave for Belem, Brazil, at 5:17 a.m., preceding the President's *Dixie Clipper* by about 45 minutes. The sunrise was observed at 6:25, and some time after eight o'clock both Clippers leveled off at 9,000 feet. The President spent the time reading, lunching, napping, and even played a game of solitaire. His other fascination was admiring Brazil's lush forest 9,000 feet below. After being airborne for approximately seven hours, the flight crossed the equator about an hour before the scheduled time of arrival in Belem. With the exception of the plane crew, Captain George Duro, Lieutenant George Fox, and Ship's Clerk Terry were the only shellbacks on board the *Atlantic Clipper* for the "Jupiter Rex" equator-crossing ceremony. A Neptune party was quickly arranged with Captain Duro sitting on the throne attired as Neptune, with Lieutenant George Fox at his left as the Royal Adviser, and Chief Ship's Clerk Terry at Neptune's right as the Royal Prosecutor.

Upon arrival at Belem, a report was handed to President Roosevelt, as follows:

To The Chief Of All Shellbacks:

It is reported that all pollywogs infesting the *Atlantic Clipper* were brought to trail this date and initiated into the Ancient Order of the Deep, with the appropriate ceremony.

Signed Captain George Duro, ATC; Lieutenant George A. Fox, United States Navy; Chief Ship's Clerk, F. J. Terry, United States Navy.

The *Dixie Clipper* did not require a ceremony, since everyone on board had already been initiated as a shellback.

One of the items presented to every Pan American passenger crossing the equator was a fully signed Jupiter Rex certificate. The certificate included the passenger's name and the date that the passenger had been taken into the ceremony. The departure and arrival information of the flight was included along with the name and signature of the captain of the flight. The time, altitude, airspeed, and weather were also recorded on the document, and in the left-hand corner was the embossed gold seal — for Pan American Airways system. A Clipper flying boat appeared in the background, in front of a large King Neptune figure.

The *Atlantic Clipper* landed in the River Para at Belem at 2:40 p.m., and President Roosevelt's *Dixie Clipper* followed 50 minutes later. The flight had covered 1,075 miles from Trinidad to Belem. The President was taken ashore at Belem and greeted by Vice Admiral Jonas Ingram and Brigadier General Robert L. Walsh.

While both Clippers were refueled to maximum capacity, President Roosevelt and his party, including Admiral Ingram and General Walsh, drove to the nearby Pan American airfield, now under the control of the United States Army as part of the Southern Air Transportation Command. They were entertained by Major L. E. Arnold, the Commanding Officer of the South Atlantic Wing Station, ATC.

Prior to the flight, the second piece of bad news of the secret mission was announced. The *Atlantic Clipper*'s Second Officer, Mervin W. Osterhout, had become ill and would be unable to continue on the journey across the Atlantic. He was replaced by Second Officer Robert H. Ellenberger, who had been stationed nearby awaiting his next assignment.

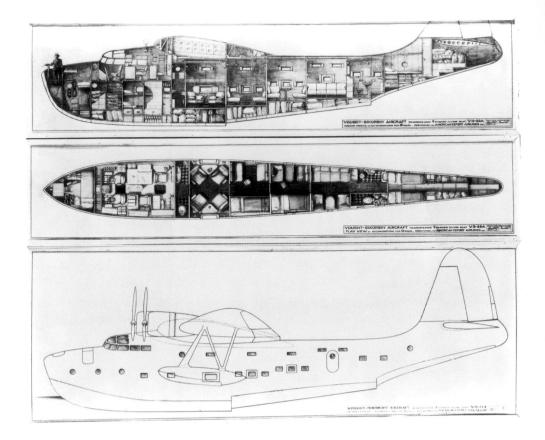

Official Sikorsky Aviation drawings of the outside and interior of the VS-44.

Igor Sikorsky Historical Archives

Three hours after landing at Belem, the *Dixie* and *Atlantic Clippers* had been refueled and checked out for the long flight across the Atlantic Ocean. Shortly after 6 p.m., the President and his party returned to the dock at Belem and embarked in the Clippers for Bathurst, Gambia, 2,100 miles to the northeast. The Clippers took off just before 7 p.m. and cruised at only a thousand feet for hours. The factor of fuel weight in such a flight, in this case 4,600 gallons, is easier to understand when it is noted that each of the Clippers burned approximately three-fifths of a ton of aviation fuel during each of the 19 hours it took to make the crossing.

Shortly after noon, Captain Cone and Mr. Harry Hopkins approached the President and sold him on the idea of becoming a "Short Snorter," a member of an exclusive airmen's club that exchanged and signed parts of dollar bills that were to be reassembled for drinks on later occasions. The President agreed to the initiation and was asked at once to give an autographed $1 bill to each Short Snorter present (Captain Cone, Mr. Hopkins, First Officer Crawford, Second Officer Hughes, Radio Officer Moore, Steward Tuinman, and Steward Garcia).

Though seven were actually on hand, Captain Cone noticed that the President had only $6 with him. Captain Cone had withheld his own personal claim. The President signed bills for the other members of the Short Snorter group. Captain Cone played with the rules since the President was short of one-dollar bills. He explained that he had only been introduced to the game a few short days earlier in New York City.

Pre-dinner drinks were served in the lounge, and gourmet meals were served by Stewards Albert Tuinman and Edward Garcia on the *Dixie Clipper* and Stewards Gustave Garreau and Philip Casprini on the *Atlantic Clipper*. A gourmet presentation of fresh fruits, vegetables, and other food had been taken on board while the aircraft were being refueled at Belem. The fresh flowers were placed on the tables. The meal that was served was a favorite of Clipper passengers: fresh melon, celery, olives, Jelly Rosa, Florida salad, hot buttered rolls, chateaubriand, parslied potatoes, string beans, a selection of various desserts, which included peach melba and petite fours, mocha, fresh coffee, and brandy.

The passengers had settled in and were walking around the aircraft in pajamas, robes, and slippers. No one changed into landing clothes until shortly before lunch. Even the President had slept in very late, but he awoke in excellent spirits and sat down with Harry Hopkins to discuss details of the upcoming conference.

That afternoon, the Clippers reached the African coast and made perfect landings in Bathurst at 4:30 p.m. Both aircraft were met by motor whaleboats from the USS *Memphis*, a light cruiser of the South Atlantic Force that normally operated out of the naval base in Natal. The USS *Memphis* had been ordered to Bathurst to provide safe and healthy quarters for the President before the last leg of the flight to Casablanca the next morning.

So perfectly had the secrecy of the mission been kept that the arrival was accepted and recognized as just another regular Clipper supply flight. As the President stepped ashore, he complimented Captain Cone and the entire flight crew for the fine trip.

The crew of both Clippers would remain for the next two weeks in Bathurst and Fish Lake, awaiting the return of President Roosevelt and the return journey across the Atlantic. The two crews would not become aware of the historical nature of the flight until their return to the United States and official press releases were provided to the various news services.

Captain H. Y. McCown, Commanding Officer of the USS *Memphis*, was on the dock to greet the President and reported that automobiles were standing by in case the President wished a tour of Bathurst and vicinity, which had been part of the original plans. Captain McCown informed the President that very little could be seen of Bathurst that was not already visible from the airport. He suggested that if the President wished to make a tour of the waterfront by boat, Commander E. F. Lawder, Royal Navy, was well informed as to points of interest and could be reached quickly. The President was determined to travel by boat rather than automobile. Commander Lawder was contacted, and a group which included himself, the President, Harry Hopkins, Admiral McIntire, Captain McCrea, and Captain McCown set off.

During the 30-minute inspection trip, many points of interest were observed along the waterfront. Several craft, including a net tender, oil tankers, and barges, passed close by. Many of the men working on the ships paid no attention to the passing whaleboats from the USS *Memphis* and did not notice their famous guest.

President Roosevelt boarded the USS *Memphis* shortly before 6 p.m. Normally, the USS *Memphis* flew the flag of the Vice Admiral Jonas H. Ingram, Commander of the South Atlantic Force. The President spent time in the Admiral's quarters with Captain McCown, ate dinner in the President's Mess, wrote several letters after dinner, and retired about 11:15 p.m.

It was noted by some of the crew and mentioned to Chief Ship's Clerk Terry that the President had come on board on the 13th day of the month, and the USS *Memphis* was light cruiser #13. No mention was made of what this omen meant.

Three camouflaged ATC C-54s would fly the President and his party to Casablanca's Medouine Airport. The first aircraft was employed as the Executive aircraft, the second would carry the secret service personnel and the third would serve as an emergency backup aircraft and carry spare parts. The President was flown past Dakar on the African coast and then inland over the Sahara Desert and the Atlas Mountains.

President Roosevelt was met by the advance party upon landing and taken by automobile to a rented villa in a residential area. The summit meeting with Winston Churchill, Joseph Stalin, and Charles de Gaulle planned the next Allied operations and listened to the vocal Stalin push for a Second Front to be opened in Southern France to relieve the pressure on the Russian forces and population. Others attending the long meetings included Lieutenant General Dwight Eisenhower, General George S. Patton, and other military commanders. One of the many items agreed to at the Casablanca Summit was that "unconditional surrender" would be demanded from the three Axis nations.

President Roosevelt took time out to meet with his two sons, Lieutenant Colonel Elliot Roosevelt and Lieutenant Franklin Roosevelt Jr. He inspected the United States Army Forces base near Rabat and traveled by car to Marrakech about 150 miles away. In the evenings, he continued a full schedule of entertaining guests, including the Sultan of Morocco. He was given a gold-mounted dagger in a beautiful teakwood case, two gold bracelets, and a gold tiara for Mrs. Roosevelt. In exchange, he presented to the Sultan a personally autographed photo, which included an engraved Presidential Seal. The item was encased in a sterling silver frame.

By early 1943, President Roosevelt was looking tired and very old for a man of 60 years. He was suffering from a very heavy cold upon his return to the United States from the Casablanca Summit and was looking forward to the return trip to Washington, DC, on the *Dixie Clipper* and a little relaxation. Upon his arrival at Bathurst, however, he insisted on taking a trip up the Gambia River. He sat in a deckchair on the USS *Aimell*, which had been sold to the British Government under the Lend-Lease Program. He then made a side trip to Liberia by aircraft and met with the President of Liberia, Edwin Barclay. Liberia was a nation of interest to the President and many African Americans, since it had been settled by slaves that had been part of a reverse migration back to the land that their ancestors had left on slave ships. He reviewed the status of American troops in the area and took several tours, including one of the Firestone rubber plantation, which was playing a pivotal role in the war effort. He reboarded the C-54 at 3:54 p.m. and was on his way back to Bathurst. He arrived at 7 p.m. and immediately boarded the USS *Memphis* once again for a late dinner.

Waiting to return President Roosevelt across the Atlantic was Captain Cone of the *Dixie Clipper* and Captain Vinal of the *Atlantic Clipper*. Both had returned from Fish Lake, where the Clippers had flown after dropping the President in Bathurst two weeks earlier.

The return flight would begin in the evening, and its first destination would be Natal, Brazil. At 11:00 p.m., the President was carried onto the *Dixie Clipper*, bathed in the glow from its interior lights. To ensure that the takeoff was safe and smooth, a group of buoyed lights had been placed in the takeoff zone by several Navy launches. Takeoffs and landings were most critical and dangerous for the Clippers, due to the inability to spot sunken objects or low water. Several had been damaged in the Pacific by coral reef obstructions. Safety on the return flight was especially important with the President on board.

The entire flight across the Atlantic was turbulent, and the passengers had to remain buckled in their seats. The motion of both aircraft made it almost impossible for the stewards to serve late-night snacks. Captain Vinal took his Clipper down from 7,500 feet

"Praised to the Stratosphere." Even Johnny Walker Whiskey was delivered on the Clippers during World War II to keep up the spirits of the troops.
Author's Collection

President Roosevelt cutting his 61st birthday cake. He had been surprised by a post-lunch birthday party. Seated next to the President is Admiral Leahy, Harry Hopkins is seated across from the President, and on the end of the table is Master Clipper Pilot Howard Cone Jr.

United States Navy Archives

to 1,000 feet and remained at the controls. A short distance out from Natal, one of the engines began to have mechanical problems. Oil began to spurt out, striking the aircraft's wing, trailing edge, and tail section. Flight Engineer Donald R. Fowler recommended to Captain Vinal that an engine should be feathered for safety reasons. It appeared that a piston had blown on the engine, and it could not continue to function and operate.

At 7:50 a.m. on January 28, 1943, Captain Cone and the *Dixie Clipper* landed at Natal, Brazil. He had departed after the *Atlantic Clipper*, but due to the other aircraft's engine problem and loss of speed, the *Dixie Clipper* had passed her. Approximately 25 minutes later, the distressed *Atlantic Clipper* set down. Due to excellent tail winds, both aircraft had gained three hours.

President Roosevelt departed and was taken aboard the USS *Humboldt*. He conferred with the Brazilian President Getúlio Vargas and later had lunch In a few short days, both men appeared in the motion picture segment *News of the World*. It featured the highlights of the events that had taken place in Natal. The next week Brazil announced that it was declaring war on the Axis powers, thus revealing what had been discussed between the two men at the luncheon meeting of January 28. Another nation had joined the war against the Axis.

Presidents Roosevelt and Vargas were also motorcaded to American and Brazilian military installations. A visit was paid to United States Navy Patrol 74, adjacent to the Pan American landing base. Once this visit was finished, President Roosevelt and President Vargas entered the motorcade to visit the United States Ninth Ferry Group, which was commanded by Brigadier General Robert L. Walsh. The airfield was filled with B-26 bombers awaiting takeoff across the Atlantic to Africa as part of the operation that Juan Trippe had established to assist the British prior to the United States entering the war. Some of the aircraft would then continue on to action in the Far East.

That evening Jefferson Caffery, the American Ambassador to Brazil, had dinner with both Presidents. The party brought up early so that President Roosevelt could be in bed by 9:45 p.m.

The *Atlantic Clipper* would require two days to repair its engine so the aircraft could continue its journey northward. Due to time constraints and the fact that President Roosevelt had been away from Washington for two weeks, it was decided to designate another Pan American Clipper to become the #2 Plane. The *American Clipper* arrived to continue the flight northward.

Orders were issued to Captain Cone and Captain Vinal to fly to Trinidad, where the President would meet them. The President and the other members of the party flew to Trinidad in a C-54 aircraft. President Roosevelt was greeted in Trinidad by Admiral Leahy, whose cold appeared to be much better. After another short tour, the President was taken to the Macqueripe Hotel.

On January 30, a major surprise greeted the President when he and his group arrived at Cocorite Airport. Captain Cone had hoisted international signals flags from atop the *Dixie Clipper* and then attached them to the radio antenna and across to the tail. In code, the message spelled out, "DNW, CAX, ELV, GUB." The message when translated read, "CinC, Birth, Day, Greetings." It commemorated the fact that President Roosevelt was about to celebrate his 61st birthday somewhere over the Caribbean.

It took less than ten minutes for the President and his company to board the aircraft, and by 7:10 a.m., the *Dixie Clipper* was aloft. The *American Clipper* followed shortly thereafter. By noon, the aircraft were over Haiti, and Captain Cone took a lazy circling to provide President Roosevelt with a fantastic view of the island.

The President was brought into the 14-seat dining lounge precisely at noon and given the window seat on the port side. The entire morning had been spent on birthday preparations to mark the special day. The tables were covered with starched linen adorned with

Martin 130 *China Clipper* outbound across the Pacific Ocean. The San Francisco coastline and the sprawling Sutro Baths pass below. The large American flag on the fuselage and wings and underside were added in 1938 to clearly indicate the nationality of the aircraft. Pan Am Clippers flew near Japanese-held islands where on one flight the *Hawaii Clipper* had disappeared with no trace. Clyde Sunderland, Pacific Aerial Surveys, HJW Geospatial Inc.

bright yellow and red tropical antheriums, tall champagne glasses, and a linen-wrapped cooler filled with ice and a large bottle of champagne.

Everyone raised their glass high to toast the President on his 61st birthday at exactly 12:30 p.m. Even the party on the trailing *American Clipper* played a part in the celebration, as the President was handed a message from Operations Chief Lieutenant Commander Leslie. Leslie was the only Pan American employee that had been aware of the real identity of Mr. Jones and where the trip was headed. Not even Juan Trippe had been informed of the President's plans. Lieutenant Commander Leslie had made the arrangements to ensure that the operation went smoothly for the President and his staff.

The message given to the President read: "Passengers and crew of Clipper #2 request to inform the President that they will drink to his health and happiness at 16:20 GMT, wishing him many happy returns on his birthday. That our Commander-in-Chief should, for the first time, be celebrating his birthday in the vast freedom of the sky seems to us symbolic of the new day for which we are all fighting with one mind and one heart."

Captain Cone presented the President with three letters: one held donations for the Infantile Paralysis Fund, the second money for the President's Birthday Ball, and the third personal letters and messages from the crew members. The President was touched by this generosity. The Infantile Paralysis Fund was very close to the President, due not only to his own situation, but also the fact that he was especially touched by the children who had the illness. Stewards Tuinman and Garcia had prepared a special dinner of caviar, celery, olives, turkey, peas, potatoes, and coffee. The last item was a large birthday cake, which had been brought aboard the *Dixie Clipper* by Captain McCrea without the President's knowledge. The President was given the honor of cutting the cake. The only

Aerial shot of the Nouméa sea base during World War II. Staging area for the Clippers and navy ships leaving to attack the various Japanese-held islands.
University of Miami, Richter Library, Pan Am Collection

Admiral Leahy and President Roosevelt admire a bound collection of vintage Trinidad prints — it was one of three birthday gifts presented to FDR.
United States Navy Archives

individual not to take a sip of champagne was Captain Cone, as aviation regulations did not permit the pilot to drink while on duty. The President was overjoyed at the surprise party and even more so when he was presented with more gifts: a rare portfolio of Trinidad prints, an engraved cigarette box, and two egg cups. The entire day's entries in the Clipper log were written in red ink under the heading "President's Birthday." He spent the entire flight talking and poring over the Trinidad prints.

The flight went smoothly and the *Dixie Clipper* landed at Biscayne Bay at 4:35 p.m. The President and party were met by an honor guard presided over by Rear Admiral J. L. Kauffman, Seventh Naval District Commander. Upon disembarking, the secret traveler stopped and spent a few minutes talking and thanking the Pan American crew for their professionalism and the success of the trip. The President was carried and placed in his chair and left for the waiting train that would take him back to his duties in Washington, DC. The train departed at 6 p.m.

Captain Cone complimented the fact that the "men and women in Pan American's shops, the crews at every station, had every detail set up. The Army Air Force and the Navy stood constant guard. The cooperation was wonderful. We take off our hats to those we had behind us. They did the hard work. Our job was easy. All we did was fly."

The two Clippers had covered 10,964 miles without a major incident. The round-trip flight took 70 hours and 21 minutes in the air and the aircraft had landed on three continents, crossed the Atlantic twice, and the equator four times. The *Dixie Clipper* had taken the first President to leave the United States by air, the first to fly an ocean, the first to touch three continents by air, and the first to cross the equator four times.

After a slight delay due to bad weather, the Clippers returned to New York City on February 1, 1943, and continued to fly commercial passengers, mail flights, and await orders for any possible mission that might be required. For the time being, their main flight plans were to cross the Atlantic to Europe, but nothing could compare to the events of January 1943.

John C. Leslie, The Atlantic Division Manager, wrote and forwarded a report on the entire mission. The conclusions were that the Clipper flights were successful and had been accomplished on schedule. The weather had been generally good. There were no mechanical difficulties on the President's aircraft, although the *Atlantic Clipper* did suffer an engine problem on its #3 engine on the leg from Bathurst to Natal. A piston had failed and a replacement aircraft was provided.

Reports received from the many passengers and, most importantly, the President found that everyone had been comfortable and enjoyed the wonderful food and hospitality. The report also stated that if the load weight and the number of passengers were kept consistent, the same comfort could be provided on any future flights. Additional load weight would result in less comfortable circumstances.

The escort aircraft was able to remain in sight of the principal aircraft during the daylight hours, but not at night or in bad weather. One problem was the short time available to refuel at Belem before sunset. Future flight schedules should allow for sufficient time to refuel, which would put less pressure on the crews to have the aircraft airborne before the sun set.

President Harry Truman presenting Juan Trippe and Pan Am Airways a plaque to recognize and honor the valiant service provided by the employees and aircraft of Pan Am during World War II.

There was also concern that the night lighting facilities were not of the quality the crew required on the return flight from Bathurst. It would have been much better if the aircraft had taken off from Fish Lake instead, due to the quality of the lighting and ground personnel.

Leslie also recommended that the air carriers be informed more fully about the nature of their task than this flight, when even Juan Trippe was not aware of the journey across the Atlantic. There should be one airline representative traveling in the same aircraft with the President's aide or whoever was acting as Trip Manager due to security concerns. It would be more efficient and safe to use the air carrier's existing ground facilities and personnel for refueling and servicing than employing Navy or Army units, which had no experience in dealing with the giant flying boats.

Consultation with the air-carrier officials would allow for the easier procurement of food and other commissary supplies en route. It was found that leaving such decisions until arrival at each destination not only created confusion, but also forced the Flight Stewards to stay up most of the night preparing the meals for the next day.

Due to the secrecy of the flight, weather information was not as detailed because personnel did not want to reveal too much information.

Lastly, it was noted that the time of the year for the area covered was the most favorable. Other times of the year might have some disadvantages that must be considered in the planning phase.

1943 would not be a kind year to the Pan American Clippers. In addition to the loss of the *Philippine Clipper* and everyone on board, other accidents would take a toll on aircraft and bring more fatalities.

The *Bermuda Clipper*, an S-42B, was destroyed while docked at Manaus, Brazil. A flight engineer had pulled the gas dump valve instead of the fire extinguisher knob to put out an engine fire. The expulsion of fuel further ignited the fire and the aircraft was engulfed in flames and burned at the dock. This marked the third sinking of an S-42 in two years. Luckily, no one was injured or killed.

With the loss of the *Philippine Clipper*, only one of the three Martin 130s still remained. There was now a shortage in the Pacific Division, so two B-314s were returned to the West Coast.

Pan American's 9,000 employees were put at the disposal of the United States Government and military. Pilots and navigators were called upon to advise and train military crews on the techniques of over-water flying. Jimmy Doolittle's famous bombing mission against Japan involved assistance from Pan American personnel.

With more resources required, Pan American crews flew twice as many hours as in peacetime. The plush interior of the B-314s were scrapped and the aircraft were used to transport tires, weapons, and other equipment. A B-314 transported the barrel and breech from the famous German Army 88 from Egypt to be tested at the Aberdeen Proving Grounds in Maryland.

Another carried mica from India and other raw materials that were required for the war effort. At least one large shipment of platinum was carried from Iran. Raw rubber and latex were carried on B-314s. The raw rubber was not one of the favorite items to be carried on the aircraft, because the constant smell of warm, moist rubber and latex would begin to make the crew feel sick to their stomachs.

Uranium was flown from the Belgian Congo. Of course on the eastward and westward flights, mail was always on board and lots of it. Mail in peace and war has played an important part in the history of Pan American Airways.

The Pan American route to Africa and the Orient became known as the "cannonball." It covered 11,500 miles from Miami to South Africa and from there on to India. It was the longest, fastest, and largest air transport route in history.

Over 542 bombers and transports were ferried, and Pan American trained more than 5,000 military pilots and thousands of mechanics. More than 200 employees lost their lives in the war effort of 1941-45. Since they were civilians, employees received very little glory and no medals. At the end of the war, however, Juan Trippe and Pan American Airways would receive the Harmon Trophy from President Harry Truman for "contribution to the military success of the Allied Powers. In a manner that could not have been equaled by any other Allied Agency. Well Done."

VS-44 on the water taxiing for takeoff. Igor Sikorsky Historical Archives

On January 17, 1942, the *Excalibur* was christened by the wife of U.S. Vice President Henry Wallace. Sikorsky had hoped that the VS-44 would become the next logical replacement aircraft for the B-314. It did not come to pass and only three VS-44s were ever constructed. One still exists in the New England Air Museum.
Igor Sikorsky Historical Archives

With the war raging, aircraft manufacturers continued to turn out flying boats for the war effort. Sikorsky Aviation even put into motion what it hoped would be Pan American Airways' next flying boat, a VS-44A called *Excalibur*. It had been developed from the United States Navy Patrol plane. The aircraft, known by the military as the "Flying Dreadnought," was the product of the United States Navy. The aircraft was a four-engine, cantilevered, high-wing monoplane flying boat. She made her maiden flight on August 13, 1937, and was flown around the same lighthouse on the Housatonic River that Charles Lindbergh and Captain Musick had test flown the S-42 around several years earlier. The zenith of flying boats had been reached, though, and with or without World War II, the days of glamour over water were coming to an end.

Only three of the giant VS-44A flying boats, the *Excalibur, Excambian,* and *Exeter,* were constructed by Sikorsky Aviation. On January 17, 1942, the wife of U.S. Vice President Henry Wallace smashed a bottle of champagne against the hull of the *Excalibur*. It refused to break until a piece of metal was held to the nose of the S-44. The inability of the champagne bottle to break may have been an omen of the end of the Golden Era of the Flying Boats.

These planes were manufactured for the United States Navy and served the military. Each aircraft carried a giant American flag painted on its bow and was painted in the navy camouflage colors of sky blue on top and light gray underneath. The three served magnificently during the war, but no other aircraft were produced.

Clipper on the water, military personnel on dock, and the PanAir boat preparing to depart. The Clippers became famous for their exploits in the South Pacific. University of Miami, Richter Library, Pan Am Collection

Ads in magazines during the war continued to focus on the end of the war and the future of commercial aviation, which was still seen as the flying boat. Only three *Excaliburs* were built; one was destroyed and the remaining two leased to the Navy. One can be found in the New England Air Museum.

Charles Lindbergh, as early as October 28, 1936, had expressed the hope that he could find a long-range aircraft to meet future needs. The day of the flying boat was coming to an end, and the future was in long-range, over-the-ocean, non-stop aircraft.

Lindbergh wrote, "I am glad that you are developing a land plane in addition to the new flying boats. I believe it is probable that the land planes will replace the flying boat on all-important routes in the future. I think the only exception will be in places where landing fields can not be obtained or where the traffic is so low that the construction of a field is not warranted. In order to protect the company's interest, I believe it is extremely important that whatever land plane you develop is capable of flying the Atlantic routes with a reasonable payload and a large fuel reserve."

Lindbergh's prediction turned out to be quite accurate. The massive construction of concrete airfields to serve the war effort would create the climate for land-based aircraft. Just as at the end of World War I, there was a surplus of trained men experienced in float plane flying. World War II would create a surplus of men experienced in long-range, overland and over-water transport flying. Long-distance transport aircraft developed during the war would become surplus. The economic boom of the post-war period would create a population wanting to travel across the United States and visit other exotic nations. Mass, inexpensive travel would become the order of the day.

For a brief time, there were beautiful, majestic flying boats, few in number, but imposing in their ability to capture the public's imagination. Gone now, they have passed into the pages of aviation history.

PAN-AMERICAN AIRWAYS "CHINA CLIPPER" ARRIVES AT SAN FRANCISCO, FROM THE ORIENT

© CLYDE SUNDERLAND

CHAPTER 9

THE MAGIC OF THE PAN AMERICAN CLIPPERS

IN THE 1930S, THE PAN AMERICAN CLIPPER FLYING BOATS were few in number, but the reach of their magic was everywhere. One would believe that there were at least a hundred flying boats, but in reality the entire total was 28, not one of which was saved for an aviation museum. The American public could not get enough information on the Clippers' latest exploits. Whenever a Clipper was departing or landing, the crowds would appear, not to see a passenger off, but just to marvel at the grace and beauty of the aircraft. The Pan American Clippers appeared in advertising, magazines, newspapers, radio, movies, cigarette cards, picture cards, and promotional giveaways and were at the center of the three major World's Fairs of the 1930s.

The Pan American Clippers evoked romance, adventure, and intrigue and became part of the American Dream. The Clippers became the focal point for everyone that wanted to have money and the ability to travel the world in style and class. The Pan American Clippers were America's aircraft, and Pan American Airways, America's national airline, even if they were not formally recognized as such. Pan American Airways was the symbol of wealth, power, and advanced aviation technology and the model of the perfect capitalist organization. The airline projected America's image of optimism and can-do to the four corners of the globe. To fly on a Clipper was to fly in luxury.

Juan Trippe used print advertising from the beginning as the major medium to bring in passengers. Advertisements appeared on the passenger trains traveling on the East Routes down to Florida. Advertisements appeared outside or inside nightclubs to entice passengers for the first flights from Key West, Florida, to Havana. Havana was the Latin hot spot for partying, gambling, and, very importantly, warm weather. Remember, when Pan American Airways was founded in the 1920s, America was in the grip of Prohibition. In 1928, one of the first Pan American Airways ads read,

> How many times have you stood on the deck of a steamer, tossing in a rough sea and enviously watched the gulls wheeling and dipping round the vessel. What swiftness and lightness, what ease, while you suffered the agonies of the endless rolling and pitching of a spiteful sea. How you longed for the smooth, quick flight of the gull.

(Left) Color postcard of the *China Clipper* on the first flight to carry mail to Hawaii. With great fanfare the M-130 departed San Francisco on November 22, 1935. The city of San Francisco is in the distance as the Clipper flies toward the Pacific Ocean and onward to Hawaii and eventually Manila.
Author's Collection

Set of 1939/40 New York World's Fair postcards. "The World of Tomorrow."
Author's Collection

These chopping crossings are as true of the Straits of Florida through which the Gulf Stream flows, as of the English Channel, which is famous for its roughness. For a steady breeze is at cross purposes with the strong current and those on the surface where wind and water meet suffer aplenty. But now man has mastered the principles of flight and may enjoy the comfort, speed and safety of aerial transportation.

As contractors for the United States and Cuban Mail, Pan American Airways, Inc., has maintained since October 18, 1927, a daily service between Key West and Havana, connecting with the Havana Special, both South and Northbound. On January 10, 1928, regular passenger service was inaugurated in accordance with the schedule shown below. The great saving in time means the best part of two days gained in the round trip to Cuba. In addition, a comfortable journey with minimum delay for custom formalities is assured. Pan American Airways, Inc., uses only the most modern and safest equipment available and employs conservative skillful pilots and expert mechanics. The United States Department of Commerce has licensed all the pilots as well as large eight-passenger Tri-motor Fokkers which are in use between Key West and Havana. Safety and service are the guiding principles of all flights over Pan American Airways.

Daily Schedule:
Leave Key West, Florida — 8:00 a.m.
Arrive Havana, Cuba — 9:15 a.m.
Leave Havana, Cuba — 3:45 p.m.
Arrive Key West, Florida — 5:15 p.m.

One way fare: $50 — includes passenger and 30 pounds of luggage, also transportation to and from the airports. Excess baggage will be carried at 25 cents a pound when the capacity of the plane permits.

Reservations can be made at any of the listed offices, by telephone or telegram. It should be noted that Pan American Airways, Inc., cannot guarantee to hold reservations made by wire, unless full fare or deposit of one-third of full fare is immediately sent. Reservations on which deposit has been made will not be held after 24 hours before intended flight, unless full payment is completed.

100 East 42nd Street, New York City —
    Telephone: Caledonia 2363
La Concha Hotel Building, Key West, Florida —
    Telephone: 377
Sevilla-Biltmore Arcade, Havana, Cuba —
    Telephone: 2222

As Pan American expanded by purchasing other airline companies and more aircraft, the advertising became more elaborate and sophisticated. The routes expanded from Latin America to the Far East and eventually across the Atlantic. Advertising focused on the beauty and magnificence of Clipper aircraft, first with the S-40s and S-42s on the Latin American route, then with the new Martin 130s and finally the Boeing 314s.

The early advertising on Latin America focused on the Lindbergh route, with the image of the famous flier appearing

1940/41 back cover of the official publication of the Boeing Aircraft Company. The back cover featured the new B-314. Boeing had hoped to sell more flying boats. Notice the new American flag that is painted on the front nose of the Clipper. The Boeing ad notes that the air has become a vital source to move men and material.

Author's Collection

on pamphlets in his *Spirit of St. Louis* leather helmet and goggles. The advertising posters became beautiful works of art in their own right. One of the most famous images is of a S-42 *Brazilian Clipper* flying over Rio with the mountains and water in the background. The posters portrayed beauty, glamour, and the lure of exotic, faraway places.

As the newer M-130s and B-314s came into service, the image on the advertising posters included the new aircraft and the 1800s Clipper sailing ship. Pan American's advertising and posters featured the image of happy travelers arriving in Hawaii and being greeted by islanders and given the traditional leis. The "Hawaii Overnight – San Francisco – Hawaii Overnight! Via Pan American to the Orient" was the work of Frank Mackintosh. His poster screams of luxury, wealth, warm and sunny climates, and good times. The brightly colored poster features the Pan American Clipper on its way to the mysterious Orient. Frank Mackintosh designed menus and posters for the Matson Shipping Line, which visited Hawaiian ports of call. The image he created can still be found in Hawaii today, on s and even T-shirts with other companies' advertising. So many of the posters of the period are credited with "artist unknown." Franklin Roosevelt's Federal Art Project was dedicated to artists and the creation of posters. Most of the brightly painted, artistic posters were of national scenes such as the Grand Canyon and Mount Rainer National Park.

The poster *There Are No Distant Lands* (1940) features a rare image of the pre-war Pan American global enterprise. A B-314 Clipper is climbing and pointed toward the many countries that Pan American served at the time.

One of the famous Paul George Lawler posters, *Flying Down to Rio/Pan American*, featured a soaring, breathtaking view of Rio de Janeiro's majestic sprawling Guanabara and Botafogo Bays as seen from the top of Mount Corcovado. An S-42 flies by in the distance. The colors are natural browns and blues with a few white clouds. Several variations of the poster exist, including one that promises, "In Five Days Via Pan American." Lawler also created *Overnight on the Honolulu Clipper*, which featured passengers disembarking in the warm sunshine and having flowered leis placed around their necks. Another famous Lawler poster featured a Clipper flying between the island mountains with a woman reclining near a grass shack below.

Leon Helguera created a large poster featuring the Pan American empire on the fateful day of December 7, 1941. Gordon Grant created Juan Trippe's favourite poster, *The Yankee Clipper Sails Again* (1939). It featured a B-314 overhead and a Clipper ship from the 1800s below.

In the 1930s, Art Deco and its "streamlined" beauty were very important to many objects or products. Even stoves, refrigerators, typewriters, toasters, phones, and posters could be beautiful objects. Juan Trippe and his marketing department were selling not just travel on aircraft, but a lifestyle. The Clipper flying boats became one of the most exclusive and expensive means of travel. After World War II, Trippe would recognize the market for travel for the masses, but in the period of the Pan American Clippers, travel

"Flying Down to Rio" in an S-42 Clipper. Advertising travel poster painted by Paul George Lawler. The 1930s color travel posters commissioned to advertise Pan American Airways and its Clippers are sought after by collectors. The colors of the images evoke a time during the Golden Age of Aviation.

Swann Galleries of New York City

1930s ad featuring the S-42. "Flying the Lindbergh Trail" focused on South America, which had been opened by Lindbergh's early survey flights in the S-38.
Author's Collection

was centered on the wealthy, and destinations were portrayed in advertising as beautiful, exotic destinations. A transpacific brochure of the late 1930s read,

Over pioneer aerial trade routes blazed by Lindbergh to the lands of the West Indies, Central and South America, high above the age-old routes of Columbus, Spanish conquistadores, swash-buckling pirateers, of Clipper ships of another generation, great Flying Clipper Ships now speed along radio-guarded highways of the sky to thirty-three countries and colonies of the Southern Americas. Linking the New World and the Old, they span the vast Pacific to Hawaii, the Philippines and China. With a record unexcelled by any other form of transportation — for schedules maintained at 99.678% over eight years — more than 750,000 passengers have flown more than three hundred million miles — thirty million pounds of mail and cargo have been carried — on these routes that link the Americas, that span Alaska, the Pacific and far-off China, and cross the Atlantic to Bermuda. Wherever you go "via Pan American," you travel in the finest equipment aviation science has produced. And "via Pan American," you travel with the supreme assurance that your capable crew — and the 4,000 trained experts along the airways — are in constant attendance on the swift, sure flight of your airliner.

Even in its early years, Pan American Airways was successful in adapting to the changing environment and altering its advertising. As the war in Europe raged on in 1941, and tensions mounted with the Japanese, Pan American Airways ads with patriotic themes appeared, and even included images of United States Navy sailors looking skyward to sight a passing B-314 with its large American flag on the front fuselage:

America's Outposts of Security and Defense — Do you know where they are? How far away? How they are reached? Important facts for every American citizen.

Right now all eyes are on America's military air power. But equally vital to this country's defense is its commercial air development. How do we stand there? You probably know that within our borders this country has an aerial network that no foreign nation can equal.

What about outside the United States? There the 75,556 mile system of Pan American Airways is the envy of the world. Its great modern Clipper ships link 55 countries, fly 98.62% on schedule. Back of this record are 13 years of "over-ocean" flying, expert pilots, modern equipment, scores of radio and weather stations and a trained loyal organization of more than 7,000 people.

What does this mean? It means that vital as is Pan American Airways role in furthering national defense, the Flying Clipper Ships are even more vital as Uncle Sam's strong right arm in furthering United States trade and good will. In the great international race for commercial air supremacy both today and after the war, America is out in front. Our job is to see that she stay there.
TRAVEL PAN AMERICAN AIRWAYS SYSTEM.

Pan American booklet and timetable for its entire system — Bermuda, Cuba, Nassau, West Indies, Mexico, Central and South America, newly added Hawaii, Philippines, China, and Alaska. Author's Collection

Hawaii — key to our Pacific defenses, is days nearer to the United States and to the sentinel isles, Midway and Wake, by Flying Clipper. From Honolulu to San Francisco is only overnight; a vital defense link.

Far East — to Hong Kong by Clipper in seven days, with Chungking only a day beyond — 9,516 miles out of California! It's eleven days faster each way than by boat — time vital to defense and diplomacy!

Indispensable — Life Lines of our nation are the routes of America's Merchant Marine of the Air. Note how Flying Clippers unite virtually every major sphere of United States trade and defense.

North Atlantic — bastions of defense are our Bermuda bases. Clippers link them to the United States — 817 miles away in five hours, providing two days faster delivery of government men, mail and materials.

Caribbean bases — 1800 miles from Florida to Trinidad, are joined by as many as 37 weekly Pan American schedules. For example, by Clipper from Miami to Jamaica its only five hours; Puerto Rico six and three quarter hours.

Pan American Airway had been successful over its 13-year history by not only understanding events as they unfolded, but being one step ahead, predicting the trends year before any other airline. The ads appearing in 1941 showcased the airline and its connection to protecting the interests of the United States. Juan Trippe would employ his favorite image, the aircraft and sailing ships of the 1800s together. During his entire lifetime, Trippe would continue to push for Pan American Airways to be declared by the United States Government as its one and only official flag-carrier airline.

New Horizon Magazine was Pan American's own. A typical headline ran, "Vital to Victory: These world air transport routes which are hastening Victory were pioneered by Pan American before Pearl Harbor." The article featured the history of the Pan American Airways system:

1927 — To Latin America — The beginning of fast, reliable air service to both coasts of South America.

1937 — To China — Pan American established the first regular, scheduled air service over any of the earth's major oceans.

1939 — To Europe — Regularly scheduled air service was established across the Atlantic to Southampton and the Continent. (A beautiful scene is pictured of a boy and girl standing on the White Cliffs of Dover as a B-314 flies overhead.)

1940 — To Australia — Pan American turned Southward from Hawaii — English speaking friends were brought closer by weeks.

1941 — To Africa — By pioneering a South Atlantic, trans-Africa route, the groundwork was laid for the vital war traffic that followed.

Another ad pointed to the fact that most of the routes Pan American World Airways had pioneered before the war were still in operation, many in cooperation and under contract with the United States Air Transport Command and the Navy Air Transport Service. It mentioned that several of the destinations — Wake Island, Guam, Hong Kong, and Manila — were temporarily discontinued.

A 1943 full-page Camel cigarette ad features Captain Joseph H. Hart: "They've Got What It Takes — 12 times across the ocean in 13 days — 'I stick to Camels — They've got more flavor and they're easy on my throat.' — First in the service — With men in the Army, Navy, Marine Corps, and Coast Guard, the favorite cigarette."

In the background is a B-314 with a large American flag painted on the side, just below the captain's window. The rest of the ad explains that Captain Joseph H. Hart has flown tons of freight and hundreds of United Nations officials across the Atlantic, and, Captain H. Hart, one of Pan American Airways' ace pilots, recently broke his own record —12 times across the ocean in 13 days and 15 hours.

New Horizons also contained a story called "America's New Lifeline to Africa," which told readers its own story. A large illustration featured a ground crew working on an aircraft and the ever-present Clipper overhead. Even though Pan American Airways was never officially declared the United States flag carrier or national airline, the majority of the flying public recognized it in that way.

Every issue of *New Horizons* featured the wealthy and famous who had flown on a Clipper in the last month. The January 1941 issue featured movie actor Robert Montgomery arriving from Europe on a Clipper. Movie actress Anna May Wong was featured as a famous actress flying on a Clipper.

The fame of the Pan American Clippers spread worldwide. The British publication *Modern Science* of September 18, 1937, contained an aviation story on blind flying. The featured two-page center spread was a color painting of the S-42 and the Martin 130 flying boats: "America's Giant Clippers — Flying Boats That Have Made History."

Other companies focused their advertising on the image of the Pan

1943 Camel ad advertising cigarettes, Pan Am, and a patriotic tone. Most ads during World War II were of this type, a combination of marketing and keeping the public appraised of war issues. B-314s sit in the water in the background. Pan Am Clippers became military aircraft during the war.
Author's Collection

American Clippers and the services or products that were on the aircraft. One ad features a Clipper with the Captain (pilot) leaning out of the cockpit window talking to a driver of a milk delivery truck. The comments mention how much fresher the milk carried on the Clipper is since it arrives right on the dock just prior to takeoff.

A Kellogg's cereal ad featured the Crew Landing Chief of a Pan American Airways Clipper eating a bowl of cereal, which he stated that he needed first thing in the morning to give him strength to blow his whistle and guide the crew.

Various tobacco companies produced aviation cigarette cards featuring Clippers. John Player & Sons of Great Britain issued a set that allowed one to receive a card album for an extra few cents and a proof of purchase seal. The album features a British flying boat flying over palm trees. The M-130 is featured on one card in the set, along with the interior shot of the S-42.

The Gerber's Baby Foods Company ran the following full-page ad:

> Feeding Baby in the Skies. If you ever have to travel with a young baby over Pan American, or United Airlines, or Transcontinental and Western Air, or via American Airlines, you can be sure that your young traveler will be well cared for. Each of these four airways provides a special feeding kit for babies, complete with bib and dishes. All four major airlines serve only Gerber's Baby Foods.

Even baby food wanted to be connected to the Clippers. Ad for Gerber's Baby Food served on the aircraft and transported as cargo to faraway destinations.

Author's Collection

In the giant Pan American Clippers, Gerber's Baby Foods are standard equipment when young travelers are aboard. In addition, Pan American Airways thoughtfully supplies Gerber's Baby Foods to its employees with children, who are stationed at bases aboard.

Companies that provided parts or equipment for the Pan American Clippers proudly trumpeted that fact in their own advertisements. Many pictured aircraft such as the B-314 *Dixie Clipper*, with its large American flag. The Synthane Corporation ran the following: "Over the Atlantic, the Pacific, over all the vast reaches of America's water front, the Clippers are winging on errands of war, mercy and business. Of many parts made from Synthane for the Clippers, probably the most important are those for the radio and electrical instruments. Synthane is valued in the air service for its many combined properties — light weight, for instance (half the weight of aluminum), excellent insulating characteristics, hardness, ease of machining, resistance to corrosion from aviation oils and gasoline, and mechanical strength."

Companies continued to advertise products connected to the Clippers during the war. A Galbestos ad has the image of a large Clipper in the hangar on a tropical island: "Where Corrosion Gnaws and Climate is Grueling: Roof and Sides of Galbestos."

Sylvania Electric Products featured a color ad: "Midget Lightships to Guide Giant Clippers Home!" A Clipper in a tropical island area is taking off in the darkness, guided by the lights of the miniature lightships. The ad explains that these items are in use in New York's Marine Terminal, Lisbon, and Eire: "The lights are the answer to a pilot's prayer."

On the lighter side, the Grace Brothers Brewing Company used the Pan American Clippers to sell beer. The company had been founded in 1873 by Frank and Joseph Grace and then hit hard times when the Volstead Act brought Prohibition. They made lager and steam beer, which was sold in bottles and barrels to local saloons and to the general public in bottles and large buckets called "growlers." Once Prohibition ended with the election of Franklin Roosevelt, the company reopened. Changing with the times, the company now sold the beer in cans, which provided a better opportunity for advertising the brand with an eye-catching painting to draw consumers to the product.

With the public crazy about anything connected to the *China Clippers*, a new brand of Grace Brothers beer hit the California market: Clipper Pale Beer. A beautiful, vivid painting of the *China Clipper* in flight over water appeared on the can. The brand sold

World War II advertisement for new building material – Galbestos by the H. H. Robertson Company. Hangars shown with the Clipper moving inside.
Author's Collection

(Below) Cigarette card sets of the 1930s manufactured in Great Britain featured the aircraft of the period. Several sets contained various Clipper types, including an S-42. Also the photo of the interior of an S-40 was reproduced in a cigarette card. Other cards featured the galleys and other aircraft. An album to place the cards in with their description was available for ten cents.
Author's Collection

World War II ad by Kodak. The ad features a crew member of a Pan Am Clipper and discusses the new V-Mail. Letters were reduced to a very small size, and therefore the giant Clippers were able to carry larger volumes of letters from servicemen and their loved ones. A Clipper appears in the distance. Author's Collection

V-Mail envelope.
Note how small. Author's Collection

well, but disappeared in 1946, as did the actual Clippers. Due to the tin metal format of the cans, very few have survived. Unlike the real Clippers, however, the cans can still be found, at both traditional auctions on eBay. The last Clipper Pale can sold for over $10,000.

During World War II, many companies published ads on the war effort and emphasized their relationship to the Pan American Clippers. International Harvester ads proudly explained how their various types of construction equipment were assisting Pan American Airways—Africa in the construction of new airfields, housing, roadbuilding and other major tasks to win the war: "International Harvester Power For Victory." The ads always included a Pan American Clipper flying overhead. Excellent public relations could be won by connecting a product or company to the Clipper aircraft.

Hollywood also picked up on the public's love for anything connected to aviation. Starting in the late 1920s, aviation movies were produced for an eager audience. The early films focused on aviation in World War I, the most famous being *Wings* (1929), which starred a young Gary Cooper, Buddy Rogers, Richard Arlen, and Clara Bow. It won the first Academy Award for Best Picture. Movies about the fearless mail pilots of the period played to large audiences.

The first movie to feature a Pan American Clipper, RKO's *Flying Down to Rio*, was made and released in 1933. The movie featured the first pairing of Fred Astaire and Ginger Rogers and is also remembered for the scene of scantily dressed showgirls dancing on the wings of the aircraft. Two versions of the movie poster had been printed. The first ran afoul of the decency rules of the movie industry in the 1930s and had to be called back from distribution. The banned poster is worth $30,000, while the censored version sells in the $10,000 range.

In 1936, Hollywood recognized the public's fascination with the new Clipper aircraft. *China Clipper* was released to nationwide movie theaters by Warner Brothers. It starred Pat O'Brien as a Juan Trippe-type character and Humphrey Bogart as the Captain Edwin C. Musick figure. The story was of a man with a dream for a transpacific aircraft to fly to the Orient and how his ambition created problems with family and friends. The script had been written by former naval aviator Frank Wead and included footage of the famous *China Clipper*. It was the first aviation movie produced without a loss of life. One scene in the movie would have delighted Pan American: after flying through a typhoon, Humphrey Bogart makes a critical deadline and saves the airline. Upon exiting the cockpit, he is greeted by Pat O'Brien, who does not even thank him. As he walks away, Bogart remarks, "I was just thinking how swell it would have been if he'd said thanks."

Other movies through the years have employed the image of the Pan American Airways Clippers in exotic locales. Charlie Chan, of the 1930s detective film series, always traveled from San Francisco to Honolulu and back again. Many of the movies referenced or featured the Pan American Clippers. The most

1933 *Flying Down to Rio,* — Hollywood blockbuster that featured the famous scene of dancing girls on the wing of the S-40. "Too Big for the World, So They Staged It in the Clouds." Author's Collection, RKO

famous, *Charlie Chan at Treasure Island,* was made in 1939 to commemorate the opening of the Golden Gate International Exposition. The film opens with Detective Charlie Chan and his son Jimmy flying into San Francisco on the *China Clipper.* The plane passes over Treasure Island before landing in Clipper Cove. A murder is committed, and the passengers eventually disembark at the Pan American Terminal on Treasure Island, and the remainder of the movie takes place in or around the island.

The film is an enjoyable piece of Pan American Airways Clipper history. Watching it, one can travel back in time and experience many of the sites of the Golden Gate International Exposition, where the Pan American Clippers were stationed.

The Charlie Chan series employed the image of the Pan American Airways Clipper in several other movies. Even though Chan was a Honolulu police detective, he and his number one son always seemed to fly first class on a Clipper. In *Charlie Chan at the Olympics,* he arrives on the Clipper from Honolulu and flies across the United States to catch the *Hindenburg* in order to reach his destination, the 1936 Olympics in Berlin.

The 1942 Universal B movie *Bombay Clipper* starred William Gargan, Irene Hervey and Charles Lang. The plot involved a thief with $4 million worth of diamonds as a passenger on the *Bombay Clipper*. The movie poster features a Clipper flying overhead as the hero and villain fight it out. Less than five minutes before the ending, the jewel thief is exposed and attempts to take over the Clipper. Cinematographer Stanley Cortez would go on to make better films with Orson Welles, including *The Magnificent Ambersons*.

In *Casablanca*, characters attempt to get exit visas so they can catch a Clipper in Lisbon. 1942's *Now Voyager* starred Bette Davis, Paul Henreid, and Claude Rains. Spinster Davis begins a life of traveling. She returns home from Latin America on a Pan American Airways Clipper. The Warner Brothers film features a nice long shot of the Clipper at the end of the dock with its four engines running and the propeller spinning.

In more recent years, *The Phantom* (1996) has a Clipper being hijacked and a passenger taken from the aircraft. Martin Scorsese's *The Aviator* (2004) concerns the rivalry between Howard Hughes' TWA Airline and his competitor Juan Trippe. Featuring Leonardo DiCaprio as Howard Hughes and Alec Baldwin as Juan Trippe, the film graphically portrays the intense dislike between the two. *The Aviator* portrayed Trippe as a very political and powerful backroom broker of deals.

The film was very accurate in this portrayal; from his first deal in the 1920s, Juan Trippe manipulated, lobbied, and employed his vast family, college, and political connections to build his dream of Pan American Airways as a global airline carrying the American flag. When Democrat Franklin Roosevelt became President in 1933, one of his first comments was to the effect that Juan Trippe and his connections to 12 years of Republican rule was about to come to an end. Eventually, there was a realization in Roosevelt's Administration that one may not like Juan Trippe and his worldwide airline empire, but Pan American Airways was vital to the outreach of the United States into all the corners of the globe.

The Aviator portrays Howard Hughes with his own flaws and focuses on his own obsession of constructing a giant wooden flying boat, *The Spruce Goose*. By the end of World War II, the flying boats' Golden Age was at an end, and *The Spruce Goose* flew for a short distance and now rests in a museum.

The weekly magazines were also filled with stories on every record or flight of the new Clippers. Juan Trippe appeared on the cover of *Time* magazine in July 1933 and then returned to its cover on March 28, 1939. *Time* honored Captain Edwin C. Musick on the December 2, 1935, cover. He was in the familiar pose of sitting at the controls of his *China Clipper*. The *Time* staff had a difficult time in putting together a story on Musick. Few outside interests, likes baseball, Buicks, apples, ham and cheese sandwiches, vacations in Manhattan, married with no children. He was a man of average height and weight, slightly stoop shouldered, with thinning black hair. He was professional and all-business.

If only the public were aware that straight-arrow Captain Edwin Musick had started his career barnstorming across the Pacific Coast as "Monseer Mussick, the famous French flier." He worked on racing cars to earn money and flew flying boats to the Bahamas and to Cuba for the over-water airline Aeromarine until the company went out of business. Then, for a time, he made money by flying liquor from offshore supply boats to clandestine airfields along the East Coast during Prohibition. He made the acquaintance of Andre Priester, and when Priester moved to the new Pan American Airways, Musick went along.

On October 20, 1941, *Life* magazine featured Trippe's Clipper on the cover. The aircraft had been photographed shortly after its arrival at LaGuardia Field when a swarm of Pan American Airways employees began to check the aircraft. The size of the men on the various areas of the aircraft gave an excellent scale of the massive size of the aircraft. Other mediums of the 1930s picked up the *China Clipper* craze. *China Clipper* became the name for all of the flying boats. A song was written by Norma Morton and Ethel Powell that one could not help but hear over and over again on the radio. Even a dance step was created from the song.

Almost every home in America had a radio by the mid-1930s, and the Clippers became the vehicle to take listeners on strange, mysterious trips. *The Shadow*, Doc Savage, *Don Winslow of the Navy,* and others on many occasions worked the Pan American Clippers into the story lines. If the story involved the Orient, there were mysterious adventures, spies, and enemy agents. On the East Coast, the spies were either traveling to Europe or returning to New York City. German agents seemed to be everywhere.

At the same time, the Pan American Clippers were involved in very real life-and-death dramas. On the *Dixie Clipper* flight from Port Washington, New York, to Marseille, France, on August 4, 1940, one passenger was on a dangerous mission. Varian Fry, a 32-year-old author, editor, and member of the Emergency Rescue Mission of New York City was traveling to Vichy, France, with $3,000 in cash. He would remain in Europe for many months, usually one step ahead of the Vichy authorities and even American authorities, who were not pleased with his mission to rescue as many Jewish intellectuals from Vichy France and Germany as possible.

Through his efforts, hundreds of Jewish intellectuals were provided with papers to travel to the United States. Marc Chagall, Max Ernst, Hans Habe, Hannah Arendt, Nobel Prize winner Otto Meyerhoff, and others would be saved. Many would assist the

China Clipper outward bound passing the unfinished Golden Gate Bridge.

United States in defeating Nazi Germany in World War II. The Pan American Airways Clipper flights were one main avenue of escape.

Unlike Varian Fry's real-life experiences, the pulp magazines were filled with aviation tales of daring flights and exploits. Aircraft model magazines offered kits to manufacture a miniature version of the *China Clipper*. Model Airplane News of June 1938 offered information and directions: "Build and Fly the China Clipper Glider. How to Create a Fascinating Flying Silhouette Model of the Trans-Oceanic Clipper from Sheet Balsa Wood." The article was written by Jesse Davidson, the well-known aviation writer and historian.

The instructions were very detailed and even went so far as to specify that the logo and name of the airline should be outlined only with black India ink, including the globe. The entire model was constructed of balsa wood, the material of the 1930s. Even the famous sponsons of the Martin 130 were described in detail, including the correct angle that each should be attached to the larger fuselage.

The builder was told to carve out four three-bladed props carefully and then twist the blades slightly so that they would whirl when the model is launched: "Glide the model indoors and out in order to observe its behavior. Should the model stall, add more foil by cementing pieces cut to the same pattern. Add as much as needed until the model glides with a long gradual descent. Choose a breezy day for outdoor gliding and always

M-130 *China Clipper* preparing to take off. Martin Aviation Historical Archives

launch into the wind. For those desiring to build a model of the *Philippine Clipper*, the dimensions above given are exactly the same for the sister ship. The license number of the *Philippine Clipper* is NC14715 and the name is placed along the bow as shown in the plans."

Companies began to issue premiums to be ordered through the mail, usually for a certain number of box tops of their product and a small sum to cover handling and shipping. In 1935, Quaker Puffed Oats and Wheat offered an assembled balsa model of the Clipper aircraft. The toy aircraft had a wingspan of 12". They also offered various *China Clipper* brass ring, wings, and even a pilot's cap with gilt braid, brass buttons and a black hatband. Not to leave out little girls, the company offered a *China Clipper* bracelet, with personalized initials on a wing design.

Boy's Life, the Scouting magazine featured a 1936 cover story on the Clippers. In 1939, Kraft Chocolate Malted Milk offered a 22-inch model of the *China Clipper* with a tin of the their milk. The H. J. Heinz Company offered "Famous Pilots" and "Modern Aviation" picture card sets. One of the aircraft featured in the "Modern Aviation" series of 25 cards was the Sikorsky S-42. It was possible to order a special album that contained information about the famous pilots and famous aircraft of the period.

A little-known radio show sponsored by Lava soap, *Davy Adams — Son of the Sea*, offered membership in the Davy Adams Shipmates Club. Member certificates and secret code rings were available along with the Davy Adams Shipmates Club Kit with Pencil.

M-130 *China Clipper*, NC14716 at rest. The *China Clipper* was the first of the three Martin 130s off the assembly line. It was accepted by Pan American on October 8, 1935.
Martin Historical Archives

The kit was offered in 1939 and contained items connected to Pan American Airways, including a radiogram bulletin, secret flying order booklet, and a mechanical pencil with a secret compartment.

Even into the early 1950s, the Kellogg's cereal company was issuing a cardboard model airplane of the historic Pan American Clipper. The Clippers were gone, but the hold on the public still remained.

Hundreds of items over the years have been offered through the mail, sold in stores, and were even available from Pan American Airways: bobby pins, wings, hats, toys, coloring books, rain caps, postcards, magazines, and other items. The items were employed as souvenir and marketing tools to keep Pan American Airways in the public's eye and to bring in future passengers: children.

There was another major event happening in the 1930s that brought aviation to the attention of the public. While the 1930s are remembered as a time of economic depression, it was also an era that has been called the "The Golden Age of World's Fairs and Expositions." No other time in history has seen as many of these international events. In 1933/34, Chicago hosted the Century of Progress, San Francisco hosted 1939/40's Golden Gate International Exposition, and New York City hosted the 1939/40's World's Fair, World of Tomorrow. The three would play a unique part in the advancement of aviation, and Pan American Airways would especially use the Golden Gate International Exposition to its advantage.

The Century of Progress in Chicago was officially opened on May 27, 1933, and ran until November 12, 1933. The Transportation Building held exhibits on the history of travel through the ages with a large focus on the new age of air travel. The covers of many of the guidebooks to the Century of Progress contained scenes of aircraft and blimps flying overhead. Postcards were sold with similar images, and one of the biggest sellers was an aerial view of the entire grounds of the event.

(Left) 1942 Pan American ad in conjunction with Kellogg's cereal. The supervisor of the docking crew starts his day with Kellogg's corn flakes. He uses a great deal of energy in blowing his whistle to give directions on berthing or launching the various Clipper aircraft.

University of Miami, Richter Library, Pan Am Collection

Late 1930s toy model of the Clipper manufactured by the Wyandotte Toy Company of Indiana. The Pan Am Clipper was everywhere. Even today the famous Corgi Toy Company has manufactured a miniature aircraft of the B-314 *Dixie Clipper*. Even the orange color on the upper wings is included. The orange paint along the top of the aircraft made it easier to be seen from the air if it was in distress on the water.

Author's Collection

Italian General Italo Balbo saluting the crowd upon landing in Newfoundland. He was in command of a formation of 25 Savoia-Marchetti SM-55X flying boats on their way to the 1933 Chicago Century of Progress. One aircraft was lost in Amsterdam Harbor when it hit a floating object. Memorial University of Newfoundland, Centre for Newfoundland Studies, Robert Tait Collection

Sadly, only one item remains from the Century of Progress, and it stands in front of Soldier Field Stadium, home to the Chicago Bears football team. The item is an ancient Roman Column that was delivered by the armada of Italian flying boats that visited the grounds in 1933. It was the tenth anniversary of Benito Mussolini's reign in Italy, and in honor of the occasion, a mass formation of 25 Savoia-Marchetti SM-55X flying boats took off from Orbetello seaplane base, 100 miles north of Rome, under the command of General Italo Balbo. One seaplane was lost in Amsterdam when the aircraft struck an object in the water. The other 24 crossed the Atlantic and arrived on Lake Michigan in mass formation on July 15, 1933. The crews had trained for a full year to master the art of not just flying a great distance, but landing and taking off from water. The Roman Column was a gift of friendship from the people of Italy to the United States.

The 24 Savoia-Marchetti SM-55X aircraft made stops in Newfoundland on the inbound leg and the return. On July 12, 1933, the aircraft landed at Cartwright Harbor and departed the next day after resting and refueling. On the return trip, the seaplanes landed at Shoal Harbor, Trinity Bay, Newfoundland. General Balbo and his 24 seaplanes departed on August 8, 1933, carrying several thousand pieces of mail back to Italy. Many letters had been stamped "1933/Gen. Balbo Flight."

An accident on the return flight at Lisbon claimed the life of another crew member and the loss of a second seaplane. Thousands turned out to greet the fliers upon their return on August 12, 1933. The 23 remaining seaplanes landed on the Tiber River. The flight demonstrated that it was possible to fly across the Atlantic Ocean in a mass formation.

The City of San Francisco and Pan American Airways would each use the success of the Century of Progress and the granting of a World's Fair to New York City in 1939/40 to advantage.

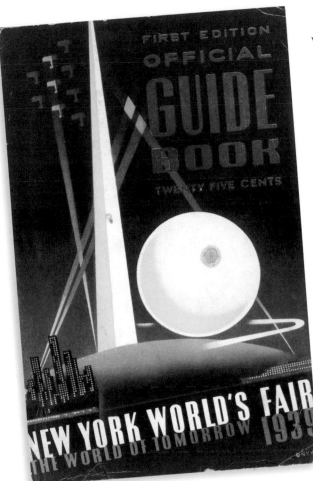

The City of San Francisco was turned down when they approached the Administration of Franklin Roosevelt to host a Golden Gate International Exposition in 1939. The government approval was denied on the grounds that money was being provided under the Public Works Programs only for the construction of highways and airports. Since San Francisco's proposal did not involve that level of construction, funding for two fairs in the same period was not possible.

San Francisco and Pan American Airways came back a few days later with a new proposal, one that included an airport. Pan American Airways would relocate its operation from Alameda to the new facilities at Treasure Island. Construction was approved for the Golden Gate International Exposition and the United States would have two fairs in 1939/40, one on each coast.

In August 1938, a 20-year lease was signed for a new Pan American Airways base to be built at San Francisco's Treasure Island. Pan American would leave its base at Alameda. First built was a hangar with a ramp railway that moved the Clippers between the hangar and the water. The new station opened with the departure of the *China Clipper* on February 5, 1939.

The Golden Gate International Exposition opened 13 days later on Saturday morning, February 18. The new Pan American Airways facility would become one of the main attractions of the Exposition. Clippers were very prominent in promotion for the event. The area of water next to the hangar was named Clipper Cove, and every map handed out to the visiting public at the Exposition not only mentioned its location on the map, but included at least one image of a Clipper flying above.

Treasure Island is manmade, built on the shoals of neighboring Yerba Buena Island. It was sold to be the first airport for San Francisco and home to the Golden Gate International Exposition of 1939/40. The island was so named for the fact that it was constructed entirely of mud dredged from San Francisco Bay and the Sacramento Delta. Since Sacramento was founded during the famous Gold Rush of the 1800s, the public relations department issued press releases announcing that the material from Sacramento could contain gold.

Treasure Island was one of 14 possible sites investigated in the San Francisco Bay Area for a land seaplane port. It was chosen since it offered the best for takeoffs and landings at 270-degree radius and had very good

The 1939 Guide Book to the sights of the 1939/40 New York World's Fair, featuring the Trylon and Perisphere and airplanes and search lights. The 1940 edition would have a muted cover since many nations did not open their pavilions that year due to the start of World War II. The excitment of the Fair just faded away. Author's Collection

1939/40 postcard from the New York World's Fair of a future airport on the water. In the background on the water is a M-130. (Bottom) 1939/40 postcard of the Trylon and Perisphere of the New York World's Fair. Author's Collection

1939/40 map of the Golden Gate International Exposition. Clipper Cove is featured along with the large Pan Am Administration Building with the control tower on top. Hangars alongside the cove. The Administration Building and two hangars still exist today. Author's Collection

(Right) Maintenance staff polishing the propeller. To maintain peak efficiency, the propellers needed to be cleaned and rubbed down prior to each flight. Since the Clippers were involved with salt water on each journey, great maintenance and care was required to lessen the effects of salt water on the aircraft. Boeing Aircraft Co., Chicago, Illinois

prevailing winds, which are so important, especially for a flying boat. The approach affords a very clear line of sight for takeoffs and landings. The air density of the area was excellent, near perfect. With a cool line of air surrounded by water, there were light, steady breezes. Fog was not a great problem in the Treasure Island area.

Three permanent buildings were built for Pan American Airways. The main building served as the Administration Building during the Exposition. Once the Exposition was over, it became a main terminal air-entrance building with a control tower on the roof. The Administration Building stands three stories high and 380 feet across.

The large building afforded room for the upper wings of the building to contain a weather station, public observation galleries, restaurants, offices, and even a dormitory. In the basement were the facilities for mail delivery, freight, and customer services. There were five ramps to load the flying boats.

Two large hangars, built of concrete and steel and over 300-feet long, were used for storage and maintenance of the Clippers. Clipper Cove allows a sheltered water area for the Clipper to take off and pull up to the floating dock. There was an area where the Clippers could be placed on a trolley and pulled onto the land for cleaning and maintenance. Flying boats require a vast amount of cleaning, since each aircraft operates in a salt water environment. Salt water can quickly cause corrosion on the airframe of the flying boat.

The International Golden Gate Exposition was a marketing tool for Pan American. Exhibits demonstrated the inner workings of the world's largest transoceanic airline company. The exhibit was seen by more than 2.5 million visitors.

One of the hangars, known as the Hall of Air Transportation, allowed visitors to observe work being done on the Clipper flying boats.

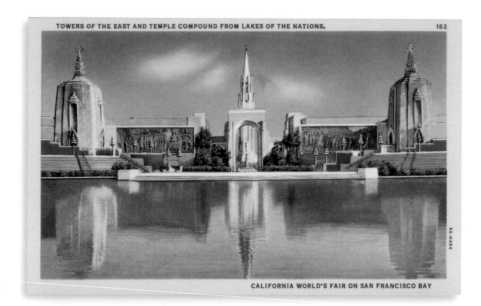

A series of postcards of the 1939/40 International Golden Gate Exposition. The Exposition opened on February 5, 1939. The 400-foot Tower of the Sun was the centerpiece along with the new Pan American Airways Terminal at Treasure Island. In addition the Exposition commemorated the new San Francisco - Oakland Bay Bridge and the Golden Gate Bridge. San Francisco had once again become the "Gateway to the Orient." Author's Collection

1939/40 Pan Am Clipper in the water in Clipper Cove, Treasure Island. PanAir tug boat in the picture. Fred Mayer

When Japan attacked the United States at Pearl Harbor, the U.S. Navy took control of Treasure Island. The Pan American Clippers remained but were taken into military service. On January 8, 1941, the day after Pearl Harbor, the first Clipper flight was underway to take various experts to the site of the destruction. The base continued to be a central part of the military structure throughout the war. To advertise the upcoming Golden Gate International Exposition, teams of young ladies were deployed in pirate costumes to attend local California events to raise public interest. One group visited Petaluma, a city just north of San Francisco, in their pirate outfits for the city's Egg Basket Days. Petaluma annually produced 45 million cartons of eggs.

(Below) 1939/40 Clipper in the water in front of the Golden Gate International Exposition grounds. The Treasure Island base would be taken over by the military during World War II and remain in their control until the early 1990s when the base became surplus. Fred Mayer

CLYDE SUNDERLAND

Clyde Sunderland (1900-1989) was a pioneer aerial photographer. Clyde took many of the fantastic photos of the Clippers over San Francisco, including shots before the Oakland Bay Bridge and Golden Gate Bridge were constructed. His photos were taken during the Golden Age of San Francisco and have been compared to Ansel Adams' nature photographs. The Golden Age of San Francisco included the construction of the Golden Gate Bridge, the Oakland Bay Bridge, the International Golden Gate Exposition, and the new ferry terminal. The other high-water mark was the arrival of the Clippers on Treasure Island.

Pan American Airways was successful in connecting Clipper Cove with the massive publicity campaign. Major companies, including Coca-Cola, were spending thousands of dollars to advertise their presence at the Exposition.

The large display model for the Exposition and its various buildings had Clipper Cove front and center: "Every once in a while, somewhere on earth there occurs an event so extraordinary that it enriches forever lives of all who witness it. San Francisco in 1939 promises just such as experience!"

Treasure Island was also referred to as Magic Island. It included 400 manmade acres, 4,000 trees, 70,000 scrubs, 700,000 plants, and a flying boat airport. When it opened on Saturday morning, February 18, 1939, the island was flooded with visitors: "A Pageant of the Pacific, on Treasure Island in the middle of the Bay of San Francisco! Avenue of the Seas, Court of the Hemisphere, Lake of All Nations, Port of the Trade Wind, Street of the World." A better advertising venue could have not been found for Pan American Airways.

China Clipper undergoing a full-scale maintenance checkup. Pan Am maintenance crew on the nose, wings, and fuselage of the aircraft. Side door hatch is fully open.

University of Miami, Richter Library, Pan Am Collection

During World War II, the United States Navy traded land for an airport in South San Francisco for the 400 acres of Treasure Island. Treasure Island became a United States Navy, Marines, and Coast Guard base. The land in South San Francisco would become Mills Field and eventually San Francisco International Airport, Gateway to the Far East.

Treasure Island was closed as a military base in 1991. The original Pan American Airways hangars are still in operation, used as movie studios and the storage facility for the city's antique fire engine collection. The first building one passes upon entering the island is Pan American's Administration Building. It sits as a reminder of the Golden Age of Flying Boats. Stepping inside is a trip back into those days of 1939, the original Art Deco paneling and hanging chandeliers still there.

Original Pan Am globe that was on Treasure Island in the Administration Building. Now on display at the San Francisco Air Museum located in San Francisco International Airport.
San Francisco Airport Museums

Some of the infrastructure from those famous days when Captain Edwin Musick and passengers boarded the *China Clipper* can still be found while around outside. The large metal hooks that held the Clippers to the docks are still cemented in the ground. The best view is to walk up the hill above the island, above Clipper Park, and look down on the island and let one's imagination travel back to those glory days of the late 1930s, when Clipper Cove was full of noise and the water filled with the famous Pan American Clippers, the hustle of planes arriving and leaving entirely on the water.

The famous world globe that occupied a prime spot in the office of Juan Trippe found a new home in the Clipper Hall. It was reported that Trippe would stand next to the globe, with pipe in mouth and a piece of string, connecting two points on the globe. This was part of the process of looking at the Pan American Airways network and planning for future expansion. The large motorized world globe that sat in the center of the Administration Building now sits in the front window of the San Francisco Airport Museum at San Francisco International Airport, restored and rotating as it did in 1939.

Since 1991, legal questions have kept the future of Treasure Island in doubt.

EVEN ON A ONE-WEEK VACATION YOU CAN
Enjoy a trip Beyond our Borders

When you go by Pan American you spend less time traveling...see more when you get there

5-DAY VACATION . . . BERMUDA

Just a hop and a skip by Clipper Ship! Only 5 hours after taking off from New York you're in Hamilton! You have four glorious days of golf, of bicycles built for two, of just plain lazin' in the sun. On longer holidays you can take a combined air-sea cruise—one way by Clipper, one way by steamer. Rates are pleasingly moderate.

21-DAY VACATION . . . PACIFIC

C'mon over! The water's fine, the Hula girls lovely at Waikiki! With Flying Clippers to whisk you on to the Philippines and Orient, you can enjoy a Hawaiian holiday—even including a sea trip from San Francisco—and still have time to spare. Beyond Honolulu you stop overnight at fascinating Midway, Wake and Guam Islands.

8-DAY VACATION . . . . MEXICO

Pick up and go! Whisk from the border to Mexico City in just a few hours—by Pan American! There's lots to do—from seeing bullfights to viewing landmarks of the old Spanish conquistadors and shopping in colorful native markets. There are also exciting all-expense air cruises which can, if desired, include nearby Guatemala and Yucatan.

AMERICA'S MERCHANT MARINE OF THE AIR

7-DAY VACATION . . . . ALASKA

All aboard for a new kind of gold rush! Within a few weeks Pan American opens its newest air route. You can "Oh" and "Ah" at mighty glaciers, fly from Seattle to Juneau in an unbelievable 7 hours, go on to Fairbanks and beyond the Yukon if you wish. Gone the remote frontier once weeks away! Now, within the limits of an ordinary vacation is a new playground—vast, unspoiled, rich in hunting, fishing and scenery.

14 DAYS . . . . . RIO DE JANEIRO

Leave a note for the milkman and you're off! Then, four days out of Miami, say hello to Sugar Loaf overlooking beautiful Guanabara Bay! Here's Clippering at its best. You fly in daytime only, miss none of the spectacular views, have almost a week in alluring Rio. You have, too, a choice of all-expense air cruises—three to eight weeks 'round South America, visiting a score of countries strung over 16,000 miles.

QUICK FACTS: *Pan American's air routes span 65,000 miles, linking 55 countries and colonies. Over them the Flying Clipper Ships have already sped 1,425,000 passengers 530,000,000 miles. There are many all-expense air tours, combination air-sea cruises, other attractive trips to choose from. For complete details consult your Travel Agent—or a Pan American office. If neither near you, write Pan American Airways, Chrysler Bldg., New York City.*

PAA
PAN AMERICAN
AIRWAYS SYSTEM

CHAPTER 10

OVERNIGHT TO HAWAII AND ONWARD TO WAKE ISLAND

THE PAN AMERICAN CLIPPER FLYING BOATS are only a memory, and with each passing day the surviving individuals who traveled on a Clipper become a smaller and smaller group. What was it like to be a passenger on a Clipper flight?

Imagine the scene in Clipper Cove on Treasure Island in San Francisco, the newly completed Oakland Bay Bridge off to one side, The Golden Gate International Exposition, "A Pageant of the Pacific," on the other. The large four-engine Clipper is sitting alongside the floating pier, making ready for departure. Uniformed staff are busy stowing large sacks of mail in the forward hold of the aircraft, many of the sacks newly arrived from other airports across the United States, almost every state in the Union. Soon the letters will be airborne, making the journey to Hawaii, Midway Island, Wake Island, Guam, the Philippines, and China.

The first-class passengers (the only class on the Pan American Clippers) have arrived by limousine, their luggage carried by stewards into the Administration Building. Every female passenger has been informed about weight limits and even provided with a list of the types of clothing that should be packed for the trip.

Pan American personnel are the best trained of any airline. Years of training, thousands of hours of flying are behind your Clipper pilot; he is an expert on engines, radio, meteorology, languages, and international law.

Personnel are attentive to your every comfort. Stewards are specially qualified. They are alert and cheerful, eager to answer questions, arrange your pillow, supply reading and writing material, or serve your first-class meals. They do not accept tips.

The Pan American Clippers are the latest, most modern aircraft. All equipment is constantly inspected and frequently overhauled, another reason why Pan American operates 98.63 percent on schedule.

Each mile of your flight is safeguarded by Pan American's worldwide meteorological system. Continuous radio contact provides flight crews with the latest weather bulletins. Nearly a thousand people man Pan American's 200 radio and weather stations.

One bell rings out. The Captain and the five Officers walk up the gangway and into their positions on the Clipper. One by one, each engine is started and checked to ensure

Pan Am luggage sticker indicating Pacific Service. As air service increased, luggage stickers became a big source of collecting. Also travelers loved to leave them on the suitcase to display their destinations. A status symbol.
Author's Collection

(Left) Late 1930s ad for Pan Am announcing how much travel can be accomplished even with only one week's vacation. When you travel Pan Am, less time is spent in traveling, which means more time for fun in the sun.
Author's Collection

that each is in proper working order. Part of the preparation has been to clean and polish each propeller prior to the starting. Two bells. "All passengers aboard!" shouts the steward.

The two stewards greet each passenger as they board the Clipper, indicate where they are to sit during takeoff so that the Clipper's load will be properly distributed during this maneuver, take hats and overcoats and put them away, check safety belts and help first-time fliers to fasten them, then sit down and fasten their own belts for the takeoff.

Passengers boarding the Clipper at Treasure Island, San Francisco. Aircraft stewards assist with carrying luggage and packages onto the aircraft. Large crowd lining the observation decks to watch the aircraft boarding. In good military fashion the crew marched onto the aircraft as if in a parade.

Dockside, a wall of handkerchiefs appear to wave the Clipper and passengers on their way. The Clipper moves slowly into the bay — a turn into the wind — the engines begin to roar as the throttle and power controls are pushed forward. Within a short time, the majestic Clipper lifts from the bay and is airborne and on its way to Hawaii, 2,500 miles away. The Clipper will arrive just in time for breakfast.

Part of the mystique of the journey is looking out the aircraft window and observing the sites of San Francisco disappearing into the bright orange glow of the setting sun. The journey to the Orient has begun.

Once airborne, the passengers begin to move about the cabin and observe the crew at work. The steward announces tea time. Looking out the window a mile above the Pacific Ocean, one can observe a ship below with lights ablaze. The ship turns on its searchlight and flashes a greeting in blue and white light.

As soon as the Clipper reaches flying altitude, the stewards really go into action. It is lunch time and there are 20 to 30 passengers to be served. The luncheon buffet has been prepared in advance of departure, and it takes only a few moments to add the last touches and invite the passengers to help themselves to cold meats, salads, relishes, bread and butter or rolls, jam preserves, and other items. Later, the stewards serve beverages and dessert.

This is the first test for the stewards: They must make certain that all passengers are served what they desire and as much as they want and at the same time keep the meal progressing on schedule, without giving the appearance of haste, so that the tables can be cleared and the galley made ship-shape.

Later, cocktail hour is at hand, the traditional ceremony on the Honolulu-bound Clippers. On the flights from Treasure Island to New Zealand, the South Seas Cocktail is the feature of the before-dinner hour: Two-fifths gin, two-fifths orange juice, one-fifth Curacao. Cracked ice. Shake vigorously and strain into cocktail glasses. On the North

Pacific run, it is the Clipper Cocktail: One pony White-Label Puerto Rican rum, one pony dry Vermouth, one half-teaspoon Grenadine. Pour over ice in mixing glass and stir. Serve with a cherry in a Clipper Cocktail glass, the rim of which has been well moistened with lemon rind.

For the passengers who do not want to experiment with unfamiliar drinks, the popular standard cocktails and highballs are available, and for those who prefer beverages of less potency, the stewards are glad to serve beer or soft drinks. Standard prices are charged. Later, passengers are seated in the lounge, transformed into a dining room by the Clipper dinner service. Every aid to gracious dining is included, the only difference being that flatware and china are somewhat lighter than those used by hotels and restaurants aground as no unnecessary weight is permitted. At midnight, a supper of sandwiches, cold cuts, and salads, with milk or hot chocolate, is served to those who are still awake.

Thereafter, the stewards have no other duties than to work on their reports and serve coffee and light lunches to the crew members who come down from the bridge when they are off watch. They usually have time to catch forty winks apiece, in relays, before it is time to awaken passengers and prepare breakfast, which again is a hearty meal, with fruit juice, cereal, eggs, toast, pastries, marmalade, jelly, and coffee or other beverages.

Upon awakening, there is time to dress, have a cup of coffee, and then look out the window to the beautiful Hawaiian Islands below. Maui is the first to arise from the sea, then the mountains of Molokai, and finally, in the distance, the big island of Hawaii. Oahu with its bright green mountains is the next site, and its clean, white beaches.

The Clipper has been tracked and guided by the direction-finding station on Makapu. Now off to one side of the aircraft is Diamond Head, Waikiki Beach, and the rolling surf. Upon arrival, one is greeted with the traditional leis and soft music and, of course, the famous Hula-dancing girls. Hawaii, just one stop on the "Sky-road to the Orient!"

The stewards have to check in with the port steward on supplies for the next day's departure; they are otherwise free to relax and catch up on their sleep until early the following morning, when they, along with other crew members and passengers, are called at their hotels to prepare for departure on the next leg of the journey.

Passengers have been known to observe that there is always food being served aboard the Clippers and to add that they are very glad

Pan Am advertisement with map showing the new service across the vast Pacific Ocean.
Author's Collection

HERE TODAY . . . HAWAII TOMORROW
[this advertisement may go down in history]

The "China Clipper" leaving San Francisco for Hawaii and the Orient

SOME DAY this page may be valuable. There is nothing unusual about its wording or appearance, but— it is the first advertisement ever published about transpacific air service!

On Wednesday, Oct. 7, 1936, at 3 P.M., the "China Clipper" left San Francisco for Manila on its first regular flight, carrying passengers as well as mail and express. You might say this flight really began nine years ago. For since the first Pan American plane flew from Florida to Cuba in 1927, we have had the experience of over a score of million miles of ocean flying over the Caribbean Sea and South Atlantic on our Latin-American air routes. And for a year and a half before any passengers were carried across the Pacific we had

flown that route with mail and express. To establish our 40,000 miles of foreign air routes we had to develop airliners greater than any in commercial service anywhere else in the world—the giant Flying Clipper Ships. We had to develop a new kind of radio direction-finder, organize our own weather bureau and network of radio stations, and build air bases in the jungle and upon hitherto uninhabited islands.

But what you, as a traveler, are interested in is that now you can make a trip to the Far East in slightly more time than it takes to cross the continent on the fastest train . . . or, if you are an exporter or importer, that trading with China is now almost as easy as trading with Canada. The "China Clipper" or

one of her giant sister ships leaves San Francisco for Far Eastern points every Wednesday at 3 P.M. You can almost set your watch by their departure.

Transpacific route of the Flying Clipper Ships—taking passengers, mail and express from Alameda (San Francisco) to Honolulu, Midway Island, Wake Island, Guam, and Manila—8,000 miles, in 5 days—all daylight flying except the overnight voyage to Hawaii.

See our nearest office for the answers to any questions you have about this service. Or ask any travel agent, air or rail ticket office about your travel plans. Information about shipments as near as your telephone. Call any office of Railway Express Agency-Air Express Division.

ROUTES OF THE FLYING CLIPPER SHIPS

PAN AMERICAN AIRWAYS SYSTEM
PASSENGERS—MAIL—EXPRESS
Passenger Reservation and Information Offices
LOS ANGELES · MIAMI · NEW YORK · BOSTON · BROWNSVILLE · CHICAGO · SAN FRANCISCO · SEATTLE · WASHINGTON

Steward serving guest dinner on the Clipper. Drinks were taken in the lounge, and dinner was served in the dining room.
University of Miami, Richter Library, Pan Am Collection

of it, because they are always hungry. They wonder, though, how they do it. The galley is no larger than the kitchenette of a one-room apartment, but it is carefully planned so that the available space will accommodate a steam table, coffee maker, sink, and shelves adequate for the job. It is supplemented by a commodious kitchen cabinet in the crew's forward compartment.

The grilled filet mignon served to Clipper passengers between San Francisco and Honolulu is delivered already 90 percent cooked and frozen as solid as a block of ice. It is removed from a freezing cold refrigerator just before being loaded on the Clipper and allowed to thaw slowly, so that it is just ready to go into the steak rack in the steam table when the stewards start preparing dinner. While they are serving appetizers, soup and salad, the steak is absorbing heat and getting the last ten percent of cooking it needs. When the plates from preliminary courses are removed, the steak is ready to be served, piping hot, along with buttered green peas and roasted new potatoes, also from the steam table. More perishable vegetables are pre-cooked and frozen like the meats. Some others may be simply pre-cooked and heated before serving.

Do Clipper Passengers Get Hungry?

Yes, according to the Commissary Department of Pan American Airways Pacific Division, but they are not permitted to stay hungry. Last year, on Clippers over the Pacific en route to Hong Kong or New Zealand, Pan American stewards served 32,760 meals to passengers and flight crew members.

At four of the intermediate stops in 1940 — Midway Island, Wake Island, Guam, and Canton — China, 231,038 meals were served in the hotels operated by Pan American Airways. The figure includes the meals provided to the ground crews.

In 1940, the Commissary Department had to supply 80 tons of meat, 20 tons of game and poultry, nine tons of pork produce (ham, bacon, lunchmeat), two tons of hors d'oeuvres, ten tons of potatoes, and 135 crates of fresh vegetables, each crate weighing 100 pounds. The hotels at Midway Island, Wake Island, and Canton received 24,530 tins of cigarettes, each tin containing 50 cigarettes.

Another question asked: Why does Pan American have stewards and not stewardesses? The answer, of course, is that the Clippers make long flights over great distances through isolated territory, and the job has always been considered a little too strenuous for a young woman.

Of the 16 stewards in the Pacific Division, the youngest is 21 and the oldest is 35. Most are younger than 30. Newly hired stewards train for six months at the Pan American School at Treasure Island, where they are taught cooking, serving, and how to survive on an island in case of an emergency. Stewards also wash floors, the plates from the galleys of returned Clippers, and unload the aircraft and bring all the equipment to the galley.

While training, they usually work 60 to 70 hours a month. The practical experience comes in working in the executive dining room. The stewards in training have to spend many months serving the executives of the company. That is the way that they learn to set a first-class table and follow proper procedures.

Before the 16 to18-hour flight to Hawaii, the steward is responsible for buying all the ingredients for the meals to be served on the Treasure Island to Honolulu trip, including beef stew, chicken a la king, fresh meat, carrots, potatoes, and eggs to fix mayonnaise and make potato salad fresh aboard the Clipper.

Since Pan American Airways operates as an ocean liner, the steward is responsible for picking the most interesting guests and having them sit at the Captain's table. This is one of the many naval traditions that operates on Pan American.

On flights on which W. A. Winston of Wendall, North Carolina, was the Captain, passengers would be entertained with card tricks. Captain Winston would perform the tricks and demonstrate how he could deal himself four aces. On other breaks when he visited the passenger compartments, he would discuss his other interest: amateur photography. He was an expert in cameras, lens, filters, and other photography paraphernalia. Captain Winston would explain to interested passengers where the best vantage points for taking photos at certain stopovers could be found.

On other Clipper flights, pilots, when not on flight deck, would visit with the passengers and answer questions about the aircraft or provide information on their own special interests that might be of value to the passengers.

When the aircraft arrived in Honolulu, the big garbage sacks were put through an agricultural inspection. No germs or bugs were allowed in the bags, so the officials used big sticks to go through it to see if it could be approved. If it passed inspection, the garbage was burned. Garbage was not allowed to be brought in to San Francisco, so about an hour before landing, in the vicinity of around 2,000 to 3,000 feet above the Farallon Islands, a window was opened in the "Honeymoon Suite" and the giant "turkey bags" were heaved out. Usually the Farallon Islands were covered with fog, so it was unknown where the bags actually landed.

Passengers enjoying a relaxing coffee and dessert on the Clipper. Everyone dressed nicely. Days when passengers dressed up to fly. University of Miami, Richter Library, Pan Am Collection

At every stopover, Pan American Airways has constructed a luxury hotel to match the luxury of the Clipper flying boat. The next destination westward after Honolulu is Midway Island. Before the Clippers, only about a hundred men had visited Midway Island. Not long after lunch, into view comes a circle of white with two dark spots within the ring: the Midway Islands. The Clipper is soon circling over a tiny atoll, a circular lake 18 miles in circumference. White coral sand and green magnolia trees come into view, followed by the buildings of Pan American Airways. Why, there is even a golf course and a dozen other buildings, staff housing, a power station, refrigeration plant, warehouse, cable relay station, windmills, and a V-shaped five-star hotel and a long pier. Due to the geography of the island, the Clipper approaches a floating dock and launches to take the passengers ashore. Automobiles wait at the end of the pier to take the passengers to the Pan American Airways Hotel.

(Top) Man on Midway Island taking a photograph of the island's famous Gooney Birds. A Gooney Bird was even on the sign that greeted passengers when they disembarked for their stopover. Pan Am had built a hotel for passengers to relax at while the aircraft was readied for the next day's flight to Wake Island.
University of Miami, Richter Library, Pan Am Collection

(Below) Two golfers in swim suits playing nine holes while the Gooney Birds watch. There were many activities on all the island stopovers.
University of Miami, Richter Library, Pan Am Collection

The flight from Honolulu to Midway Island is a short nine hours. With the change in time, passengers arrive at Midway Island at 2 p.m. While your luggage is carried to your private room by staff, there is time to see what is available. Lunch is being served, some guests are swimming in the sheltered cove's crystal-clear water. Or one can search for souvenirs from one of the ancient shipwrecks on the island, fish on the beach or from a boat, or visit with the famous Gooney Birds of the island. The Gooney Birds are there to greet guests at the Pan American Hotel or on other parts of the island. Take a picture as a souvenir. There is a sand golf course to play on, accompanied by a Gooney or two.

The Clipper departs from Midway Island in the early morning and turns westward to Wake Island. Two days out from San Francisco and the Clipper will be crossing the "International Date Line," where the passengers cross from one day to the next. Finally, 5,000 miles from the mainland of the United States and only eight hours from Midway Island, appear Wake Island, Wilkes Island, and Peale Island. The three islands resemble a horseshoe with brilliant white sand and turquoise water. Wake Island was unheard of until Pan American Airways made it one of the legs in its island-hopping system developed for the Clipper flying boats.

Approximately a mile long and less than half a mile wide, Peale Island is where the Pan American Airways Hotel and operations are located. From the veranda of the hotel, one can look out at the beautiful lagoon to marvel at the crest of the surf beating on the coral reefs. Magnolia trees line the walking paths to the living quarters of the Pan American staff. Further along is the power plant, refrigeration building, hospital, and a pergola containing a beautiful collection of the atoll's lore: bits and pieces of wrecked sailing ships, seashells, coral, and other items native to the area. The Clipper flying boat bobs in the crystal-clear, sheltered water of the lagoon.

Passengers could view the exotic tropical fish in the water or try their skills at bow-and-arrow fishing or attempting to spear a fish for dinner. Launches were available to take passengers out for deep sea fishing if so desired. Situated across the lagoon was the famous "Wilkes Island Railroad," which ran for an entire two city blocks. The railroad was built to haul all the building materials and supplies required on the island.

Wake Island was an unspoiled land until it became a tourist destination due to the arrival of the Clippers. Situated at 19 degrees 15 North and 166 degrees 31 East, Wilkes, Peale and Wake Islands are coral atolls surrounding a shallow lagoon. Their total area contains 2,600 acres, with the highest point of elevation 21 feet. The atoll is entirely surrounded by a reef, and the only small boat entrance is a short distance southwest of the channel, between Wilkes and Wake Islands. The group of atolls was discovered by Prince William Henry in 1796 and was visited and charted by United States expeditions under the leadership of Captain Wilkes in 1841. Eventually, the atolls were claimed for the United States by Commander Taussig in January 1900. The area was not visited again until the surveyor Tanager visited in July and August of 1923. In 1927, a second American expedition aboard the USS *Beaver* did a second survey. A third survey by crew members from the USS *Nitro* was undertaken in 1935. In early spring 1935, the first Pan American Airways construction workers landed on Wilkes Island, which would become home to the Pan American Hotel and Administration Building and other facilities. Materials were unloaded and the actual construction work began in early April 1935. The first Pan American flying boat arrived from Midway Island on August 17, 1935, at 12:29 p.m. local time.

Away from the hustle of the modern world, the Pan American traveler reaches the land that is reserved for those who fly. Comfort and convenience are as much a part of your stay as the breath-taking sunsets, the soft thundering of the sea and its magnificent 30-foot surf. Not soon can one forget these rainbow waters, soft deep sands, the friendly sun, and the cool, sweet trade winds blown from across the broadest sea.

On the stopover at Wake Island, passengers were greeted and given information about the wonderful, fantastic entertainment opportunities that awaited them on their brief stay. Hunting was available. Amusement could be found in the famous Wake Island expedition that hunted down the atoll's famous rats. Only the most intrepid were recommended to take part in the sport. Air rifles and ammunition were available at the Pan American Airport Office.

For those not interested in hunting, attractive shells or pieces of coral could be found on the sandy beaches. Multicolored glass balls of different sizes from the nets of Japanese fishing boats could be found on the beach. Some Japanese fishing boats were

Passenger on the beach collecting Japanese fishing net balls. One major item that washed up on the shores of Midway Island were glass balls of various sizes and colors that had separated from Japanese fishing nets. Of course some of the fishing was accomplished to spy on the military defenses that were being constructed.

University of Miami, Richter Library, Pan Am Collection

Part of a large article on the various legs of the Clippers' travels across the Pacific. The starting point was Treasure Island, the end Canton, China. This section focuses on the flight to Guam. Author's Collection

probably on spying missions, as on the other side of the atoll, the United States Marines, Navy, and civilian contractors were busy constructing a military airfield and fortifying the atoll.

Lucky explorers might find a piece of metal from the old barque *Libelle*, which met its fate off Wake Island. Passengers didn't even have to pack any souvenir items, as the objects only had to be left at the Airport Office and the Pan American Airways staff would ensure that the objects were packed correctly and taken with you on the next leg of your journey. On the back page of the small guidebook provided each passenger was the often-used section for autographs.

For the passengers who just wanted to relax or sightsee, a small points-of-interest handout was provided. The ruins of the old Japanese settlement, which was abandoned in 1908, was only a 15-minute walk from the end of the dock. There was a colony of Sooty Tern with their young on the most easterly point of Peale Island. The natural rock seawall, protecting the island from the northeast, was a five-minute walk along the trail from the point of the direction-finding station.

If one wanted a nice, warm swim, water goggles could be provided at the Airport Office. Field glasses could also be borrowed and taken to the Observation Tower. Trips on the lagoon and to Wake and Wilkes Islands could be arranged. Be at the Airport Office at 5 p.m. and watch the flightless Laysan Duck being fed.

Many fish were to be found in the lagoon and on the outer coral reefs. Large Rock Cod could be found by turning over many of the rocks in well-shaded locations, while Ulua would rise to the surface. A large green fish, variety unknown, could be found in the reefs. Sharks were plentiful and would afford much thrill for a short struggle. Large morays could be encountered, but it was recommended to cut them loose, "as they will be most troublesome if brought ashore." It was stressed that the smaller, White Eel should be avoided as they would attack an individual if cornered and could do great damage. Fishing tackle, bait, and helpful tips could be found at the Airport Office. A stay could be as busy or relaxed as each passenger desired.

In a very brief time, the picture-postcard descriptions of the islands in the Pan American Airways Clipper island chain would become home to some of the fiercest fighting in the Pacific theater. The Battle for Midway Island, which commenced on June 4, 1942, would be the high-water mark for the Japanese Empire. With its defeat and the destruction of the large aircraft-carrier force that had hoped to invade and secure Midway Island, the tide in the Pacific had turned. Pan American Airways island bases had played a major role.

ALASKA CLIPPER

For a very brief period, a Pan American Airways S-42 known as the *Alaska Clipper* operated on a route from Seattle, Washington, to Juneau, Alaska. The inaugural flight was on June 20, 1940. This first flight was for dignitaries and the press corps. The first scheduled passenger service commenced on June 24, 1940. The service was short-lived, due to the lack of passengers and the cost of operating the aircraft in a colder climate. The *Alaskan Clipper* was transferred and its name changed to the *Hong Kong Clipper*. The *Hong Kong Clipper* was sitting on the water on December 8, 1941, in Hong Kong and became the first civilian aircraft destroyed in the Japanese attack. A bomb hit the aircraft and destroyed it.

Alaska Clipper on the water in Alaska. Off in the distance are snow-covered mountains, a large difference from the lush, green vegetation of its Pacific destinations.

University of Miami, Richter Library, Pan Am Collection

SIKORSKY S-40 FLIGHT TEST RESULTS

INTER-OFFICE CORRESPONDENCE
SIKORSKY AVIATION CORPORATION

To: Mr. I. I. Sikorsky
cc: Mr. Neilson
    Capt. Sergievsky
    Mr. S. Gluhareff
    Mr. N. Sinitzin
    Files (2)
Date: August 31, 1931
From: M. Gluhareff
Subject: Flight report on S-40 amphibian — gross weight 32,000 pounds
Weather: Clear, approximately 12 wind (NW)
Temperature: 75
Barometer Pressure: 30.04
Time: Start 2:15 p.m., Finish 4:13 p.m.
Takeoff time on the water — 30 seconds
Cruising on 1650 RPM all engines — average speed 100.5 MPH
Cruising on 1750 RPM all engines — average speed 107.75 MPH
High speed, full throttle, 2010 RPM all engines — average speed 130.25 MPH
Crosswind interfered with the speed test flight; it was exactly 90 degrees to the C.
The fairing on the landing gear axles came off, building a screen about 12 square feet flat plate area on each side.

Charles Lindbergh and Igor
Sikorsky discussing aviation
while in flight.

Igor Sikorsky Historical Archives

Landing at New Haven Harbor about 3:20 PM the fairings from the axles were removed.

Climb to Altitude	Time	Speed Ind.	RPM
500	30 sec.	90	1850
1000	1 min. 17 sec.	95	1800
2000	3 min. 7 sec.	95	1820
3000	4 min. 40 sec.	96	1820
4000	6 min. 25 sec.	95	1800
5000	8 min. 10 sec.	97	1800
5800 - 6000	10 min.	B	——

At 6000 feet altitude — three engines — flight was tested — rate of climb approximate 200 feet per min. (RPM 1830)

At 2000 feet altitude — two engines — flight was tested — during five (5) minutes 600 feet were lost (RPM 1820)

At 2000 feet altitude — three engines — flight was repeated — during one minute exactly the ship gained 200 feet, from 2100 to 2300 feet (RPM 1820)

Pilot: Captain Sergievsky

Observers: S. Gluhareff, M. Gluhareff

Signed

M. Ghuhareff

THE SIKORSKY S-42: THE DEVELOPMENT AND CHARACTERISTICS OF A LONG-RANGE FLYING BOAT

SPEECH GIVEN TO THE ROYAL AERONAUTICAL SOCIETY, LONDON, ENGLAND, ON NOVEMBER 15, 1934, BY IGOR I. SIKORSKY

ALMOST A DECADE AGO, with the rapid world-wide development of air transportation, came the demand for new types of aircraft. It became evident that a plane capable of operating from land or water was the logical step needed to open up larger areas for air transportation. The proximity of water compared with the remoteness of available landing fields to the centers of population was the deciding factor in amphibian development.

While the advantages of the amphibian are obvious, the limitations and difficulties of creating an efficient plane of this type are evident. Compared to the seaplane or land plane, the amphibian must take care of the extra weight and parasitic resistance, as well as solve various other problems connected with combining the characteristics of the land and seaplane in one aeroplane.

In order to overcome these difficulties and produce an amphibian that would compare favorably in performance with the best land or seaplane, it was necessary to make the utmost effort to refine all basic elements. In other words, it was necessary to create highly efficient power plant, wing, and control surface units so that a wide margin of increased performance would be obtained that would compensate for extra weight and resistance of the amphibian.

Evolved from painstaking study and research came the S-38. Its history is the conception of Pan American Airways, the air yacht of the private owner, and the pioneering aircraft of exploration into hitherto inaccessible regions of Central and South America and Africa.

Over a five-year period more than 100 of these aircraft were delivered, and the majority of them are still in service. As the characteristics of this aircraft became more and more evident, the hazy dream of large aeroplanes materialized into a definite plan. With the increasing business of Pan American Airways, their fleet of S-38s became inadequate. Upon their request, the big flying boat idea became a reality.

The three Clipper flying boats that now fly over the South Americas are the results. In our minds, at the time of designing, was a flying boat diverting in outline from the usual Sikorsky outrigger design, but it was felt that radical changes were not advisable, particularly because the large plane was to be an amphibian. Knowing what the S-38 could do, it was felt that a large-size edition of this type would be the logical jump from an eight to a 40-passenger ship.

A considerable amount of work, research study, and experimentation was spent in the development of the S-40. The theoretical work, design, stress analysis, and research required the full time of the Sikorsky Organization for more than two years. The Sikorsky Company realized that upon the experience that this model would give, an even more efficient amphibian would be based.

Even then this new amphibian was gathering shape in the minds of Sikorsky designers.

From its first flight, the S-40 was a success. Capable of carrying 40 passengers over a considerable range, the S-40s dovetailed with the need of larger equipment to meet an ever-increasing passenger list. The engineers who built the S-40 watched the performance very closely.

In November 1931, when the first "Flying Clipper" made its cruise from Miami to Colombia and the Panama Canal Zone and return, the designer was on board and had several conferences with Colonel Charles A. Lindbergh, technical adviser to Pan American Airways and Chief Pilot in charge of this flight, wherein the basic ideas and main requirements for a new type large flying boat were set down.

Immediately afterwards the engineers of the Sikorsky Company started actual research and development of a seaplane along these lines. The endeavor was to obtain a much higher all-round efficiency that would permit a much greater flying range and higher cruising speed, as well as to introduce various other improvements and refinements. In the meantime, Pan American Airways had placed in extensive service the second and third Clipper aircraft. The experience obtained from millions of miles of commercial flying gave Pan American Airways excellent data for the development of a very complete set of detailed specifications for a plane that would cover the needs of further expansion and the possibilities of a commercial line across the Atlantic. Written into the specifications were requirements that were seemingly far in advance of the progress of aviation.

Gathering impetus from the reality of the S-42, power plant development advanced with great rapidity, so that when the question of engines and propellers became imminent, the Pratt and Whitney Aircraft Corporation was ready with its greatly improved Hornet model, and Hamilton Standard Propeller Company had to offer what was considered by the Collier Trophy Committee an outstanding advance in the aviation world, a practical controllable-pitch propeller.

Knowing the difficulties that are encountered in the endeavor to coincide the desired with the practical, close cooperation between Pan American Airways and the Sikorsky Company was necessary. Every detail from design to final fabrication was an approval based on careful criticism and study; every phase that forms a part of the commercial airline was considered, including cost of operation, maintenance, durability, and passenger comfort. Design work again required over two years. Reports, records, and tests, in seemingly endless procession, were culled of their best ideas, and these were incorporated as far as was practical.

Stress men spent tireless hours figuring structural strength that would meet high self-imposed safety factors and still allow for simplified construction and low weight. Their complete analysis covers almost a thousand pages of closed-type matter with no consideration to the countless pages that contributed to the final figures.

Because of the stringent requirements of the contract calling for a useful load-to-gross-weight ratio of 47:53, a rigid weight control was set up. A threefold system was employed — one, an estimation from the design figures allocating to each unit a certain

Pan American constructed hotels at its island stopovers. In 1936 hotels that had been prefabricated in the United States were placed on Midway and Wake Islands. Each hotel contained 45 rooms, hot and cold running water, showers, lounges, and dining rooms to make the short stopover as comfortable as possible for the first-class passengers.

University of Miami, Richter Library, Pan Am Collection

share of weight; another calling for calculations from the finished drawings and a comparison with the estimate; and the third, a program of actual weighting of parts. The value of this triple control is shown in the 48:52 ratio obtained.

No drawing was approved until is passed through the manufacturing department for a check against complicated design that would involve expensive fabrication or that would require undue maintenance when put into operation.

THE S-42

In its very outline, the S-42 represents simplicity. Diverting sharply from the past Sikorsky designs, external bracings have been reduced to a minimum. The tail, instead of being supported by outriggers, is attached directly to the hull.

The one-piece wing with tapering tips is attached to the hull by means of a superstructure. The necessary, large external struts brace from the hull to the outer portion of the wing. These struts are the largest streamlined duralumin sections ever extruded. With a span of 114 feet, 2 inches, the wing has an area of 1,330 square feet. Spars and compression members of modified Warren Truss design are constructed of extruded duralumin shapes. Stressed metal skin covers the major portion of the wing surface. Flush-type rivets are used throughout the external surface.

S-42 resting on calm water while several maintenance workers make repairs.
Igor Sikorsky Historical Archives

Extending along the full straight portion of the rear spar is the hydraulically controlled flap. The flap is me chanically operated by means of a substantial hydraulic piston. The piston is actuated by an electrical pump that is controlled from the pilot's compartment. For emergency use, a manually operated pump is provided. The angular position of the flap can be altered in accordance with the altitude of flight, thus changing the performance of the whole wing. Ailerons of conventional design, tampering in conformity with the wing plan, are hinged to the rear spar outboard of the flaps. The power plant units, consisting of four Pratt & Whitney 700-horsepower geared Hornet engines, together with the necessary accessories, are attached to the front spar by means of welded-steel tubular nacelles. Completing these units are the three-bladed variable-pitch propellers, the largest of this type ever produced by the Hamilton Standard Propeller Company.

The full anti-drag rings and nacelle cowls merge into the wing at the front spar. Recessed into the leading edge are powerful landing lights. The lenses of these lights follow the curvature and form part of the leading edge. Eight sections of the leading edge, one on either side of each engine, fold down and form engine-servicing platforms. Along the interior of the leading edge run the control cables, electrical conduits, and other control and fuel units. All installations are made suitable for easy inspection and maintenance. Cradled between the spars and compression members are eight elliptical fuel tanks of a total capacity of 1,240 gallons and four similar-shaped oil tanks of 74-gallon capacity. Holding these in place are metal straps, which are covered with thick padding to ensure vibration insulation.

Removable panels above the fuel and oil tanks and on the entire center of the lower surface afford access for inspection and servicing. The refueling system in the center portion of the wing is an interesting time-saving device. A single intake pipe directs fuel under pressure to any one or all tanks by means of a series of control valves. Equal in importance with the wing are the parts that make up the body group. The two-step, long stern-type hull measures 67 feet, 8 inches from bow to stern. Deep keel, transverse frames which are widely spaced in order to facilitate maintenance, and heavy stringers form the hull skeleton. Keel and frames are of plate, girder type. Duralumin shapes and sheeting are used throughout.

The skin covering has the appearance of a smooth, unbroken surface. This has been obtained by the use of a filler in the skin seams and in the impressions of the slightly dented flush-type rivets. Nine watertight doors separate the various compartments. Marine equipment is located in the bow compartment. This compartment has been designed especially large to afford easy handling of a convenient anchor winch and to facilitate rapid mooring operations.

The pilot's compartment following averages eight feet wide and seven feet from bulk-head to bulkhead. An aisle 20 inches wide separates the pilot and copilot seats. These seats are extra roomy and are adjustable. They are designed to supply the maximum of comfort for long flights. Both pilots have an unobstructed view of the complete flight instrument board. Special requirements as to making all instruments and parts readily removable for checking and servicing have been rigidly adhered to.

To the rear of the pilot's seat is located the flight mechanic's quarters. From his position, the mechanic can readily attend to all the details under his control. Grouped on a separate panel directly in front of the mechanic's seat are all the instruments pertaining to power plant operation. Opposite the mechanic's quarters and in an uncrowded space is the radio receiving and sending station.

Surface controls are of the dual type, featuring ease of operation. Controls are hooked up to the automatic pilot unit located beneath the floor. Dials and instruments for setting and regulating the automatic pilot are on the center of the flight instrument board within easy reach of either pilot.

Engine control units are centered overhead, comfortably reached by either pilot and the mechanic. It affords either unit control for all engines or selective control for each engine. Next to this unit are the engine fire extinguisher controls. A twist of a dial directs extinguishing gas to one or all engines.

Reached from the outside by a hatch large enough to accommodate large packages and permitting for passenger exit, located between the pilot's compartment and passenger cabins, is the front baggage compartment. The allowable baggage space is 157 cubic feet. Here are also stored two life rafts and various tools. A strongbox for valuables is located under the floor.

At the main passenger stairway in the rear are located additional baggage compartments with a total capacity of 95 cubic feet. Large packages find ready access through the main passenger entrance that measures 25 inches by 72 inches. Between the front and rear baggage compartments are located the passenger cabins and the lavatories. The four passenger cabins, measuring 76 inches by 110 inches each, seat eight passengers. More than sufficient space is allowed for wide aisles and comfortable legroom. The distance from the floor to ceiling is well over six feet.

Tubular racks suspended from the bulkheads support the seats. This construction eliminates chair legs, thus permitting an unobstructed space beneath each seat for luggage. Seats are adjustable to meet individual comfort. High headrests afford complete relaxation.

Accessories, including carpets, removable tables, magazine racks, and curtains, harmonize with the decorative scheme.

Sound and vibration have been the subjects of careful study. Thick pads of sound-proofing material fill in the space behind the walls and ceiling. Because of their vibration, springs have been replaced in cushions by a special material that is proving more service-able and comfortable. Windows are held in place by a clincher-type rubber ring, without the need of fasteners that would cause shattering. In any passenger cabin, conversation may be carried on in a normal tone.

S-42 coming straight at the viewer. In the background the Dinner Key Terminal and the hangars of the airport.

University of Miami, Richter Library, Pan Am Collection

237

UNITED STATES
BAHAMAS
WEST INDIES   MEXICO
CENTRAL AMERICA
SOUTH AMERICA
ALASKA
HAWAII   PHILIPPINES
CHINA
NEW ZEALAND
BERMUDA NEWFOUNDLAND CANADA
EIRE   PORTUGAL   AZORES
FRANCE   ENGLAND

Travel PAN AMERICAN AIRWAYS *System*
THE LINE OF THE FLYING CLIPPER SHIPS

Front part of the folder that contained passenger tickets. 1940/41 version of the folder includes Portugal and France as destination spots.

Author's Collection

A concealed ventilating system supplies upwards of 30 cubic feet of air per passenger per minute. Auxiliary to this is an efficient exhaust system. Installation fittings on walls, ceiling, floors, and seats are such that an entire passenger cabin can be stripped to its bare structure within 40 to 50 minutes and reinstalled in a similar period.

Each cabin is equipped with safety belts, and life belts are distributed throughout the boat; in convenient locations are fire and emergency equipment. The two life rafts in the front baggage compartment and the two located rearward of the main stairway are suitable for carrying a full-capacity crew and passenger list.

The superstructure, already mentioned, also serves as a passageway for items of control that pass from hull to wing. Entrance is afforded to this structure from the inside of the cabin as well as from the outside. The internal space of this structure is such as to allow a man to work with comfort.

Every external part of the hull may be reached by a center-ridge walkway that extends from bow to stern. This walkway, together with the wingways and the engine platforms, makes it possible to conduct almost any inspection or servicing operation without the need of outside scaffolding. The economic feature of this is obvious.

Pontoons, hinged from the wing on two streamline struts and braced by cross wires, follow similar construction design as the hull. Easy handling from sea to land, or vice versa, is offered by the beaching gear. This is a three-part unit consisting of two twin wheels on strut carriages that attach to special fittings on the front of the hull and a single tail wheel that fits into a socket at the stern of the hull. All carriages may be turned on their axes so that motion is possible in any direction. Seven to ten minutes is required to attach or detach the entire gear.

Even more important than the structural characteristics of the S-42 is its performance. Reports on performance were handed in by three of the outstanding pilots in the aviation world: Captain Boris Sergievsky, holder of numerous world records and Chief Test Pilot for Sikorsky Aviation Corporation; Mr. Edwin Musick, Chief Test Pilot for Pan American Airways and an airman of outstanding experience and ability; and the final stamp of approval by Colonel Charles A. Lindbergh. Thirty-two flights on an average of over two hours each filled in the five-month period of performance testing.

In no way, however, has the high performance reduced the practical purposes of this boat. The weight ratio of useful load to gross weight of 38,000 pounds, a useful load of 18,236 pounds, is obtained. This ratio is then in the nature of 48:52, or the useful load equals 48 percent of the gross weight.

The weight allocations for a gross weight of 38,000 pounds and a range of 1,200 miles fit commercial requirements. The fuel and oil for this range weighs 7,995 pounds, equipment weighs 2,181 pounds, and payload equals 7,060 pounds. Should consideration be given to using the S-42 for fast freight delivery only, practically all the 2,181 pounds of equipment, plus the chairs, wall and ceiling trim, and soundproofing can be dispensed with, giving a payload of approximately 10,000 pounds over a range of 1,200 miles. For a range of 3,000 miles, cruising at 145 miles per hour and at 6,000 feet altitude, the allowable payload will be 1,500 pounds. Thus the S-42, keeping well within the safe limitations of the structural strength, capable of maintaining a high ceiling with only three motors, and at the same time carrying a reasonable payload, is entirely suitable for the establishment of transoceanic routes.

If equal payloads are considered, that is, 7,500 pounds, the range for the S-40 is 479 miles and the S-42 is 1,130 miles, an increase of 651 miles. The extensive test made with the S-42 made it possible to make some interesting comparative measurements. With the engines of the S-42 throttled down to 575 bhp to conform with the bhp of the S-40's Hornet "B" engines, the speed obtained was 163 miles per hour, as against 137 miles per hour obtained from the S-40.

The improvement in efficiency of the S-42 is better exemplified if a study is made of the cruising speed of the S-42 against the S-40, using equal horsepower in each case. Using 432 bhp per motor, the S-40 cruises at 115 miles per hour, while with the same power and an increased gross weight of 4,000 pounds, the S-42 cruises at 145 miles per hour, an increase of 30 miles per hour.

From an economic viewpoint, that is, comparing load carried against fuel consumed, an important deviation is found. Each plant using the same horsepower and the fuel consumption per hour of the S-42 being 144 gallons and that of the S-40, 140 gallons, the following ton mile per gallon is given:

Payload in Tons: Miles per gallon (1,000) miles ton mile per gallon.

S-40 0.82 3300/2000 ' 1.65 1.35

S-42 1.0 8505/2000 ' 4.25 4.25.

In view of the fact that operating and maintenance costs are based on flying hours, consideration is here given to that item. Equal in size, the S-40 is again taken for our analysis. The unit of maintenance and operating costs per hour being considered equal, we find that for each flying hour, the S-40 is credited with (1.65 tons x 115 miles) 169.75 ton miles, and the S-42 (4.25 tons x 145 miles) 616.25 ton miles.

It is quite clear that, in this consideration of payload ton miles, that operation and maintenance cost vs. load carried would be decreased in the same proportions. In reality, the decrease will be substantially greater because of the refinement for fast and simplified inspection, servicing, and maintenance incorporated by the Sikorsky engineers in conjunction with the staff of Pan American Airways.

GENERAL CONSIDERATIONS

Because of the general cleanliness of the S-42, due to the careful study of the aerodynamic interference of parts, the total parasite resistance at a cruising speed of 160 miles per hour is only 3,620 pounds. At the time of designing, careful consideration was given to the cantilever wing, but it was felt that the increase in profile resistance, due to the greater thickness of the center section of the wing, would be greater than the drag of external struts. Research also revealed that the structural weight of the cantilever wing would be greater than the present wing and struts.

The table attached gives the curves of the original estimated performance compared with data measured during test flights. It should be noted that actual performance is in general accord with the figures estimated by the more liberal, simplified method in which the profile drag of the wing and the resistance of engines are taken as having a constant value subject to the square of speed. It is believed that the slight excess of actual performance over the original estimate is due partly to greater scale speed effect than the one that was considered, and partly due to the smooth surface created by flush riveting. It is evident that the ship with full load is able to maintain flight easily, using much less than half the power available. It is shown further that the best LID ratio of the whole aeroplane is above 13. The data on which the table is based were recorded during test flights with calibrated intake manifold pressure gauges mounted on all the engines. The reading of these instruments, plus careful observation of the RPM, permitted the accurate establishment of the power used at various conditions of speed and load.

Late 1930s advertisement featuring the *Hawaii Clipper* and the individuals that fly on the Clipper. One of the reasons that the public turned out in large numbers for the takeoff and landing of a Pan Am Clipper was to observe which famous celebrities might be leaving or coming. Author's Collection

After a careful study of the conditions under which this ship would operate, it was decided to have a high-wing loading. The ship was designed primarily for high cruising speed and operation over long transoceanic routes. A service of this character offers no immediate landing possibilities, and in view of the distances and duration of flight, the ship must be able to withstand varying weather conditions. Good airworthiness in stormy weather was considered most essential. A simple aerodynamic study showed that the action of a squall or of a vertical air gust becomes more violent as the wing loading decreases. Therefore, a heavy wing loading of 285 pounds, combined with ample hp per square foot of 2.1 bhp, was found desirable.

One of the refueling barges for the Pan American Clipper fleet. In addition to constructing bases on various islands, Pan American developed refueling barges that allowed the Clipper to pull up and tie off in the open water. The service crew would then refuel the aircraft from this floating gasoline filling station.
University of Miami, Richter Library, Pan Am Collection

Flight tests confirmed this decision. The S-42 flies easily and smoothly in the roughest of weather. The comparatively small and rigid wing has the added advantage of safely weathering strong wind and heavy squalls while afloat, particularly with the flap in a neutral position. Added approval of this consideration is given by nature. It is interesting to note that large birds that fly over the sea, having long distances to traverse before being able to alight in case of stormy weather, have a much heavier wing loading than birds of similar size that fly over land.

The disadvantages of heavy wing loading, namely, difficult takeoff and fast landing, were avoided by the use of specially designed flaps. After a very careful wind-tunnel study of several types of auxiliary surfaces, preference was given to the straight flap that now fills up the rear of the wing between the ailerons. This flap produces an increase in lift of about 40 percent. When placed at a 40-degree angle, the flap affords an actual stalling and landing speed of 65 miles per hour. Tests showed that the best position for takeoff is with the flap set at +10 degrees to +12 degrees. Carrying a definite test load, the ship with the flap in neutral position took 12 seconds for takeoff. Landing immediately, the flap was set at +10 degree and the takeoff time was reduced from 12 seconds to 7 seconds, indicating that the flap decreased takeoff time by nearly 40 percent.

FUTURE CONSIDERATIONS

The results achieved with this new seaplane are encouraging for the future development of large planes. They prove that it is now possible to make accurate estimations of structural weights, performances, and all general characteristics for planes of even more substantial size and advanced design. It is, therefore, permissible to make a forecast of the future development, design, and operation of large aircraft.

In the past, it has been intimated that efficient planes of large size would be impractical. It was argued that with increasing size the structural weight would increase beyond reasonable proportion to the gross weight, so that the ratio of useful load to gross weight would become progressively worse. It is claimed, however, that if careful study is made to distribute the power plant weight and other units of weight along the wing, stresses decrease, and an efficient structure becomes possible.

As previously mentioned, the structure weight of the S-42 is only 52 percent of the gross weight, but at the same time, the ship is built not only in strict conformity with the load factors as set down by the United States Government but, in many cases, has even wider margins of safety.

In view of these considerations, it is reasonable to conclude that efficient planes of still larger size and weighing hundreds of tons are not only possible, but practical. With respect to structural limitations, the hydro- and aerodynamic advantages of large planes, particularly flying boats, may be pointed out. As the size of the boat hull increases, the displacement and therefore the normal loading grows as the cube of the linear dimensions, while the air resistance increases substantially less than the square. This is due to the scale effect and because many auxiliary parts, such as pilot windows, doors, handles, and many other items, do not increase in proportion to the size. In line with this, the water characteristics improve as the size increases, and high aerodynamic efficiency, offering high cruising speed, becomes entirely possible for the large seaplane.

Clipper at the dock of the Marine Air Terminal, LaGuardia Field, New York. The PanAir launch is on the other side of the dock.

Passenger comforts would increase with the size of the ship. In a seaplane of 100,000 pounds or more, it would be possible to have the individual cabins, dining rooms, smoking lounges, etcetera, entirely comparable in comfort and luxury to those of a modern ocean liner. There is no doubt that planes of great weight, capable of nonstop ocean flights, cruising between 150 to 200 miles per hour, can be designed at this time and be ready for service within two and a half to three years. Greater cruising speeds are possible, but the size of the earth does not warrant greater speeds.

The progress of air transportation will benefit more if designers will give more attention to increased passenger comfort and ways and means to lower transportation costs rather than greater speed. It is expected that within the next five years great strides will be made in this direction.

How high will the luxury airliner of the future fly? A few years ago nearly everyone pointed to the stratosphere as the height. While this is possible, the writer believes that the contingent limitations and difficulties will permanently keep the major part of air traffic below the stratosphere. The need of an airtight plane for stratosphere flying brings up a very serious consideration. Should a leak occur, allowing a momentary release of the oxygen in the ship, disaster would result. Possible safeguards against this condition would mean large increases in structural weight. This consideration, together with the well-known basic complications of the stratosphere plane, will probably limit its use to a few exceptional services.

The flying altitude of the commercial airlines will be between 12,000 to 20,000 feet. At this altitude, the plane will be clear of the majority of air disturbances and will be capable of cruising at considerable speed.

This discussion is based on the results of present-day achievements. Projected from them will be the future of great airliner. Present aerodynamic experience predicts aircraft of long ranges, carrying many passengers with comfort, safety, and dispatch over routes will reach to the far corners of the world.

Another company advertisement proudly discussing the item that they provide to the famous Pan American Clippers. The advertisements enhanced the named company, and the image of the Clipper was a wonderful advertisement for Pan American. Companies worked hard at selling to Pan American so that their company would receive recognition from the famous aircraft known worldwide.

Author's Collection

PERFORMANCE DATA

IGOR SIKORSKY

Performance Data on the Sikorsky, Martin, and Boeing Flying Boats

	SIKORSKY S-40	SIKORSKY S-40A
TYPE	AMPHIBIAN	AMPHIBIAN
LENGTH	77 FEET	77 FEET
SPAN	114 FEET	114 FEET
WING LOADING	C	–
HEIGHT	24 FEET	24 FEET
GROSS WEIGHT	34,010 POUNDS	34,600 POUNDS
ENGINES	PRATT & WHITNEY HORNET BX4	PRATT & WHITNEY HORNET T2DIX 4
HORSEPOWER	575 HP	660 HP
RANGE	800 MILES	800 MILES
FUEL CAPACITY	1,040 GALLONS	1,060 GALLONS
USEFUL LOAD	10,870 POUNDS	11,400 POUNDS
CRUISING SPEED	115 MPH	120 MPH
SERVICE CEILING	13,000 FEET	12,500 FEET
CLIMB RATE	712 FEET PER MINUTE	712 FEET PER MINUTE
PASSENGERS	34	40

	SIKORSKY S-42	SIKORSKY S-42A
TYPE	BOAT	BOAT
LENGTH	68 FEET	68 FEET
SPAN	114 FEET	118 FEET
WING LOADING	28.5 POUNDS/SQ. FT.	29.9 POUNDS/SQ. FT.
HEIGHT	17 FEET	17 FEET
GROSS WEIGHT	38,000 POUNDS	40,000 POUNDS
ENGINES	PRATT & WHITNEY X2	PRATT & WHITNEY X2
HORSE POWER	700 HP	750 HP
RANGE	1,200 MILES	1,200 MILES
FUEL CAPACITY	1,240 GALLONS	1,240 GALLONS

USEFUL LOAD	18,000 POUNDS	18,000 POUNDS
CRUISING SPEED	150 MPH	160 MPH
SERVICE CEILING	16,000 FEET	20,000 FEET
CLIMB RATE	800 FEET PER MINUTE	800 PER MINUTE
PASSENGERS	38	38
CREW	5	5

M-130 in flight over San Francisco Harbor.

University of Miami, Richter Library, Pan Am Collection

	SIKORSKY S-42B	MARTIN 130
TYPE	BOAT	BOAT
LENGTH	68 FEET	90 FEET
SPAN	118 FEET	130 FEET
WING LOADING	31.3 POUNDS/SQ. FT.	–
HEIGHT	17 FEET	25 FEET
GROSS WEIGHT	42,000 POUNDS	51,000 POUNDS
ENGINES	PRATT & WHITNEY X4	PRATT & WHITNEY TWIN WASP X4
HORSE POWER	750 HP	800 HP
RANGE	1,200 MILES	3,000 PASSENGER MI., 4,000 MAIL MI.
FUEL CAPACITY	1,240 GALLONS	4,000 GALLONS
USEFUL LOAD	18,000 POUNDS	22,784 POUNDS
CRUISING SPEED	155 MPH	157 MPH
SERVICE CEILING	15,000 FEET	20,000 FEET
CLIMB RATE	800 FEET PER MINUTE	–
PASSENGERS	24	43 (18 SLEEPERS)
CREW	5	7

In 1997 the Pan Am Clipper was featured as part of a series of historical aviation postage stamps issued by the United States Postal Service.
Author's Collection

(Right) Each Clipper passenger was treated to autographs by the crew members and, if the flight involved crossing the Equator, a certificate. The certificate had the passenger's name, date of the flight, the time of the crossing, altitude, air speed, and weather conditions. The certificate was signed by the Captain (pilot) of the Clipper and in the bottom left corner appeared a gold seal containing the Pan Am logo. Juan Trippe believed in making flying an experience and building upon the airline's reputation.
Author's Collection

	BOEING 314	**BOEING 314A**
TYPE	BOAT	BOAT
LENGTH	106 FEET	106 FEET
SPAN	152 FEET	152 FEET
WING LOADING	–	–
HEIGHT	28 FEET	28 FEET
GROSS WEIGHT	82,000 POUNDS	84,000 POUNDS
ENGINES	WRIGHT CYCLONE X4	WRIGHT CYCLONE X4
HORSE POWER	1,500 HP	1,600 HP
RANGE	3,500 STATUTE MILES	4,275 STATUTE MILES
FUEL CAPACITY	4,200 GALLONS	5,448 GALLONS
USEFUL LOAD	23,500 POUNDS	31,360 POUNDS
CRUISING SPEED	150 MPH	150 MPH
SERVICE CEILING	21,000 FEET	21,000 FEET
CLIMB RATE	–	–
PASSENGERS	74 (34 SLEEPERS)	74 (34 SLEEPERS)
CREW	10-16	10-16

From the Illimitable Vastness of the Hyperterrestrial Firmament,
the Empyrean Realm of

Jupiter Rex

King of the Heavens, Lord of the Sun, Moon, Planets, Stars and Nebulae, Ruler of the Winds and Weather, Master of Lightning and Thunder; Supreme Potentate of all things above the Surface of the Earth

Know All Ye By These Presents That:

Sidney Martin Blair

on this **8th** day of **April** in the **40th** year (flying time) was borne on the wings of an airliner of the **Pan American Airways** System across the Equator en route from **Africa** to **S. America**

And, therefore, for this good and sufficient reason, let it be known that **S. M. Blair** has been accepted into the Empyrean Realm of His Exalted Majesty Jupiter Rex, and shall now and forever after be known as Condor **Blair**, R.O.J.R., K.O.H., F.O. M.A.S.O.T.S., and shall receive of all men below the profound Privileges and Immunities of our Aerial Realm.

Given Under My Hand and Seal

W. A. Winston

Captain and Plenipotentiary Extraordinary R.O.J.R.

Time **0700** Altitude **8000'** Air Speed **120** Weather **Cloudy**

PAN AMERICAN AIRWAYS FLYING BOATS

THE CLIPPERS, named for the large sailing ships of the mid-1800s that brought Juan Trippe's family their large fortune, only numbered a total of 26 aircraft, but the aircraft have become the most famous in aviation history. Listed below is the type of each Clipper aircraft with their registration number, name and year placed in service, the region the aircraft served, and the final outcome of each aircraft.

A Sikorsky Clipper being pulled by a tow tractor at the Dinner Key, Miami, facility.
University of Miami, Richter Library, Pan Am Collection

SIKORSKY S-40 (3)

NC80V — *American Clipper*
— entered service in October 1931. Took the first inaugural flight on November 11, 1931. Served in the Pacific and was eventually scrapped.

NC81V — *Caribbean Clipper*
— entered service in November 1931. Served in the Pacific and was eventually scrapped.

NC752V — *Southern Clipper*
— entered service in August 1932. Served in the Pacific and was eventually scrapped.

SIKORSKY S-42 (10)

NC822M — *Brazilian Clipper*
— entered service in May 1934. Served in Latin America. Renamed the *Colombia Clipper* and employed on the Pacific survey flights to chart new routes. Scrapped on July 15, 1946.

NC823M — *West Indies Clipper*, renamed *Pan American Clipper*, then *Hong Kong Clipper*
— entered service in December 1934. Employed on Pacific survey flights. Sank at Antilla, Cuba, on August 7, 1944.

NC824M — The aircraft was never christened and given a name
— entered service in May 1935. Employed in Latin America. Crashed at Port-au-Spain, Trinidad, on December 20, 1935.

(Left) On November 11, 1945, the B-314 *Honolulu Clipper* was forced to land in the Pacific Ocean. Towing the aircraft failed, and eventually the decision was made to destroy the *Honolulu Clipper* by naval gunfire. It took more than 1,300 20mm shells to sink the gallant aircraft. One of the last chapters in Clipper history closed as she slid beneath the water.
University of Miami, Richter Library, Pan Am Collection

NC15373 (S-42A) — *Jamaica Clipper*
— entered service in July 1935. Employed on Latin American flights.
Scrapped on July 15, 1946.

NC15374 (S-42A) — *Antilles Clipper*
— entered service in December 1935. Employed on Latin American flights.
Scrapped on July 15, 1946.

NC15375 (S-42A) — *Brazilian Clipper*
— entered service in February 1936. Later the *Colombia Clipper*.
Employed on Latin American flights. Scrapped on July 15, 1946.

NC15376 (S-42A) — *Dominican Clipper*
— entered service in April 1936. Employed on Latin American flights.
Lost in an accident in San Juan Harbor, Puerto Rico, on October 3, 1941.

NC16734 (S-42B) — *Pan American Clipper II*, renamed the *Samoan Clipper*
— entered service in September 1936. Employed as the survey aircraft for Pan
American's Chief Pilot, Captain Edwin C. Musick. The *Samoan Clipper* was lost
with its entire crew on January 11, 1938, near Pago Pago.

NC16735 (S-42B) — *Bermuda Clipper*
— entered service in September 1936. Served on the Atlantic and Pacific routes and
Baltimore to Bermuda route. Renamed the *Alaska Clipper* in 1940 and later *Hong Kong
Clipper II*. Served on the Manila to Hong Kong route. Sunk on December 8, 1941, in
Hong Kong Harbor by attacking Japanese aircraft. This Clipper became the first
American aircraft destroyed in World War II.

NC16736 (S-42B) — *Pan American Clipper III*
— entered service in 1937. Employed on North and South Atlantic survey flights.
Transferred to the Bermuda route in 1940 and renamed the *Bermuda Clipper*.
Destroyed at Manaus, Brazil, a thousand miles up the Amazon River on July 2, 1943.

MARTIN 130 (3)

NC14714 — *Hawaii Clipper*
— entered service in March 1936. Employed on the Pacific routes. First scheduled transpacific passenger service on October 21, 1936. Lost over the Pacific without a trace on July 29, 1938.

NC14715 — *Philippine Clipper*
— entered service in 1935. Serviced the Pacific routes. Sold to the United States Navy in 1942 (Navy Number 48230). Crashed into a mountain between Ukiah and Boonville, Northern California, on July 21, 1943.

NC14716 — *China Clipper*
— entered service in October 1935. Carried the first transpacific mail on November 22, 1935. Sold to the United States Navy in 1942 (Navy Number 48231). Crashed near Port-au-Spain, Trinidad, on January 8, 1945.

B-314 moving slowly through the calm water after landing. The side hatch has been opened.
University of Miami, Richter Library, Pan Am Collection

(Left) S-42 picking up speed as it skims across the water.
University of Miami, Richter Library, Pan Am Collection

BOEING 314 (12)

NC18601 — *Honolulu Clipper*
— entered service in January 1939. Served the Pacific routes. Collided with United States Navy ship USS *San Pablo* while under tow. The *Honolulu* was destroyed by cannon fire on November 11, 1945.

NC18602 — *California Clipper*, renamed *Pacific Clipper*
— entered service in January 1939. Employed on the Pacific routes. Sold to the United States Navy in 1942 (Navy Number 48224). Sold to World Airways after World War II. Scrapped in 1950.

NC18603 — *Yankee Clipper*
— entered service in February 1939. First transatlantic airmail delivery in 1939. Sold to the United States Navy in 1942 (Navy Number 48225). Crashed and sank in the River Tagus near Lisbon, Portugal, on February 22, 1943.

NC18604 — *Atlantic Clipper*
— entered service in March 1939. Employed on the Atlantic routes. Sold to the United States Navy in 1942 (Navy Number 48226). Salvaged for spare parts in 1946.

NC16805 — *Dixie Clipper*
— entered service in April 1939. Employed on the Atlantic routes and carried the first transatlantic passengers. Sold to the United States Navy in 1942 (Navy Number 48227). Became the official aircraft of President Franklin Roosevelt. He celebrated his 61st birthday on the *Dixie Clipper* on January 30, 1943. Sold to World Airways in 1946 and scrapped in 1950.

NC18606 — *American Clipper*
— entered service in June 1939. Employed on the Atlantic routes. Sold to the United States Army Air Force in 1942 (Army Air Force Number 88631). Later sold to the United States Navy (Navy Number 99083). Sold to World Airways in 1946. Scrapped in 1950.

NC18607A — Ordered by Pan American Airways but sold to the British Government on request from the United States Government —entered service in April 1941 (British Purchasing Commission Number 18607). The NC18607A changed to G-AGBZ, and the aircraft was renamed *Bristol*. Sold to World Airways in 1948. Eventually scrapped.

NC18608A — Ordered by Pan American Airways, but sold to the British Government on request from the United States Government — entered service in April 1941(British Purchasing Commission Number 18608). The NC18608A changed to G-AGCA, and the aircraft was renamed *Berwick*. Sold to World Airways in 1948. Eventually scrapped.

NC18609A — *Pacific Clipper* — entered service in May 1941. Employed on the Pacific routes, replacing the *California Clipper*, which was being redeployed to the Atlantic routes. Sold to the United States Army Air Force (Army Air Force Number 42-88632). Sold to the United States Navy in 1946 (Navy Number 99084). Navy sold the aircraft to Universal Airlines. Aircraft damaged in a storm and salvaged for spare parts.

Three young ladies watching a Clipper moored at the Marine Air Terminal, New York City.

University of Miami, Richter Library, Pan Am Collection

(Right) Painting of the *China Clipper* in its final approach to landing in Hong Kong.

University of Miami, Richter Library, Pan Am Collection

NC18610A — Ordered by Pan American Airways but sold to the British Government on request from the United States Government — entered service in April 1941 (British Purchasing Commission Number G-AGCB) and named *Bangor*. Sold to World Airways in 1948. Eventually scrapped.

NC18611A — *Anzac Clipper* — entered service in June 1941. Employed on the Pacific and Atlantic routes. Sold to the United States Army Air Force (Army Air Force Number 88630). Later sold to the United States Navy (Navy Number 99082). Sold to American International Airways after World War II. Sold to World Airways in 1948. Sold to unknown parties in 1951 and destroyed in Baltimore, Maryland.

NC18612A — *Capetown Clipper* — entered service in August 1941. Employed on the Atlantic routes. Sold to the United States Army Air Force in 1942 (Army Air Force Number 42-88622). Later sold to the United States Navy (Navy Number 99081). Sold to American International Airways in 1947. Sunk at sea by the United States Coast Guard as a hazard after it collided with a boat on October 14, 1947.

PAN AMERICAN CLIPPER ACCIDENTS

JANUARY 11, 1938: the *Samoan Clipper* (S-42A) disappeared near Pago Pago, American Samoa. Believed the aircraft, piloted by Pan American's Chief Pilot Captain Edwin C. Musick, exploded in midair. The entire crew of seven perished.

July 28, 1938: the *Hawaii Clipper* (M-130) disappeared between Manila and Guam. No trace of the aircraft or the 15 people on board was found.

January 21, 1943: the *Philippine Clipper* (M-130) slammed into a mountain near Ukiah and Boonville, Northern California, on a flight from Pearl Harbor, Hawaii to Treasure Island, San Francisco. Wreckage was not found for a week. All 19 people on board perished.

February 22, 1943: the *Yankee Clipper* (B-314) crashed while attempting to land at Lisbon, Portugal. Left wingtip made contact with water while making a descent prior to landing. Twenty-four were killed and 15 survived. Among the dead was famous novelist Ben Robertson, and seriously injured was singer Jane Froman.

August 8, 1944: the *Hong Kong Clipper* (S-42) crashed and sank on takeoff at Antilla, Cuba. There were 31 passengers and crew; 14 survived.

January 8, 1945: the *China Clipper* (M-130) crashed while attempting to land at Port-au-Spain, Trinidad. There were 30 crew and passengers on board; only 7 survived. The *China Clipper* was the last surviving M-130; the other two, the *Hawaii Clipper* and *Philippine Clipper*, had also met tragic fates.

PAN AMERICAN EARLY FIRSTS

Photo of the wreckage of a Pan Am Clipper.

1927 — Mail delivery between Key West, Florida, to Havana, Cuba. Key West was the first airfield of Pan American Airways. Later operations would be relocated to Dinner Key, Miami.

1928 — First American airline to use radio communications.

1928 — First American airline to carry emergency lifesaving equipment.

1928 — First American airline to employ multiple flight crews.

1928 — First American airline to develop an airport and air traffic control system.

One of four engines from a Clipper that met a terrible fate. The reality of the fleet of S-40s, S-42s, M-130s, and B-314s is that none survived to be placed in an air museum. Crashes or destruction was the fate of each one.

University of Miami, Richter Library, Pan Am Collection

1928 — First American airline to order and purchase aircraft built to its own specifications (the Sikorsky S-38). Pan American would continue to provide specifications for aircraft to meet its transoceanic requirements.

1929 — First American airline to employ cabin attendants and serve meals while in the air.

1929 — First American airline to develop a complete aviation weather service.

1929 — First American airline to start expanded passenger service to Latin America: Port-au-Spain, Mexico City, Nassau, Santo Domingo, St. Thomas, Guatemala City, Buenos Aires, Santiago, and Montevideo.

1930 — First American airline to offer international air express service.

1930 — Service expanded in Latin America: Rio de Janeiro, St. Lucia, Caracas, Maracaibo.

1931 — First American airline to purchase and operate four-engine flying boats.

1932 — First American airline to sell all-expense international air tours.

1932 — Service expanded to Port-au-Prince, Haiti.

1933 — Service started to Tampa, Florida.

1934 — Service expanded in the United States to Los Angeles, California, and Orlando, Florida.

1935 — First American airline to develop and employ its own long-range weather forecasting system.

1935 — First American airline to install onboard facilities for heating food on an aircraft in flight.

1935 — First American transpacific mail service on November 22, 1935 (San Francisco, California, to Honolulu). Aircraft piloted by Captain Edwin C. Musick and navigator Captain Fred Noonan.

1936 — Pan American Airways President Juan Trippe accepted the Collier Trophy from President Franklin D. Roosevelt on August 6. The award was given to Pan American Airways for "the establishment of the transpacific airplane and the successful execution of extended over-water navigation." Pan American Airways had flown six million passenger miles without an accident or canceled flight. The trophy is awarded each year for "the greatest achievement in aeronautics or astronautics in America, with respect to improving the performance, efficiency, and safety of aircraft."

1937 — Service expanded to New York, Bermuda, and Sao Paulo.

1939 — First airline to operate regularly scheduled transatlantic passenger and mail service.

1939 — The first scheduled passenger flight across the North Atlantic.

1940 — Service expanded to Seattle/Tacoma, Washington.

1942 — The first airline to operate international service with all-cargo aircraft.

1943 — Service started to Dakar, Senegal.

1944 — First airline to propose a plan for low-cost, mass transportation on a worldwide schedule once World War II ended.

1945 — The end of the Golden Age of Pan American's Flying Boats. Pan American becomes the first airline to employ high-speed commercial land planes on transatlantic routes.

Several of the Clippers became part of the World Airways Inc. air fleet. For a brief period, several were employed in passenger and various other tasks. The lack of spare parts for aircraft no longer being manufactured caught up to World Airways Inc., as did pressing financial problems. By 1949, the aircraft known as the Clippers had passed into aviation history. Not one had been saved and preserved to place in an aviation museum.

Strange stories have survived over the years concerning last flights and whereabouts of some of the aircraft. Some involve the smuggling of illegal immigrants; another tells of parts of one aircraft being buried on one of the islands in the Caribbean. Even when extinct, the Clippers provided stories of strange and exotic happenings.

The days of the beautiful Clippers were at an end. World War II had created new land airfields, miles of runways and, very importantly, new large and efficient long-distance aircraft.

Wing and engine lifted out of the water.

University of Miami, Richter Library, Pan Am Collection

Part of the legacy of the Pan American Clippers was the development of equipment and techniques for other types of flying boats, including many military versions. The 1955 *Popular Mechanics* shows a flying boat beaching rig. The rig was developed to handle the Clippers. Author's Collection

REMEMBERING THE PAN AMERICAN CLIPPERS

THERE ARE MANY ARCHIVES ON PAN AMERICAN AIRWAYS across the United States. The largest collection was donated by Juan Trippe and his wife to the Richter Library at the University of Miami. Sadly, most of the collection is still unsorted. Memories of the short, glorious reign of the Pan American Clipper flying boats can still be found at a fantastic collection housed in the International Terminal at San Francisco Airport. The museum does not contain any full-size aircraft, but does contain a fantastic collection of papers, articles, history, and photos of the company. Special focus has been on the Pan American Clippers that flew to worldwide destinations from 1931 to 1945. The museum has been compiling oral histories from as many former Pan American Clipper employees as possible.

What memories individuals have of the glorious time of the Clippers. Every individual has one special memory of a flight or event to recount. Many have photos of not just the passengers and crew, but scenes of individuals watching a Clipper take off or even the men in Port Washington, New York, who fished in the shadow of the wing of the B-314 and employed it as a giant sun umbrella.

"Whenever a B-314 overnighted anywhere, an anchor 'watch' was used to hold the airplane in case a strong wind came up and the anchor started dragging. At Shediac, New Brunswick, Canada, a junior pilot and myself were assigned such duty, as there were not enough station personnel. So the two of us rowed a rowboat and tied up to the B-314. Soon it became cold, and he had to run around to find some blankets because there was no source of heat. Then we became hungry and the nearest source of food was a lobster/fish shop where we bought some lobster that had just been cooked. After rowing back to the B-314, we found the shell to be so hard that we had to get the engineers to open them up. At dawn we rowed ashore, thoroughly chilled, to find that the rest of the crew had attended the Saturday night dance in town. That was the first and last time that I volunteered to perform the anchor 'watch.'"

The golden sun glistens off the front of the Administration/ Passenger Terminal built at Treasure Island for Pan American and the Golden Gate International Exposition and still in use. The inside and outside contain the original Art Deco figures and artwork from 1939. In the corner of each end of the outside building is the figure of a Neptune figure holding an M-130 in his hands. Visiting Treasure Island is a step back into the days of the Golden Age of Aviation.
Treasure Island Museum Association

"Any waterborne aircraft has problems in a crosswind. The wind is trying to tip the downwind wing into the water, and if this happens to a B-314, the outboard propeller hits the water and bends right up. Pan American Airways developed a system where the extra crew members go out on a 'catwalk' inside the wing to balance the engine on the high wing to help move the wing to a horizontal position. The location was very noisy even at low power, but the engine on the high wing had to use lots of power to overcome the weathervane effect of the three-fin sponsons ... Sailing knowledge was very valuable in these conditions. After all, it was a flying boat."

"One of the tricky operations was at Horta, a harbor on an island in the Azores. It is a small harbor surrounded by mountains. Landings could be made toward the mountains, but the longer takeoffs and small rate of climb meant takeoffs were made toward the open ocean. The design of the B-314 limited the waves to three feet in height, because of the high stresses as the B-314 hit the tops of the waves. The Engineer's job was to read the Captain's accelerometer. During night takeoffs, this was especially hard, because we couldn't let our hooded flashlight spoil the darkened cockpit. This duty was normally performed by the Second Flight Engineer kneeling between the pilots. There are many photos of many B-314s waiting in Horta harbor for the waves to subside. I clearly remember the skill of our Horta employees in handling the thin-skinned B-314. They are seafaring people."

View from the back of a motor boat near the Marine Air Terminal, LaGuardia Field, with a Clipper riding on the waves.

University of Miami, Richter Library, Pan Am Collection

"Aluminum and salt water corrode rapidly. Boeing's great Engineering Department minimized this by specifying Alclad, anodized, zinc chroma-sheet aluminum. We had special brushes and chemicals to remove the white powdery corrosion and then we coated the wetted areas with lanolin. We realized the life of the airplane would be short. The bilge, or the bottom, was especially affected, because they were a series of water-tight, unvented compartments. One had the fuel transfer pumps."

Pan Am's base at Sumay on Apra Harbor, Guam. It had been the flying boat base of the United States Marine Corps. The buildings and area were heavily damaged and destroyed during the Japanese attack and capture of Guam.
University of Miami, Richter Library, Pan Am Collection

"A significant part of Pan American's reputation came from our Flight Service. On the B-314, they often chose the food, cooked it and served it in courses on linen tablecloths, using specially designed silverware. We engineers were close to Flight Service because we fixed their galleys and controlled the temperature, fixed clogged toilets, etc. They were all males until the end of World War II. They were even trained to help with engine changes. They were in charge of the ship's papers and smoothed our entry through the various customs, immigration, and public health in unfriendly countries. Certain countries required bribes for short entry times. Since they made many shore contacts, the pleasure of layovers in a man's city like Lisbon depended on how well you got along with the purser. They knew everybody."

"The B-314's departure from a small floating dock at Garden Bay Marine Terminal at LaGuardia Field was complicated by the hazard of fire during the engine start with the passengers aboard and only one exit door to get out of. The two flight engineers are already doing their checklists. The rest of the 12 crew members now formally marched aboard. There was a hawser from the bow to an underwater pulley and then to shore to a tractor that had a special fitting that accommodated a quick release fitting that could be released by a beaching crew member, who tied his rowboat to the same fitting, awaiting the signal to release the stern line. After the four engines started, the passengers walked aboard. The entry door was shut. The captain signaled to be released. The tractor started pulling on the bow rope, and when it was taut, the man in the rowboat released the tail rope and the B-314 moved away carefully from the dock. When the bow rope was loose, the pilot threw the bow post, retracted them, and closed the hatch. On one cold, windy day, the man in the rowboat could not untie his rope, and because the captain did not know this, he started taxiing out of the bay in the usual crosswind. This was always tricky in the narrow bay. The alarmed man in the rowboat began beating on the fuselage above him. A passenger looking out saw what was happening and informed the purser, who relayed this to the captain on the deck above. They apparently solved the problem, because there was never a report of a B-314 arriving at Botwood, Newfoundland, with a man hanging on."

"The B-314 wingspar was made from a round tube of aluminum that was rolled into an almost square shape. During this process, some undetected crack may have occurred. During flight, the flight engineers were required to inspect all of the B-314 that were accessible, every two hours. The wings were large enough to accommodate a crawlway to the #1 and #4 engines. We carried wrenches and a flashlight so we could repair any

problem on the spot. Why, one of our engineers did change a defective magneto during flight. He took a good magneto and installed it on the defective engine. This 'can-do' attitude was typical of Pan American Airways in those days."

USS AVOCET (AVP-4)

The USS *Avocet* has an important place in early American aviation history. The seaplane tender was stationed in the Pacific during the 1930s. On July 2, 1937, the USS *Avocet* was one of the ships that searched for the missing Lockheed Electra piloted by Amelia Earhart and navigated by Fred Noonan. Fred Noonan was the Pan American Airways navigator on the first flight from San Francisco to Hawaii on November 22, 1935.

On January 11, 1938, the USS *Avocet* was sent to the search an area around Pago Pago for Pan American Airway's Chief Pilot Captain Edwin C. Musick and his crew. The S-42 *Samoan Clipper* was on a survey flight to chart new routes for Pan American Airways when it reported a problem with an oil leak. The USS *Avocet* found no sign of the six-man crew and very little wreckage.

On December 7, 1941, the USS *Avocet* was moored at Pearl Harbor, Hawaii, near the battleship USS *California*. The USS *Avocet* opened fire with its lone .50 caliber machine gun and shot down a Japanese Kate torpedo bomber. The Kate had just launched her torpedo at the *California*. The aircraft burst into flames and crashed near the United States Naval Hospital.

During the engagement, the USS *Avocet* departed her mooring at the Naval Air Station dock and sailed into the harbor to assist in keeping the USS *Nevada* afloat. At the end of World War II, the USS *Avocet* was scrapped.

USS *Avocet*: Hull Number AVP-4
Displacement: 1,695 tons (standard), 2,800 tons (full load)
Waterline Length: 300 feet
Length Overall: 311 feet
Maximum Beam: 41 feet
Maximum Draft: 13 feet, 5 inches
Armament: 1 x 3" .50 caliber machine gun
Laid Down: September 13, 1917, at Baltimore, Maryland
Named: November 17, 1917
Launched: March 9, 1918, at the Baltimore Drydock and Shipbuilding Company by Miss Frances Virginia Imbach, daughter of the manager of the upper plant of the Baltimore Drydock and Shipbuilding Company
Commissioned: September 17, 1917, at Norfolk Navy Yard, Lt. Christian Crone in command

A 1950s photograph of a mother, father, and two children looking at many items that were key to the history of Pan American. The first engine, a wicker chair from the first aircraft, and the large globe where Juan Trippe plotted out with string the next exotic destination for the Clippers.
University of Miami, Richter Library, Pan Am Collection

(Left) The original engine from the historic first mail flight from Key West, Florida, to Havana, Cuba, in 1927.
University of Miami, Richter Library, Pan Am Collection

THE LEGACY OF THE PAN AMERICAN AIRPORTS

As Pan American Airways grew in the early 1930s, its base of operation was moved from Key West to Dinner Key, a small island in Biscayne Bay. It had been joined to the mainland during World War I to provide a training facility for the United States Navy. After World War I, the base continued to be used as a nonscheduled airfield. It was destroyed by a hurricane in 1926. In 1930, Pan American Airways acquired the New York to Rio to Buenos Aires airline, which flew twin-engine Commodores from Miami to Buenos Aires.

Pan American Airways selected Dinner Key as its base for inter-American operations with the first inaugural flight to Panama on December 1, 1930. The first passenger terminal at Dinner Key was a houseboat purchased in Havana, towed to Miami, and anchored to pilings with large barges at each end. Additional land was obtained and filled, and a deeper channel was dredged. The dredging of the channel was a milestone event, marking the first time that the Congressional Rivers and Harbors Committee had approved dredging to create a navigable channel for marine aircraft. Also constructed were a terminal building and several additional aircraft hangars.

The Dinner Key Terminal served as the model for other Pan American facilities. The terminal was dedicated on March 25, 1934, and swiftly moved into operation. The terminal contains four sun, and rain-shielded walkways to keep the passengers dry and make it easier to board the aircraft. Dinner Key served as the model for observation decks, providing spectators an excellent opportunity to view incoming and outgoing Clippers. The observation decks were usually packed, as the spectators wanted to find out which famous celebrity or politician was departing or arriving. The observation area was a key feature in the Pan American facilities in New York City, Treasure Island, and Rio de Janeiro.

James E. Young, the attorney for Pan American Airways, accepting a check for $25,000 from the Miami City Manager, A. B. Curry. This was the first payment in the sale of the Dinner Key Terminal to the City of Miami for a total price of $1,050,000.

University of Miami, Richter Library, Pan Am Collection

The facility served as a base for the United States Navy during World War II, as well as a commercial airport facility. Pan American Airways' final flight departed Dinner Key on August 9, 1945. The two-storey Terminal Building is rectangular in shape, with one-storey extensions on each side, white stucco exterior walls, and a flat roof. Extending around the building is a frieze of winged globes and rising suns, connected at the corners by sculptured eagles, the symbols of Pan American Airways. Takeoffs and landings were observed from an outer promenade on the second floor. At the first-floor level were the waiting rooms, an international mail office, customs, public health offices, immigration services, and a ticket counter. The famous and enormous 3.5-ton revolving world globe in the lobby once attracted thousands of visitors to the building. The ceiling of the building depicted the signs of the zodiac, and murals near the ceiling showed the history of flight from Leonardo da Vinci to the Pan American Clipper flying boats.

In May 1939, Pan American Airways signed a lease for a new marine base with the City of New York. A hangar and terminal were constructed at a cost of $40 million. It would officially be named LaGuardia Airport.

Pan American Airways paid a heavy price in lives and money to open a route to New Zealand. Captain Musick and his crew were lost, and the service only operated for a short period before the attack on Pearl Harbor in 1941.

The landing site at Kingman Reef was not very functional. It was an atoll that sits a little underwater and is awash the majority of the day. It was not even a good spot for refueling due to the terrain of the area. Kingman Reef was abandoned and a new site picked at Canton Island. There was a question regarding whether or not it was a U.S. possession. The United States sent a warship to take over the island, and the British built a mail hut on the other side of the island to protect their claim.

Pan American built a hotel in the same style as on Midway and Wake Islands. Nouméa in New Caledonia was not Pan American's first choice for a terminus. Original plans called for the stop to be at Pago Pago, American Samoa. The approach to the harbor at Pago Pago was very difficult and was unprotected from the elements. It was here that Captain Musick and his crew were lost. Nouméa has a better harbor and was chosen instead.

Pan Am ad from 1970 pointing out that the company's passenger aviation experience reached back to the Clippers of the 1930s. In fact Pan Am was the airline featured in the famous 1968 science fiction movie *2001: A Space Odyssey.*
Author's Collection

OTHER FLIGHTS

The story of Pan American Airways usually focuses on the passenger flights, but before the passenger flights could proceed, survey flights came first, followed by a mail flight to test the surveyed route and then passenger travel. The first flight to Hawaii on April 17, 1935, was a survey flight. The survey flight would be followed by the first mail flight on November 22, 1935. Hawaii Post has issued commemorative stamps and first day covers for the historic survey flight.

A second survey flight from Alameda, California, to Honolulu was undertaken on June 12, 1935, commanded by Captain R. O. D. Sullivan. The aircraft reached Honolulu three minutes ahead of schedule. It departed the next day for a survey flight to Midway Island. The aircraft carried fresh fruit and supplies. The major excitement of the flight was when the entire crew wanted to see the famous Gooney Birds of Midway Island up close. There were safety concerns as the Gooney Bird is a member of the albatross family and able to soar, thus a menace to takeoffs and landings.

On October 5, 1935, the final survey flight was undertaken to complete last technical details. Sullivan left Alameda and landed at Sumay Point in Guam's Apra Harbor on October 11. The total westbound flight had taken 45 hours and 47 minutes. As with the other two flights, aerial surveys were undertaken and completed and instrument landings were practiced, employing the new radio tower that had just been completed.

Sullivan and his crew returned to San Francisco on October 24 and announced that the route was operational and ready. The new Martin 130 had been delivered and was named the *China Clipper.* The aircraft, infrastructure, and mail were set for the first flight on November 22, 1935.

An early S-40 in flight. Note the rear wheel on the aircraft. The S-40s had landing gear.

University of Miami, Richter Library, Pan Am Collection

The Atlantic survey routes were started on June 25, 1937. Pan American had been approved for stations at Shediac, New Brunswick; Botwood, Newfoundland; Foyes, Ireland, and Southampton, England.

The first flight flew from New York to Shediac, New Brunswick, but did not land. The first flight was to check radio, sun sights, and the impact of the coastline on radio bearings.

The second flight on June 27 saw the Clipper land at Shediac and Botwood before flying back to New York the next day. On this flight, the night sky was studied for its effects on radio and navigation.

Captain Gray and his crew left Botwood, Newfoundland, on July 3, 1937, with an S-42B, climbed to 8,000 feet, crossed the Atlantic, and landed at Foyes, Ireland. On hand to greet the crew was Eamon de Valera, the President of Ireland.

Pan American Airways had conquered the Pacific and the dangerous Atlantic. Juan Trippe's dream of founding and controlling a worldwide airline had been achieved. If history is a loop, then just maybe the day of the flying boats will return. In June 2006, New York City Mayor Michael Bloomberg "floated" the idea of seaplanes, recalling Juan Trippe's testimony in the 1930s that New York City needed the Marine Air Terminal. Bloomberg noted that the ground facilities in New York are overcrowded and the solution may be to bring back the flying boats to relieve the congestion. He argued that at least for short hops, the flying boat is a possible answer to the problem.

Not everyone is buying into the idea: Michael Boyd of Boyd Group, an aviation consulting firm, agreed it was a good idea, as soon as the *Hindenburg* is brought back.

Whether any type of flying boat will appear in the future is very much open to debate. For a very brief time in aviation history, though, there were magnificent flying boats that flew the skies. The Pan American Clippers operated as ships of the air. The crews wore naval uniforms and passengers were treated royally. The captain and crew of the aircraft marched to the aircraft as if boarding a luxury ocean liner. Selected passengers ate at the Captain's table as if they were on a ship on the high seas. One captain even performed card tricks to amuse the passengers on a leg of the journey.

Today, when passengers are crowded into aircraft as sardines in a can and even have to brown-bag their own meals and drinks, it can be easy to forget that there was a brief time when flying was not only an adventure to exotic places, but a traveling experience like no other.

REQUIEM FOR THE CLIPPER

Aye, tear her once proud ensign down
Long has it flown on high.
For many an eye has danced to see
Clipper ships in the sky.
Beneath her flowed the frenzied waves
Above the big jets roar.
The Clippers of the ocean air
Shall sweep the clouds no more.
The Clipper flew to Wake and Guam
And had its day at Pearl
And Lindy pioneered the routes
That grew around the world.
Her boats were seen in Shanghai's ports,
No more will fly the wide-eyed child
Nor hope-filled refugee,
For the harpies of the shore shall pluck
The eagles of the sea.
So give her routes to foreign flags
Her ships to rot and ruin,
Her people to the jackals
Who fax fat on the Clippers doom.
The better that the shattered fleet
Should sink beneath the wave,
Her engines shook the mighty deep
And there should be her grave.
Fix to her side her country's flag,
Set every wing and tail.
And give her to the God of Storms,
The lightning and the gale.

— *Jim Boland*

Two Clippers on the water in San Francisco Bay with a new transoceanic Constellation flying overhead. The Golden Era of the Pan American Flying Boats had come to an end.

University of Miami, Richter Library, Pan Am Collection

Clipper tied off and being pulled into the service area of the Marine Air Terminal, LaGuardia Field, New York City. University of Miami, Richter Library, Pan Am Collection

BOOKS

Banning, Gene. *Airlines of Pan American Since 1927: Its Airlines, its People, and its Aircraft.*
McLean, VA: Paladwr Press, 2001.

Bender, Marilyn. *The Chosen Instrument: Pan Am, Juan Trippe, the Rise and Fall of an American Entrepreneur.*
New York: Simon and Schuster, 1982.

Chapman, Francis Allan. *Talking to the World from Pan Am's Clippers.* Newton, NJ: Carstens Publications, 1999.

Cohen, Stan. *Wings to the Orient: Pan American Clipper Planes 1935-1945: A Pictorial History.*
Missoula, MT: Pictorial Histories Pub. Co., 1985.

Conrad, Barnaby, III, *Pan Am: an Aviation Legend.* Kansas City, MO: Andrews McMeel Universal, 1999.

Culbert, Tom, and Andy Dawson. *PanAfrica: Across the Sahara in 1941 with Pan Am.*
MacLean, VA: Paladwr Press, 1998.

Daley, Robert. *An American Saga: Juan Trippe and his Pan Am Empire.* New York: Random House, 1980.

Davies, R. E. G. *Charles Lindbergh: An Airman, his Aircraft, and his Great Flights.*
McLean, VA: Paladwr Press, 1997.

Davies, R. E. G. *Pan Am: An Airline and its Aircraft.* New York: Orion Books, 1987.

Dunning, Eugene J. *Voices of my Peers: Clipper Memories.* Nevada City, CA: Clipper Press, 1996.

Gandt, Robert L. *China Clipper: The Age of the Great Flying Boats.* Annapolis, MD: Naval Institute Press, 1991.

Kauffman, S. B. *Pan Am Pioneer: A Manager's Memoir from Seaplane Clippers to Jumbo Jet.*
Lubbock, TX: Texas Tech University Press, 1995.

Leopard, Dave. *Rubber Toy Vehicles Identification and Value Guide.* Paducah, KY: Collector Books, 2003.

Mosley, Leonard. *Lindbergh, a Biography.* Mineola, NY: Dover Publications, 1976.

Rydell, Robert W. *World of Fairs: The Century-of-Progress Expositions.* Chicago: University of Chicago Press,
1993.

Trippe, Betty. *Pan Am's First Lady: the Diary of Betty Stettinius Trippe.* McLean, VA: Paladwr Press, 1997.

OTHER PUBLICATIONS

Other publications consulted include the Outline of the History of Pan Am Airways Inc.,
Latin American Division, 1927-1942, and the *Clipper Newsletters.*

Passengers arriving at LaGuardia in 1939
on the Boeing B-314 *Atlantic Clipper*.

Page numbers in italics refer to illustrations.

Passengers and crew on the doomed *Honolulu Clipper* had to evacuate the aircraft by rubber raft. Note the departure by way of the floatation wing. Eventually, when towing it failed, the *Honolulu* would be sunk by the USS *San Pablo*.

University of Miami, Richter Library, Pan Am Collection